The Mercier Companion to Irish Literature

The Mercier Companion to Irish Literature

Sean McMahon

Jo O'Donoghue

MERCIER PRESS

Published in 1998 by Mercier Press
PO Box 5 5 French Church Street Cork
Tel: (021) 275040; Fax: (021) 274969
e.mail: books@mercier.ie
16 Hume Street Dublin 2
Tel: (01) 661 5299; Fax: (01) 661 8583
e.mail: books@marino.ie

Trade enquiries to CMD Distribution
55A Spruce Avenue
Stillorgan Industrial Park
Blackrock County Dublin
Tel: (01) 294 2556; Fax: (01) 294 2564

© Sean McMahon
and Jo O'Donoghue 1998

ISBN 1 85635 216 1

10 9 8 7 6 5 4 3 2 1

A CIP record for this title is available
from the British Library

Cover painting courtesy of Anne Yeats
and the National Gallery, Dublin
Cover design by Penhouse Design
Printed in Ireland by ColourBooks,
Baldoyle Industrial Estate, Dublin 13

Introduction

The Irish who once were known with justice and pride as the 'fightin' Irish' could with greater justice be called the 'writin' Irish'. How else to explain the popularity and success of Bob Welch's magisterial *Oxford Companion to Irish Literature*, Bob Hogan's opulent two-volume *Dictionary of Irish Literature*, the high literary content of Louis McRedmond's *Modern Irish Lives*, all published in 1996, and the latest writer-filled edition of Henry Boylan's *A Dictionary of Irish Biography* (1998). Indeed with such excellent reference books available, why 'another damned, thick, square, book!' as the Duke of Gloucester said to Edward Gibbon about *The Decline and Fall of the Roman Empire*? Why indeed! Except that it is smaller than these giants and in paperback and can be read in the bath without fear of doing it irreparable damage.

The range of Irish writers from the saints and scholars of the early centuries to the poets, novelists, and dramatists of today is impressive. Interest and pride in the scribblers of our land is the sincerest and least harmful form of chauvinism. The pen may be mightier than the sword, as Bulwer-Lytton says, but Irish writers have rarely been murderous, preferring the roles of critics and celebrators of the land that gave them birth and now gives them shelter. The days when the lovely land sent its writers and artists into banishment are thankfully over but the damaging and hurtful aspect of the censorship laws that characterised more than three shameful decades in the country's recent history was that the shortsighted and narrowminded legislators did not realise how necessary and hygienic the work of these holders of the mirror up to nature, these abstract and brief chroniclers of the time.

Inevitably, any book of lists lays itself open to charges of unforgivable omissions and even more unforgivable inclusions. In a country with a dense literary history, one where new and gifted writers are discovered every day, it is impossible to please (or include) all. Idiosyncrasy, ignorance – even prejudice – all come into play, no matter how hard the drudging lexicographer may try to eschew them. The field is vast and the space limited. The book tries within its limits to be representative and sound. It is based upon many years of reading and much pleasure, and is offered to the many who may not realise how widespread the Irish *cacoethes scribendi* is, has been and will, in spite of microchipped Jeremiahs, continue to be.

We take this opportunity to thank Francis J. D'Arcy of Derry for help, advice and salutary criticism. We are also grateful to Peter Sirr of the Irish Writers' Centre, to Chris Kelly of the Mercier Bookshop for helping out with queries, and to publishers and individuals too numerous to mention who provided us with information. We are grateful too to Cormac Deane, Sarah Marcus, Rachel Sirr and Christy Ward, all of whom worked on the book in an editorial capacity and contributed to its inclusiveness and accuracy. Where the compilers had personal acquaintance with an author's work, we tried to give some sense of its quality or preoccupations; however our attempt to be as inclusive as possible of contemporary writers made this impossible in some cases.

Abbreviations

BBC NI	British Broadcasting Corporation Northern Ireland
CBS	Christian Brothers Schools
DCU	Dublin City University
DIAS	Dublin Insitute for Advanced Studies
DMP	Dublin Metropolitan Police
ENT	Ear Nose and Throat
FCA	Forsa Cosantais Áitiúil (Local Defence Force)
FRSM	Fellow of the Royal Society of Medicine
IAOS	Irish Agricultural Organisation Society
Inst	Royal Belfast Academical Institution
IRA	Irish Republican Army
IRB	Irish Republican Brotherhood
NI	Northern Ireland
NIHE	National Institute for Higher Education, Limerick (now Limerick University)
NUU	New University of Ulster
OM	Order of Malta
QUB	Queen's University Belfast
RDS	Royal Dublin Society
RIA	Royal Irish Academy
RIC	Royal Irish Constabulary
RNT	Royal National Theatre
RSC	Royal Shakespeare Company
RTÉ	Radio Teilifís Éireann
TCD	Trinity College Dublin
UCC	University College Cork
UCD	University College Dublin
UCG	University College Galway
ULT	Ulster Literary Theatre

UU	University of Ulster
UWC	Ulster Workers' Coalition
WEA	Workers' Educational Association
WWI	First World War
WWII	Second World War

A

ABBEY THEATRE, THE (estd. 1904) opened in Dublin with *On Baile's Strand* and *Cathleen Ní Houlihan* by W. B. Yeats* and *Spreading the News* by Lady Gregory*. Yeats, Gregory and Edward Martyn, the founders of the Irish Literary Theatre, gladly accepted it from the generous Miss A. E. Horniman*, and it was to become the main focus of the Irish Literary Revival*. The strongest acting element came from the Fays of the Irish National Theatre Society, with Sarah Allgood as principal actress. Its early years saw some controversy, with Synge*'s *The Playboy of the Western World* (1907) and O'Casey*'s *The Plough and the Stars* (1926) causing rioting. The early ideal of poetic drama gave way to mainly rural prose realism with effective work by Padraic Colum*, St John Ervine* and Lennox Robinson*, while the earlier plays of Sean O'Casey showed that a heady combination of urban wit and backstreet poetry existed in the capital city. In 1925 a government grant (*see* Ernest Blythe*) made it the first subsidised theatre in the English-speaking world and by the late 1930s actors were required to be bilingual in order to perform an increasing number of Gaelic plays. The original premises were destroyed by fire in 1951 and the company had a fifteen-year Babylonian exile in the Queen's Theatre in Pearse Street. The new Abbey opened in 1966 and continues a policy of presenting new Irish and internationally known plays. Its 'other place', the Peacock, uses greater auditorium flexibility to stage mainly experimental material.

Abraham, James Johnston (1876–1963), surgeon and writer, was born in Coleraine, County Derry, and educated there and at TCD where he studied Medicine. After service with the Serbian army and in the Middle East during WWI, he became a Harley Street specialist. He wrote a novel, *Night Nurse* (1913), and several volumes of autobiography. He was FRSM and winner of the Arnott Medal in 1949.

Adamnán (*c*. 625–704), abbot and hagiographer, was born in Donegal and was abbot of Iona from 679 until his death. He wrote *Vita Sancti Columbae*, the biography of its first founder Colum Cille*, and *De Locis Sanctis*, an account, according to tradition personally dictated, of the visit of Bishop Arculf to the Holy Land. Adamnán's name is also associated with law reform and with the attempt to reconcile the Celtic Church with the rules determined for the universal Church at the Synod of Whitby (664).

Æ (George William Russell) (1867–1935), poet, editor and mystic, was born in Lurgan, County Down, but moved to Dublin when he was eleven. After attendance at Rathmines School he became a clerk in Pim's Drapery in South Great George's Street but furthered his artistic education at the Metropolitan School of Art and the RHA. Here he met W. B. Yeats*, who became one of his closest friends. They shared other interests besides painting: both became interested in theosophy. Æ had already had mystic experiences in the form of daytime dreams, and the cult seemed to accommodate such visions. In 1898 he married Violet North, a fellow adept, who was tolerant of his necessary journeys around the country, often by bicycle, establishing the Irish Agricultural Organisation Society (IAOS) which he helped to run for Sir Horace Plunkett (1854-1932). He became editor of the IAOS journal, the *Irish Homestead* (1905-23), and later of the *Irish Statesman* (1923-30), and welcomed to their pages many aspirant Irish writers, including Padraic Colum*, Seumas O'Sullivan*, Eva Gore-Booth* and Alice Milligan*. His play *Deirdre* (1902) was one of the first offerings of the Irish Literary Theatre and it was followed by many volumes of poetry and prose, usually of mystic content. His house in Rathgar Avenue was a forum for all interested in the literary and economic life of the nation. Bereft by the death of his wife (in 1932) and having no relish for the anticipated life in de Valera's Ireland, he went to live in England in 1933 and died in Bournemouth two years later.

aisling, [lit. dream] type of poem in Irish favoured by the Jacobite poets of the eighteenth century (*see*, for instance, Aogán Ó Rathaile*, Seán Ó Tuama*) although having its roots in much earlier prose and verse, both political and amorous. In it the poet encounters (sometimes in a dream) a beautiful woman who is neither human nor fairy but a *spéirbhean*, the personification of Ireland. She bewails the pitiful state of her people and looks forward to the return of the country's rightful masters, the Stuart kings. In the hands of poets such as Ó Rathaile and Eoghan Rua Ó Súilleabháin*, this form, although conventional, was a vehicle of surpassing lyricism and energy.

Alexander, Annie French (1825–1902), novelist, was born in Dublin, the daughter of Robert French, a solicitor. She published in all forty novels which ranged from high romance to Gothic mystery. Her best known work was *The Wooing O't* (1875). Of one of her mysteries, *Blind Fate*, a publisher's hack composed the following deathless lines: 'In Mrs Alexander's tale/Much Art she clearly shows/In keeping dark the mystery/Until the story's close.'

Alexander, Cecil Frances (1818–95), poet, was born Humphreys in Eccles Street, Dublin, spent her girlhood in Wicklow and moved to Strabane, County Tyrone, in 1833 when her father became land steward to the Duke of Abercorn. In 1851 she married William Alexander and eventually moved to Derry when he was made Bishop of

Derry and Raphoe. She wrote much verse, most of it sacred, but her *Hymns for Little Children* (1848) contains the three pieces which have made her name famous: 'All Things Bright and Beautiful', 'Once in Royal David's City' and 'There Is a Green Hill Far Away'. She died in Derry and is buried there.

Allingham, William (1824–89), poet and diarist, was born in Ballyshannon, County Donegal, and worked as a customs officer in different posts in Ulster until he settled in England in 1863 and eventually (1874) became editor of *Fraser's Magazine*. His early poems were published anonymously and sold as halfpenny broadsheets. He was an associate member of the Pre-Raphaelite Brotherhood and a friend of Carlyle and Tennyson. *Poems* (1850) contains most of his best known work, including 'The Fairies'. A longer poetic work, *Laurence Bloomfield in Ireland* (1864), on the subject of philanthropic landlordism, and his *Diary* (1907) are useful nineteenth-century sources. He married Helen Paterson the artist (1848-1926) in 1874. Though Protestant, he found the 'Kelts' very congenial but could not bring himself to write a history of Ireland: 'lawlessness and turbulency, robbery and oppression, hatred and revenge, blind selfishness everywhere – no principle, no heroism. What can be done with it?' (*Diary*, 11-xi-1866). He died in Hampstead and was buried, in accordance with his wishes, in Ballyshannon.

All Souls' Night (1948), play by Joseph Tomelty* which deals with poverty and thrift in a fishing family on Strangford Lough. Katherine Quinn has by miserliness acquired a substantial sum of money on which she will not even touch the interest. Her husband John and son Michael are forced to carry on their perilous trade with inferior equipment and a dangerously small boat and she refuses to provide money for a deposit on a better vessel. At the Feast of the Dead, as the locals call it, Michael's older brother Stephen, who was lost at sea, is prayed for, and Michael, heading out on a hazardous job of salvage, is also drowned. He returns, speaking an effective poetic language devised by the author, and it becomes clear that Stephen too was driven to death by his mother's avarice.

Amongst Women (1990), novel by John McGahern*, tells the story of Moran, a violent and repressive ex-freedom fighter who cannot adjust to life in the new Ireland, which, he feels, betrays everything he fought for in the War of Independence. A domineering patriarch, he exerts huge psychological pressure on his children and second wife Rose, eventually driving all but her away from him. Such is the hold that Moran has over his daughters that they are never truly free until he dies, when they seem to absorb his strength. *Amongst Women,* with its measured, unadorned and beautifully crafted prose, was a major critical and popular success.

Amory, Thomas (c. 1691–1788), novelist, was born in Ireland and educated at TCD. He studied Medicine for a while before retiring to live an urban life of leisure in Dublin (where he was a friend of Swift*) and London. His main works are *Memoirs of Several Ladies of Gt Britain* (1755) and *The Life and Opinions of John Buncle* (1756 and 1766), both mixtures of biography, fiction and philosophy. He was a Unitarian, like the philosophical hero of his second book who marries seven beautiful women. His later life, spent in London, was reclusive. He died there.

Anderson, Paris (c. 1790–1860), novelist, was born most likely in Kilkenny and served in the militia there. He wrote essays for the *Kilkenny Moderator* which were later published as *Nooks and Corners of the County Kilkenny* (1914). His novel *The Warden of the Marshes*, which is set in the county in the fourteenth century, has as one of its characters the famous witch Dame Alice Kyteler.

ANGLO-IRISH WAR, THE (1919–21), the War of Independence, fought mainly guerilla-style and largely in Dublin and the south, with Michael Collins as commander of the IRA. With the RIC unable to cope, two forces were recruited, the execrated Black and Tans and the even more ruthless Auxiliaries ('Auxies'). Hostilities ceased in July 1921 and an Anglo-Irish Treaty was signed on 6 December 1921. A section of Republicans, led by Éamon de Valera, repudiated the Treaty and the Civil War* ensued.

annals, the, manuscript sources for Irish history, generally dating from between the fourteenth and the seventeenth centuries. They were usually compiled by scholars of learned families to preserve the dynastic and political details of their kingdoms or regions. They include the *Annals of Clonmacnoise, Annals of Connacht, Annals of Inisfallen, Annals of Loch Cé, Annals of the Four Masters*, *Annals of Tighearnach* and *Annals of Ulster*.

Annals of the Four Masters (*Annála Ríoghbachta Éireann/Annals of the Kingdom of Ireland*), history of Ireland compiled between 1632 and 1636 at the Franciscan friary at Bundrowse, County Donegal by Franciscan brother Micheál Ó Cléirigh and three other scholars. These were the 'four masters*' of the popular title, the other three being Cúchoigríche Ó Cléirigh, Fearfasa Ó Maolchonaire and Cúchoigríche Ó Duibhgeannáin. The history was a deliberate attempt to salvage from various records the story of Gaelic Ireland after the collapse of the old order with the Battle of Kinsale (1601) and the Flight of the Earls (1609). The *Annals* range from 'forty days before the Flood' to AD1616. They have been invaluable as a source for Irish history since the coming of Christianity and particularly for the period from 1500 to 1616.

AOSDÁNA, set up in 1983 and administered by the Arts Council, is a government-supported group of artists. Its 200 members are entitled to a substantial annual tax-free *cnuas* (subsidy): the sum is £8,500 in 1998. Up to five members may be elected as *Saoi* (wise person). *Saoithe* so far elected have included Sean O'Faolain*, Mary Lavin*, Benedict Kiely* and Seamus Heaney*.

ARAN ISLANDS, three islands, Inis Mór, Inis Meáin and Inis Oírr (resp. 'great', 'middle' and 'east' islands), which lie northwest-southeast across the mouth of Galway Bay, about thirty miles from Galway city. Rich in mainly monastic archæological remains from pre-Christian, early Christian and medieval times, the islands have played a significant part in modern Irish literature. Synge*, who spent some weeks each summer from 1898 until 1902 mainly on Inis Meáin, found the source of much of his work there and devised an appropriate Hiberno-English in which to express it. *The Aran Islands* (1907) describes his time there and he set his play *Riders to the Sea* (1904) on Inis Meáin. Liam O'Flaherty* was born on Inis Mór, as were his nephew Breandán Ó hEithir* and the poet Máirtín Ó Direáin*. Robert Flaherty made his film *Man of Aran* there in 1935. Its modern laureate is the cartographer Tim Robinson.

ARANMORE, island off west Donegal, seven miles northwest of Dungloe, which supplied the main topography of three of Peadar O'Donnell*'s novels: *The Storm*, *Islanders** and *Proud Island*.

Armstrong, George Francis Savage (1846–1906), poet, was born in County Dublin and educated at TCD. He was Professor of History and English literature at Queen's College, Cork, and died in County Down. His poetic reputation rests on *Stories of Wicklow* (1886). He was very interested in his mother's family, the Savages of Ards, wrote their history in 1888 and added Savage to his name. His verse was so highly regarded by the end of the century that on Tennyson's death in 1892 he was proposed as Poet Laureate by the Irish press.

Arnold, Bruce (b. 1936), novelist, art historian, political and literary editor, was born in London and educated at Kingham High School, Oxfordshire, and TCD, graduating in English and French. He has been a literary and political journalist, both staff and freelance, with many Irish papers and magazines and is at present literary editor of the *Irish Independent*. He is the author of the four novels of the Coppinger sequence, *A Singer at the Wedding* (1978), *The Song of the Nightingale* (1980), *The Muted Swan* (1981) and *Running to Paradise* (1983), which presents a gripping picture of youth and manhood in the two postwar decades, as much informal social history as fiction. Other works reflect Arnold's preoccupations and expertise, with much writing on art, literature and politics, and include *Orpen: Mirror to an Age* (1969), *Mainie Jellett and the Modern Movement in Ireland* (1991), *The Scandal of Ulysses* (1991) and *Haughey: His Life and Unlucky Deeds* (1993).

As I Was Going Down Sackville Street (1937), the first and best of Oliver St John Gogarty*'s books of reminiscence about his Dublin life from 1900 to 1930. Gogarty was successfully sued for his portrayal of an antique dealer and he left Ireland soon after. It was typical of his grand manner that he should use the old name of Dublin's main thoroughfare.

At Swim-Two-Birds (1939), Flann O'Brien*'s first and best novel, which incorporates much parody of Gaelic literature and many narrative modes, from pulp fiction to intrusive author, the structure complicated by the fact that the main character, a less than industrious undergraduate at UCD, is writing a book about a man writing a book, and believes that fictional characters are entitled to lives of their own. The book, which had a cult following in Ireland, has now become an internationally appreciated text about texts.

Autumn Fire (1924), T. C. Murray*'s best known play, about the attraction between a widower, Owen Keegan, and a local girl, Nance Desmond. The possible match is strongly resisted by Keegan's daughter Ellen and his son Michael, who wants Nance for himself.

B

Ballad of Reading Gaol, The
(1898), prison poem written by Oscar
Wilde* and detailing mainly the
reaction to the hanging of a murderer
during his time there. It also indicates
Wilde's own response to his imprisonment and 'that little tent of blue/That
prisoners call the sky'.

Banim, John (1798–1842) and
Banim, Michael (1796–1874),
novelists, were born in Kilkenny and
together wrote a series of novels (the
attempted equivalent of those of Sir
Walter Scott) that aimed to present the
Irish in an acceptable light to the
British. It was John who, after the
severe trauma of a tragic love affair,
suggested writing the O'Hara tales.
Twenty-four books followed, of which
thirteen were done by Michael. Though
overly sentimental and with Irish lo-
cutions embarrassingly rendered, they
gave an honest picture of post-Union
Ireland, with its tithe and repeal
struggles and its violent secret society
culture, that showed the way for better
writers. Of most significance are the
contemporary tales, for example
Croboore of the Billhook (1825) and
The Mayor of Windgap (1835), both by
Michael, and *The Nowlans* (1826) by
John who also wrote the historical
novel *The Boyne Water* (1826). In *The*

Croppy (1828) Michael, by now a
prosperous Kilkenny merchant and
briefly mayor of the city, tended to play
down the violence and question the
wisdom of the United Irishmen. John,
who died prematurely of the spinal
tuberculosis that blighted his life, is also
the author of the well known poem
'Soggarth Aroon'.

Banville, John (b. 1945), novelist, was
born in Wexford and educated at St
Peter's College. He has been a journalist
since 1969 and is at present literary
editor of *The Irish Times*. His first book
Long Lankin (1970) is a collection of
linked stories with a novella which incorporates most of the characters, the
effect being a kind of literary Tarot
pack. *Nightspawn* (1971) is a deliberately confusing novel about Greece in
1967, the year of the Generals'
takeover. *Birchwood* (1973) is a piece
of Irish Gothic set in a Big House at an
uncertain date and including a spon-
taneous combustion. Banville's next
four novels are a consideration of the
imaginative lives of such scientists as
Copernicus, Kepler and Newton. *The
Book of Evidence* (1989) and *Ghosts*
(1993) deal with the moral life of a
confessed murderer, Freddie Montgomery, who, having 'explained' his
action in the first book, finds himself on

an island full of noises. Banville is a modern novelist in the critical sense, exploring the meaning and nature of fiction as he creates his often cold cerebral characters. His most recent novel is *The Untouchable* (1997).

Banville, Vincent (b. 1940), novelist, short story writer and critic, was born in Wexford and educated at UCD. He taught in Nigeria, using his experiences there in *An End to Flight* (1973), a powerful novel about the Biafran War written as by 'Vincent Lawrence'. He also contributed some striking short stories for David Marcus's 'New Irish Writing' page in the *Irish Press*. Subsequently, on retirement from teaching, he produced a number of funny, subversive children's books featuring his resourceful creation Hennessy and some excellent hardboiled thrillers, the mean streets being Liffeyside.

Barber, Mary aka 'Sapphira' (*c.* 1690–*c.* 1757), poet, and wife of an English-born Dublin tailor, began to write verse as part of her children's education and became one of Swift*'s circle. Her *Poems on Several Occasions* (1734) did not sell, but the Dean allowed her to publish his *Polite Conversations* (1738), the proceeds of which enabled her to live in frugal comfort in spite of chronic arthritis and gout.

Barrington, Margaret (1896–1982), novelist and short story writer, was born in Malin, County Donegal, in 1896 and educated in Dungannon and TCD. She married Edmund Curtis the

historian in 1922 and Liam O'Flaherty* in 1926. She wrote many short stories, a selection of which was published in *David's Daughter, Tamar* (1982) five months after her death, and a semi-autobiographical novel, *My Cousin Justin* (1939). She worked as a left-wing journalist in London during the 1930s and spent the last forty years of her life in west Cork.

Barry, Michael Joseph (1817–89), poet and journalist, was born in Cork and became a barrister and an enthusiastic Young Irelander, being imprisoned in 1843. In later life his politics changed and he became a police magistrate. His verses 'The Arms of 'Eighty-Two' and 'The Wexford Massacre', written for *The Nation**, are appropriately patriotic but he wrote much comic verse as well, often using the pseudonym *Bouillon de Garçon* (Broth of a Boy) and anticipating Percy French's refrain, 'Ses he.'

Barry, Sebastian (b. 1955), poet, playwright and novelist, was born in Dublin, the son of actress Joan O'Hara, who has often appeared in his plays, including the latest, *Our Lady of Sligo* (1998), based upon stories told about a grandmother he never knew. Barry studied Latin and English at TCD and spent most of his twenties in France and Greece. His novels include *Macker's Garden* (1982), about adolescence, *Time out of Mind* (1983), about a 1930s loveless marriage, and *The Engine by Owl-light* (1987). His play *Boss Grady's Boys* (1988) is a study of ageing and sibling rivalry set in Kerry, and *Prayers of Sherkin* (1990) describes the decay of a fundamentalist sect on Sherkin Island, near Cape Clear in County Cork. *The Steward of Christendom* (1995), about the memories of the former head of the DMP as he lies in a lunatic asylum, was one of the most significant Irish plays of the 1990s. Barry has also published two volumes of poetry. Another novel, *The Whereabouts of Eneas McNulty*, appeared in 1998.

Bax, Sir Arnold (1883–1953), composer and man of letters, was born in London and eventually became a distinguished composer and Master of the King's Musick (1942). He came to Ireland in 1905 and became in effect an Irish writer, calling himself 'Dermot O'Byrne' and making friends not only with the literary figures but also with the 1916 leaders. His banned poem 'A Dublin Ballad – 1916' contains the lines: 'To all true Irishmen on earth/Arrest and death come late and soon.' He wrote verse, plays and stories about Ireland and died in Cork.

Beckett, Mary (b. 1926), novelist and short story writer, was born in Belfast and worked as a teacher until 1956, when, on marriage to a civil servant, Peter Gaffey, she went to live in Dublin. Her early stories were printed in *Threshold**, *Irish Writing** and *The Bell** but it was not until 1980 that a selection of them was published as *A Belfast Woman*. This was followed by the award-winning novel *Give Them Stones* (1987) and *A Literary Woman*

(1990). She has also written beautifully crafted stories for children.

Beckett, Samuel (1906–89), novelist and playwright, was born in Dublin and educated at Portora Royal School*, Enniskillen, and TCD. He taught French in Campbell College, Belfast, and English in Paris, where he became a kind of amanuensis to Joyce*. He lectured for some time in TCD and, after a period of depression and much travelling, settled in Paris in 1937. He elected to remain in France during the German occupation, working with the French Resistance and earning the Croix de Guerre. Back in Paris, Beckett wrote his best novel, *Molloy* (1951), a depiction of life's hopelessness and the myth of reality, which was applauded by the Parisian élite and followed by two other books, *Malone Dies* (1951) and *The Unnamable* (1953), to form a trilogy with the same preoccupations. Much more popular was *Waiting for Godot** (1949) which caused equal amounts of approval and dismay. (Its English language première was presented at the Pike Theatre* in Dublin.) Other plays, notably *Endgame* (1957), *Krapp's Last Tape* (1958) and *Happy Days* (1961), used disease, physical disability and various forms of restraint to convey aridity and ultimate dissolution, the last-named requiring one of the two characters to remain largely silent while the other, his wife Winnie, talks incessantly while buried up to her waist in sand (to her neck in Act II). Later work grew ever more terse but was still done in well-wrought prose with a remarkable number of Irish allusions. The short plays, often directed by himself and featuring such actors as Jack McGowran and Billie Whitelaw, had stage directions as sacrosanct as the text. The bleak austerity in Beckett's work was matched by a personal reticence; he did not attend the ceremony for the award of the Nobel Prize in 1969 and resolutely refused to be photographed, filmed or interviewed, none of this detracting from his reputation as a modern master.

Behan, Brendan (1923–64), playwright, was born in Dublin and educated by the Christian Brothers and his own well-read and heritage-saturated family. He joined Fianna Éireann, the cadet branch of the IRA, while learning the trade of painting from his father, who had been interned during the Civil War*. He was arrested in 1939 for taking part in a bombing campaign in England and spent three formative years at borstal in Suffolk. On his release he returned to Ireland and in 1942 was sentenced to fourteen years in prison for attempting to kill a detective. He was released after serving five years and resumed his trade, although determined to be a writer. One of his earliest pieces 'I Become a Borstal Boy' appeared in *The Bell** in June 1942 and Behan was strongly encouraged to write by Sean O'Faolain*. The years of incarceration eventually yielded Behan's best book *Borstal Boy* (1958) and his finest play *The Quare Fellow**(1954), which had already been offered to the Abbey as *Casadh Súgáin*

Eile (*A Curtsy to Hyde*) but which was first performed in the Pike Theatre*. Because of the success of *The Quare Fellow* in London and some lively television appearances, Behan, who had had a following at home because of *Irish Press* pieces (published as *Hold Your Hour and Have Another* in 1964) and a Nighttown reputation for drink and wit, became public property. *The Hostage* (1958), which was adapted by Joan Littlewood until the original play (staged as *An Giall* in An Halla Damer) was almost lost in a revue, increased his worldwide reputation. The years of success were marked by alcoholism and sadly neglected diabetes, and though Behan made many attempts to dry out, he died prematurely. The tape-recorded books of his later years were edited by an indulgent secretary, Rae Jeffs, seconded from his publisher Hutchinson.

Bell, Sam Hanna (1909–90), novelist, short story writer and broadcaster, was born in Glasgow of Scots-Irish parents but, after the death of his journalist father, came 'home' to live in County Down and later in Belfast. After many different occupations, including nightwatchman, he joined the BBC in Belfast in 1945 and was Senior Features Producer till 1969. He wrote many radio features and some plays, and did much to collect the vanishing folklore of the province, but his most important work was as a writer of historical fiction in which he portrays, as no other writer, the psyche of the Ulster working-class Protestant, both rural and urban. His first and most famous novel *December*

Bride*(1951), set near Strangford Lough, the scene of his adolescence, describes a notorious *ménage à trois*. It was later successfully filmed. *The Hollow Ball* (1961) is set in the poverty-stricken Belfast of the 1930s; *A Man Flourishing* (1973) is concerned with the growth of Belfast from radical village to conservative Victorian industrial city; and *Across the Narrow Sea* (1987) is a romance after the manner of Scott about the seventeenth-century Ulster Plantation. His collection of short stories, *Summer Loanen,* appeared in 1943. Other work includes *Erin's Orange Lily* (1956), an account of Ulster folkways, and *The Theatre in Ulster* (1972).

BELL, THE (1940–54), a monthly literary and cultural journal founded by Peadar O'Donnell* and Sean O'Faolain*, who was its editor until 1946, when O'Donnell, who had been business manager, took over. It published material from many contemporary Irish writers, including Brendan Behan*, Mary Beckett* and Sam Hanna Bell*, whose earliest work appeared there, and it actively encouraged contributors from the North. As well as poetry and fiction from professional writers, the editor asked for pieces from anyone with a wish to write – 'You who read this know intimately some corner of life that nobody else can know' – and helped to realise that wish. The journal showed an isolated, somewhat smug Ireland its own face, challenged set attitudes of Church and State and prepared the ground for the growth of a more liberal country.

Bergin, Osborn (Osborn Ó hAimhirgín) (1872–1950), poet, editor and scholar in Irish, was born in County Cork and educated at UCC, where he joined the Gaelic League and lectured for a time, and in Germany. He was appointed Professor of Irish in UCD in 1908. His scholarly work included writings on bardic poetry and an edition of parts of Seathrún Céitinn*'s *Foras Feasa ar Éirinn** but he is also remembered for the much-anthologised poem 'Maidin i mBéarra' which was published in a collection of the same name and may be sung to the air of 'Danny Boy'.

Berkeley, George (1685–1753), philosopher and Anglican Bishop of Cloyne, was born in County Kilkenny and educated at Kilkenny College and TCD, becoming a Fellow in 1707. He was appointed Dean of Derry (which he never visited) in 1724, and with the money left him by Esther Vanhomrigh in despite of Swift*, tried to establish a seminary in Bermuda in 1728. He lived for three years in Rhode Island waiting for the grant. It was here that he wrote his poem 'On the Prospect of Planting Arts and Learning in America', the first line of which is: 'Westward the course of empire takes its way'. He returned to Ireland in 1731 and was appointed Bishop of Cloyne in 1734, retiring because of ill health in 1752. He died in Oxford the following year. Berkeley was friendly with all the great literary figures of the time and had a keen social conscience. His major philosophical work is *A Treatise concerning the Principles of Human Knowledge* (1710) and his concerns about the condition of Ireland are to be found in *The Querist**.

Berkeley, Sara (b. 1967), poet and short story writer, was born in Dublin and educated at TCD. Two precocious collections of poetry, *Penn* (1986) and *Home-Movie Nights* (1989), marked her out for special praise. She spent some time working in California after taking her degree and subsequently published a collection of short stories, *The Swimmer in the Deep Blue Dream* (1991), and two further collections of poetry, *New and Selected Poems* (1994) and *Facts About Water* (1995). She is one of the most individual and original voices among the young Irish poets.

Bennett, Ronan (b. 1956), novelist, was brought up in Belfast. He is the author of three novels, *The Second Prison*, *Overthrown by Strangers* and *The Catastrophist* (1998), an accomplished work set in 1959–60 in the Congo at the time of the post-colonial civil war but with a kind of relevance to Northern Ireland. He has also written books of non-fiction, including *Double Jeopardy*, about the Guildford Four affair, and screenplays for film and television.

Binchy, Maeve (b. 1940), novelist and journalist, was born in Dublin and educated at UCD. She spent some years teaching before joining the staff of *The Irish Times* in 1969, where her droll, honest articles made her very popular. Her first books were collections of well written, engaging stories set in London and middle-class Dublin, but it was with *Light a Penny Candle* (1982), about the friendship between two girls, Aislinn and Elizabeth, from strikingly different backgrounds in the arctic Ireland of the 1940s and 1950s, that she made her name. She has written many bestselling novels since, including *Firefly Summer* (1987), *Silver Wedding* (1988), *Circle of Friends* (1990), which was made into a successful film, *The Glass Lake* (1992), *Evening Class* (1996) and *Tara Road* (1998), all noted for readability, humour and excellent character sketching.

Birmingham, George A. (pseudonym of Canon James Owen Hannay) (1865–1950), novelist and playwright, was born in Belfast and educated at Haileybury and TCD. He was ordained in 1889 and served as rector in Westport, County Mayo, from 1892 till 1913. He became an army chaplain in 1916, vicar of Mells, Somerset, in 1924, and after his wife's death in 1933 served in a quiet London parish. His prolific writing began as a means of supplementing his stipend, and from *The Seething Pot* (1905) to *Two Scamps* (1950) he wrote sixty novels out of a total of eighty published works. Many of these are frothy but very entertaining humorous books, and the ones set in Ireland give a genial but accurate account of the author's country. In spite of a unionist background he was a nationalist and counted among his friends Horace Plunkett*, Arthur Griffith, Standish James O'Grady* and Douglas Hyde*. When his play *General John Regan* (1913) was done by a touring company in Westport in 1914, the rector had the unsettling experience of seeing himself burnt in effigy in his beloved town by Catholics he took to be his friends. This naïvety (or determined satiric purpose) was shown again in the dedication of his novel *Up the Rebels* (1919) to 'any friends I have left in Ireland'. (The novel, written two years after the Easter Rising*, was a humorous account of a bloodless Irish insurrection.) His understanding of the Ulster Protestant temper was precise, as his novel of the United Irishmen's rising of 1798, *The Northern Iron* (1907), showed, and his dark comedy about the UVF, *The Red Hand of Ulster* (1912), was partially prophetic about inevitable partition. Like many another liberal, wounded by the intransigence of the Irish 'situation', he found life in England, especially in neo-Trollopean close quarters, more congenial than at home.

Blackburne, E. Owens (pseudonym of Elizabeth Casey) (1848–94), novelist, was born in Slane, County Meath. She lost her sight as a child but regained it after an operation by Sir William Wilde* when she was eighteen. This enabled her to graduate from TCD and begin a career in journalism in London in 1874. Her first novel *In at the Death* was serialised in *The Nation** and published as *A Woman Scorned* (1876). It had the theme of many of her score of novels: the difficulties faced by professional and other women in a male-dominated society. The novels *Molly Carew* (1879), *The Glen of the Silver Birches* (1880) and *The Hearts of Erin* (1883) have Irish heroines and deal with such contemporary problems as the Land League

and relations between Ascendancy and native Irish. Her concern for women was evidenced in her publication of a collection of short biographies, *Illustrious Irish Women* (1877), the first work of its kind. She returned to live in Ireland and died in a house fire at Fairview, Dublin.

Blacker, William (1777–1855), Orange poet, born in Carrickblacker near Portadown, became, like his father, a colonel in the Seagoe Orange Yeomanry (raised to counter the United Irishmen). He remained happily anti-Catholic and became a kind of laureate of Orangeism, acquiring a proverbial fame as the author of ' . . . put your trust in God, my boys, and keep your powder dry' from the poem 'Oliver's Advice'. *Ardmagh* (1848) is a verse chronicle of the Protestant cathedral in Armagh from earliest times to the Act of Union. His poem 'Carmel' sees the Famine as 'the correcting hand of God'.

Black List, Section H (1971), autobiographical novel by Francis Stuart* in which H, the protagonist, lives out Stuart's own life, including his internment after the Civil War*, his marriage to Iseult Gonne, his time in Germany during and after WWII, his meeting with the woman who became his second wife. The novel depicts his extreme suffering as a kind of forge for his art.

Blackwood, Caroline (1932–96), novelist, was born in County Down, the daughter of the Fourth Marquis of Dufferin and Ava. She married Lucien

Freud and later became Robert Lowell's third wife. Her first book *For All That I Found There* (1974) is a fascinating collection of autobiography and exotic reportage. Her novels include *The Stepdaughter* (1976), a wry tale of the emotional neglect of a girl by a deserted wife, *Great Granny Webster* (1977), an Ulster Big House black comedy with lots of madness and cruelty, and *Corrigan* (1984), about a charismatic and therapeutic con-man. Other works include *In the Pink* (1987) and *Last of the Duchess* (1996).

BLASKET ISLANDS, group of islands southwest of the Dingle peninsula in County Kerry, traditionally reached by currach from Dunquin. The largest, the Great Blasket, *An Blascaod Mór*, was inhabited until 1953, when all remaining inhabitants were moved to the mainland. The islandmen and women eked out a living from rocky ground and treacherous sea but the Irish they spoke and their cultural traditions were very rich and ancient, and the island became a mecca for folklorists, ethnographers and Irish-language enthusiasts. Native laureates included Tomás Ó Criomhthain* (*An t-Oileánach* : *The Islandman*, 1929), Muiris Ó Súilleabháin* (*Fiche Blian ag Fás*: *Twenty Years a-Growing*, 1933) and Peig Sayers* (*Peig*, 1936), all of which have been translated into English. English scholar Robin Flower was a regular visitor to the island, translated many island writers including Tomás Ó Criomhthain and wrote a classic account, *The Western Island* (1945).

Blythe, Ernest (1889–1975), politician, theatre administrator and Irish-language activist, was born in Lisburn, County Antrim. Despite his Protestant background he became an Irish language enthusiast and republican, a member of the Gaelic League* and the IRB, and a participant in the 1916 Rising*, the War of Independence* and the Civil War*. He was a Cumann na nGaedhal minister in the Free State government until he lost his seat in 1933. He was responsible for making the Abbey Theatre* the first government-granted theatre in the West but his fanatical devotion to the revival of Irish hampered artistic development during his management of the theatre (1941–67) and he has been severely blamed for the shortcomings of its productions. Blythe also founded the government-funded Irish-language publishing venture, An Gúm*, and encouraged the Galway-based Taibhdhearc* theatre. He published a collection of poetry and two volumes of autobiography.

Bodkin, M[athias] McDonnell (1849–1928), novelist, was born in Tuam, County Galway, and educated at Newman's Catholic University (later UCD). He was Nationalist MP for North Roscommon and became a county court judge in Clare. He wrote humorous stories and novels of the kind that a more straitlaced age would with unnecessary sensitivity call 'stage-Irish'. These included *Poteen Punch* (1890), *Patsy the Omadhaun* (1909) and *Kitty the Madcap* (1927). He also wrote historical novels about Lord Edward Fitzgerald and Robert Emmet. His pseudonym was 'Crom a Boo' and his book of memoirs, *Recollections of an Irish Judge*, was written in 1914.

Boland, Eavan (b. 1944), poet, was born in Dublin, the daughter of F. H. Boland, sometime President of the United Nations General Assembly. She was educated in London, New York and Dublin, graduating from TCD and briefly lecturing there. She is one of Ireland's leading poets, formally concerned with the position of women in Irish society, and a kind of laureate of urban domesticity. The story of Ireland's past and its modern reverberations inevitably play their part in her work. Her published collections include *New Territory* (1967), *The War Horse* (1975), *In Her Own Image* (1980), *Night Feed* (1983), *Outside History* (1990) and *In a Time of Violence* (1994). She has also published a book of prose, *Object Lessons* (1995). A *Collected Poems* appeared in 1995. She is married to the novelist Kevin Casey* with whom she has two daughters.

BOLG AN TSOLÁIR (1795) was a single edition Irish-language magazine, compiled by the Gaelic scholar Patrick Lynch and published by the *Northern Star*, the Belfast paper of the United Irishmen. Its effect on the later fortunes of the Irish language was significant.

Bolger, Dermot (b. 1959), novelist, poet and playwright, was born in the north Dublin suburb of Finglas and worked as a factory hand and librarian before becoming a writer and publisher.

The district of his birth and the nearby countryside play significant parts in his fiction. The novel *Night Shift* (1985) was based upon his industrial experiences, while *The Woman's Daughter* (1987, revised 1991) deals with incest and violence, and moves freely between the present and the Victorian past. The novel, in triptych form, is darkly erotic and, like *Emily's Shoes* (1992) and *A Second Life* (1994), has male obsession as its main preoccupation. In the latter book a man saved miraculously from certain death after a car accident uses his second life to find the mother who gave him up for adoption. The world of Bolger's imagination is dark and unforgiving, and there is in his work a sense of social injustice and loss of childhood innocence (identified with the numinous topography of his chosen region). He founded the Raven Arts Press in 1979 and continues to foster Irish writing in New Island Books, of which he is editorial director. His most recent novel is *Father's Music* (1997). He has had four plays produced in Dublin theatres, of which two, *April Bright* and *Blinded by the Light*, were published in 1997.

BOOKS IRELAND, monthly periodical founded by Jeremy Addis in 1976, which provides comprehensive coverage of books of Irish interest in Irish and English. Shirley Kelly and Alan Titley are contributing editors and the publication is valued for trenchant and sometimes provocative independent reviews.

Boran, Pat (b. 1963), poet and short story writer, was born in Portlaoise, County Laois. His poetry collections include *The Unwound Clock* (1990), *Familiar Things* (1993) and *The Shape of Water* (1996). He has also published a volume of short stories *Strange Bedfellows* (1991). He has been editor of *Poetry Ireland Review* and Writer in Residence for Dublin Corporation.

Boucicault, Dion[ysius Lardner] (1820-90), actor and playwright, was born in Dublin to the sister of the poet George Darley* who had separated from her husband, Samuel Boursiquot, a Huguenot wine merchant, a year before Dion's birth. His father, Dr Dionysius Lardner, was a lodger in the mother's Lower Gardiner Street house and became the boy's guardian. After a year at London University the young Boucicault became an actor, using the name 'Lee Moreton' and by 1841 had written his first great success, *London Assurance*. He became one of the most prolific of nineteenth-century playwrights, being credited with 150 plays. They were mainly melodramatic adaptations which used the 'sensation' effects that were becoming available in the larger theatres: buildings collapsing in fire, trains, horse races, ships that sailed across the diorama, and mobile transparent ghosts. In 1844 he married a rich aristocratic French woman who died in mysterious circumstances four years later. His second wife was the actress Agnes Robertson and she played the lead in his most famous plays, *The Colleen Bawn* (1860) – adapted from Gerald Griffin*'s *The Collegians* (1829) – *Arrah na Pogue* (1864) and *The Shaughraun* (1874). *The Octoroon* (1859) was the first play to deal with the black population of the United States and *The Poor of New York* (1857) could with simple titular adjustment play in Liverpool, Dublin or Boston. In 1885 he eloped to Australia with Louise Thorndyke, an actress less than half his sixty-four years in age. He died in comparative poverty in New York. Boucicault, who was a brilliant comic actor, appeared in most of his own plays. His works were particularly popular in Ireland, in spite or because of their 'stage-Irishism', and among those who learned dramaturgy from them in the Queen's Theatre in Dublin were, at different times, Shaw* and O'Casey*. One scene in *Arrah na Pogue*, including some dialogue, was taken over by Shaw for *The Devil's Disciple* (1897).

Bourke, P[atrick] J. (1883–1932), playwright, was born in Dublin. He was attached to the Queen's Theatre as actor, company manager and eventually playwright. His works were essentially romantic patriotic melodramas which dealt mainly with the heroes and heroines of 1798, notably *The Wexford Rose* (1910) and *For the Land She Loved* (1915). He also wrote and produced one of the first Irish films, *Ireland a Nation* (1913). Like Boucicault* and O'Keeffe* he used music to good effect in his plays, devising a form between melodrama and comic opera.

Bourke, Ulick J. (1829–87), Irish language activist, was born in Castlebar County Mayo in 1829 and ordained at Maynooth for the Tuam archdiocese in 1858. While still a student he published *College Irish Grammar* (1856) and was appointed Professor of Irish, Logic and Humanities at his old school, St Jarlath's, becoming president in 1865. He became parish priest of Claremorris in 1878 and remained there till his death. He devised simple lessons in Irish which were published in *The Nation**. He was first Chairman of the Society for the Preservation of the Irish Language (SPIL) at its founding in 1876, and at the inevitable split went with David Comyn to found the Gaelic Union in 1880 and to edit *Irisleabhar na Gaedhilge* (*The Gaelic Journal*). Both these societies were necessary forerunners of the Gaelic League*.

Bowen, Elizabeth (1899–1973), novelist and short story writer, was born in Dublin into an Anglo-Irish family that had settled in Doneraile, County Cork, in the seventeenth century. (The house at Bowen Court was burned during the War of Independence.) She left school at seventeen, published her first book *Encounters*, a collection of short stories, in 1923, and married Alan Cameron, an educationalist, the same year. In all she wrote seven novels noted for their poetic sensitivity and their impressive understanding of adolescent girls. *The Last September* (1929) and *A World of Love* (1955) were set in Ireland, the first dealing with the emotional awakening of Lois Farquahar, niece of the Naylors of Danielstown House in Tipperary, during the Troubles of 1920, the second with the eventually relieved obsession of young Jane Danby with the dead Guy Montfort, the former owner of a Big House. Her finest novel *The Heat of the Day* (1949), like the short story collection *The Demon Lover* (1945), gives a remarkable picture of wartime London in which she served as an air-raid warden. She was a frequent visitor to Ireland during those years, on semi-official business for the Ministry of Information, with a brief to report on national attitudes to the war. Of her ninety stories the ten set in Ireland, though small in number and written comparatively late, show her as a significant writer on Irish themes.

Boyd, John (b. 1912), playwright, was born of working-class parents in east Belfast and educated at Inst, QUB and TCD. Like Sam Hanna Bell* and John Hewitt*, he became a committed socialist in the 1930s and helped found in 1943 the magazine *Lagan**, which blazed its intellectual light amid the encircling sectarian and philistine gloom. He gave up teaching in 1947 to join BBC NI as a producer. On retirement in 1972 he became literary adviser to the Lyric Theatre*, edited its journal *Threshold** and wrote a number of plays about the sectarian and violent nature of NI, including *The Flats* (1971), *The Farm* (1973) and *The Street* (1977). He has written two volumes of autobiography, *Out of My Class* (1985) and *The Middle of My Journey* (1990).

Boyd, Thomas (1867–1927), poet, was born in Carlingford, County Louth, and worked as a solicitor in Manchester and London. His poetry, romantic and mainly based on Celtic legends, some of it written originally for Arthur Griffith's *United Irishman*, was published in *Poems* (1906) and regularly anthologised.

Boylan, Clare (b. 1948), novelist and short story writer, was born and educated in Dublin and until 1984 worked as a journalist and magazine editor. Her first book, *A Nail in the Head* (1983), was a collection of stories, lively and wry, mainly about disappointments in love. This was followed in the same year by *Holy Pictures*, a blackly comic novel about growing up in Dublin which introduced Nan Cantwell, whose forebears appear in *Home Rule* (1992). The title of the former refers ambivalently to old icons and new movies. Other work includes the novels *Black Baby* (1988), *The Stolen Child* (1996) and *Room for a Single Lady* (1997) and collections of stories such as *Concerning Virgins* (1989) and *Another Family Christmas* (1997).

Boyle, Patrick (1905–82), novelist and short story writer, was born in Ballymoney, County Antrim, and educated at Coleraine Academical Institution. He spent forty-five years in service with the Ulster Bank, twenty of them in County Donegal, where many of his stories are set. His first collection *At Night All Cats Are Grey* (1966) was published when he was already in his sixties and it was followed by his only novel, *Like Any Other Man* (1966), a mordant rework-ing of the biblical story of Samson. Other collections of stories, all marked by dark humour and an acceptance of the existence of cruelty in life, are *All Looks Yellow to the Jaundiced Eye* (1969) and *The View from Calvary* (1976). He became a bank manager in Wexford and retired in 1968.

Boyle, William (1853–1922), playwright, was born in Dromiskin, County Louth, and worked as a customs officer. His stories are collected in *A Kish of Brogues* (1899) but his claim to literary fame subsists in three plays written for the Abbey Theatre*, *The Building Fund* (1905), *The Eloquent Dempsey* (1907) and *The Mineral Workers* (1907), all documentary comedies dealing natural-istically with small-town Irish life. The character of Jerry Dempsey, the time-serving publican in *The Eloquent Dempsey*, a play Yeats* found 'inexpres-sively vulgar', struck a chord in con-temporary audiences, and Dempsey's wife's charge, 'You're like Lanna Machree's dog – a bit of the road with everyone', has become proverbial.

Breathnach, Pádraig (b. 1942), novelist, short story writer and essayist in Irish, was born in Moycullen, County Galway. He is lecturer in Irish in Mary Immacu-late Training College, Limerick. He has published several collections of stories, including *Bean Aonair* (1974), *Úosla agus Scéalta Eile* (1992) and *An Pincín agus Scéalta Eile* (1996), and a novel, *Gróga Cloch* (1990). *The March Hare and Other Stories* (1994) is a collection of his stories translated by Gabriel Rosenstock*.

Brennan, Rory (b.1945), poet and critic, was born in Westport, County Mayo, grew up in Dublin and was educated at TCD. He worked in broadcasting and as administrator of Poetry Ireland and for a time lived with his family on a Greek island. His first collection, *The Sea on Fire* (1978), won the Patrick Kavanagh Award. He has published two further collections, *The Walking Wounded* (1985) and *The Old in Rapallo* (1996).

Broderick, John (1927–89), novelist, was born in Athlone, the only son of a prosperous baker. Financial independence allowed him a freedom that other Irish writers of the time could not usually attain, to write as he chose about the dark side of Irish sexuality and small-town life. Broderick was bisexual; there is in all his books an interest in the epicene and homoerotic, and his view of women, especially in his early novels, *The Pilgrimage* (1961), *The Fugitives* (1962) and *The Waking of Willie Ryan* (1965), tends towards the misogynistic. He eventually found Ireland oppressive and spent the last years of his life in comfortable if lonely exile in Bath. He retained an interest in Irish affairs, especially in the changes of Church attitudes and in the fortunes of the Irish in England, as *The Trial of Father Dillingham* (1975), *The Pride of Summer* (1976) and *London Irish* (1979) show. The NI Troubles upset and fascinated him – *The Fugitives* dealt with IRA activity in the late 1950s – and themes of murder and madness, as in *The Rose Tree* (1985), began to appear in his later work. His last completed novel, his eleventh, was *The Flood* (1987), intended to be the first of a 'Bridgeford trilogy' and set somewhat nostalgically in the Athlone of the 1930s. It viewed the world with a more benign eye – that glimpsed in the comparatively light *Don Juaneen* (1963) – and the mood was of forgiveness and a sense of kinder times. He died before the trilogy could be completed; the second volume, the unfinished *The Irish Magdalen*, was published in 1991.

Brooke, Charlotte (?1740–93), Irish language enthusiast, was born in Rantavan, County Cavan, the only one of the twenty-two children of Henry Brooke (?1703-83) to survive him. (He had some reputation as a playwright, poet, novelist and pamphleteer, whose anti-Catholic writings, associated with his fear of possible support for the Young Pretender, changed in time to pamphlets against the Penal Laws*.) She was brought up in County Kildare, educated by her father and encouraged by him to study Irish. She devoted any time left over from acting as secretary and later nurse to her father to collecting and translating many kinds of Irish verse (including material from the ancient sagas) and in 1789 published *Reliques of Irish Poetry*, which includes her own paraphrases and original text. After Henry's death unwise investments reduced her to near poverty but the publication of *Reliques* and her edition of his works somewhat restored her fortunes. Some of her translations were published in *Bolg an tSoláir** (1795).

Brown, Christy (1932–81), novelist, was born in Crumlin, Dublin, severely handicapped with athenoid paralysis. He revealed a remarkable intelligence when, after being for years considered mentally retarded, he began drawing on the floor with a piece of chalk gripped between his toes. He was taught to speak by his mother and given effective speech and coordination therapy by Robert Collis, who encouraged him to publish in 1954 an autobiography called *My Left Foot*, typed pedally on an old typewriter. *Down All the Days*, a novel of childhood, followed in 1970. Brown continued to be the main argument of his book, other novels about middle-class characters being less effective. His first volume of poetry *Come Softly to My Wake* (1971) was, like his first two books, a bestseller. He married a Kerry nurse in 1972 and lived with her in Kerry and Somerset, where he died suddenly. Jim Sheridan's film of *My Left Foot* (1989) with Daniel Day-Lewis in the leading part, won many awards.

Brown, Stephen (1881–1962), bibliographer, was born in Holywood, County Down, and after education at Clongowes was ordained a Jesuit priest in 1914. He founded the Central Catholic Library in Merrion Square, Dublin, in 1922, already having compiled two invaluable bibliographical surveys: *A Guide to Books on Ireland* (1912) and *Ireland in Fiction* (1919), a fuller version of *A Reader's Guide to Irish Fiction* (1910). The manuscript of a second volume of fiction summaries, unfinished at the time of his death in a car accident, and dealing with the years 1918–60, was completed by the bibliographer Desmond Clarke (1907–79) as *Fiction in Ireland* (1985). His accounts of works by Irish authors and other books about Ireland have critical comments in which, not unexpectedly, literary considerations take second place to moral ones.

Browne, Frances ('The Blind Poetess of Donegal') (1816–79) was born in Stranorlar, the seventh of twelve children of the local postman, and lost her sight as a result of an attack of smallpox in infancy. She nevertheless attended school in the town, having Isaac Butt* as one of her fellow pupils, and acquired an education through hearing the other children repeating their lessons. She became a prolific author, publishing poetry, novels and a remarkable collection of fairytales, *Granny's Wonderful Chair* (1856), which was republished a dozen times, most recently in 1995. She moved first to Edinburgh in 1847 and later to London in 1852 (helped by a gift of £100 from the Marquis of Lansdowne) where she lived until her death of a heart complaint. She published an autobiography, *My Share of the World*, in 1861.

Buchanan, George (1904–89), novelist and poet, was born in Kilwaughter Rectory, County Antrim, the 'son of a country clergyman', and educated at Campbell College, Belfast. He became a journalist in London and served in the RAF during WWII. Collections of poetry include *Conversation with Strangers*

(1959) and *Inside Traffic* (1976), which have as one of their main themes the soullessness of urban life. His first significant novel was *Rose Forbes* (1937), which was enlarged in 1940. It describes the life of an Ulsterwoman who seeks fulfilment in three husbands and occasional affairs. The uneasy, sectarian life of the early years of the NI state are well conveyed but the book and its successor *A Place to Live* (1952) suffer from a stilted and mannered style. This latter novel is partially based upon Buchanan's wartime experiences. His version of his own life, *The Green Seacoast* (1959), describes mainly his childhood in the troubled decade 1910–19.

Bulfin, William (1864–1910), journalist, was born in Derrinlough near Birr in County Offaly, and educated in Birr, Banagher and Galway Grammar School. Emigrating to Argentina in 1884, he was a pampas cowboy for four years before becoming a contributor to and eventual editor of the *Southern Cross*, a paper run for the Irish community in Buenos Aires. Returning to Ireland in 1902, he became a strong supporter of Arthur Griffith* and travelled about Ireland on his bicycle. The pieces written about his tours for the *United Irishman* and *Sinn Féin* were collected in the slightly misnamed *Rambles in Eirinn* (1907). The book is nationalist, showing a strong bias against northern Protestants and West Britons, and contains some of the unthinking anti-Semitism of the day. He died at his birthplace.

Bullock, Shan F[adh] (1865–1935), novelist, was born at Crom, County Fermanagh, son of the land steward of the Earl of Erne. He was educated in Westmeath and became a civil servant in London. His quasi-Gaelic Christian names he took from a character in Carleton*'s *Traits and Stories*, changing them from John William in a gesture of solidarity with Catholic neighbours in Fermanagh whom he felt were socially and economically disadvantaged by the Orange Order. His Irish novels and stories, *By Thrasna River* (1895), *Dan the Dollar* (1902) and *The Loughsiders* (1924), are set on Lough Erne in Fermanagh and urge a non-sectarian community spirit among the hard-working small farmers of the area. They are characterised by precise observation of both traditions and their emotional and economic interdependency and by a nostalgia for the simple, goodly, industrious life remembered from a happy childhood. Bullock collaborated with Emily Lawless* in a novel of the French invasion of Connacht in 1798, *The Races of Castlebar* (1915).

Bunbury, Selina (1802–82), travel and fiction writer, was born in Kilsaran, County Louth, the daughter of a Methodist clergyman who went bankrupt when she was seventeen. To supplement the family income she became a schoolteacher and began writing sketches for the various journals of the time. Her first books, *A Visit to My Birthplace* (1820), *Cabin Conversations and Castle Scenes* (1827), *Early Recollections* (1829) and *Tales of My*

Country (1833), give an interesting picture of pre-Famine Ireland and though good-humoured are firmly proselytising. She moved to Liverpool and lived with (and kept) her twin brother until his marriage in 1845. Here her evangelistic tendency became muted. She became an energetic traveller in later life and wrote about her journeys in successful travel books. She is credited with up to a hundred titles which include historical romances and devotional tracts for children. She died in Cheltenham.

Bunting, Edward (1773–1843), collector of Irish music, was born in Armagh and went on his father's death in 1782 to live in Drogheda with his eldest brother Anthony who was an organist and music teacher. He discovered a precocious musical talent in himself and was established in Belfast as a teacher while still in his early teens, living in the house of Henry Joy McCracken, the United Irishman. Bunting's name is especially associated with the Belfast Harp Festival which was held in 1792, since he transcribed the traditional airs which might otherwise have been lost. His interest was so stimulated that he travelled in Ulster and Connacht on collecting expeditions, producing in 1796 the *General Collection of the Ancient Music of Ireland*, which contained sixty-six airs. (Thomas Moore* adapted many of these to fit his verse in the *Irish Melodies*.) His second collection, published in 1809, contained seventy-seven airs, most taken down from Denis Hempson, the blind harper of Magilligan, County

Derry, who was a hundred years old. A final volume, *Ancient Music of Ireland*, containing 120 new airs, appeared in 1840. Bunting was by that time living in Dublin, having moved there in 1819 on his marriage to Mary Ann Chapman. He continued to teach music and was organist of St Stephen's, Mount Street. He is buried in Mount Jerome.

Burke-Kennedy, Declan (b. 1944) was born in County Offaly. A founder-director of Dublin's Focus Theatre, he has had several plays produced, including *The Trespasser* (1973), *Hood* (1975–76) and *The Day of the Mayfly* (1980). Since 1980 he has worked for the *Irish Times*. His novels are *Robert's Alibi* (1988) and *Leonie* (1995).

Burke, Edmund (1729–97), orator and political philosopher, was born in Arran Quay, Dublin, the son of a Protestant lawyer and a Catholic mother, Mary Nagle from County Cork. Educated at TCD, he moved to London as a young man and produced a number of works of serious but varied character, among them a philosophical treatise on aesthetics (1757) and an incomplete history of England. He undertook from 1758 the editing of the *Annual Register*, a record of the events of the time. Opting for a career in politics, he spent a period back in Ireland in the 1760s and was later elected to parliament in Westminster, which led to his production of a long series of pamphlets and speeches on contemporary crises and problems. Particularly notable were his *Thoughts on the Causes of the*

Present Discontents (1770) and some outstanding speeches in favour of conciliating the American colonists, such as *On American Taxation* (1774) and *On Conciliation with America* (1775). Two other causes engaged his attention: the government of India and the state of his native land, particularly the disabilities of the Catholic community. These resulted in speeches such as those impeaching Warren Hastings (1778), and his *Letter to Sir Hercules Langrishe* (1792). It was the issue of the French Revolution that evoked Burke's most widely read and contraverted work, especially *Reflections on the Revolution in France* (1790) and *Appeal from the New to the Old Whigs* (1791). In these his ferocious opposition to the revolutionaries, his upholding of religion and his defence of the privileges of the different orders of society were clearly displayed. Even towards the very end, his power and pugnacity in riposte were evident. In his final years he was deeply engaged in trying to make the Irish administration adopt a more conciliatory policy towards the Irish Catholics, fearing what might happen. He may very well have been the most eloquent Irishman who ever employed the English language.

Burnside, Sam (b. 1943), poet, was born in mid-Antrim and educated at UU at Coleraine and Magee College, Derry. He taught for some years before becoming WEA organiser for the northwest. He was the founder of the Verbal Arts Centre in Derry and was editor of and contributor to *The Glow*

upon the Fringe (1994) a celebration of many writers who originated in the area. He has published two books of verse: *The Cathedral* (1981), really a single poem, which won a Hennessy Award, and *Walking the Marches* (1990), a personal response to life in the North.

Butler, Hubert (1900–90), man of letters, was born near Bennetsbridge, County Kilkenny, and educated at Charterhouse and Oxford. After some teaching in Egypt and the Balkans he travelled in Asia Minor and America. He helped to revive the Kilkenny Archaeological Society in 1945. His writings against the conservatism of the Ireland of the 1940s and 1950s and his exposure of the ethnic attacks by Catholic Croatians against Serbians during WWII made him unpopular but he maintained his intellectual independence. He was associated with *The Bell** during Peadar O'Donnell*'s editorship and in time began to be appreciated for his courtly integrity and the excellence of his essays, which were collected in *Escape from the Anthill* (1985), *The Children of Drancy* (1988) and *Grandmother and Wolfe Tone* (1990).

Butt, Isaac (1813–79), statesman, was born in Cloghan, County Donegal, the son of a Protestant rector who moved to Stranorlar a year later. He was educated in the Royal School, Raphoe, and at TCD which he attended at age fifteen having come first in the entrance examination. His father died while he was still an undergraduate and his university career was beset by the drudgery of teaching private pupils. In 1838 he became Professor of Political Economy and was called to the bar, becoming a QC in 1844. He gave up the academic life in 1841 for the richer pickings of the courts but he never became even comfortably off, once serving a term in prison for debt. His conservatism and opposition to O'Connell* were mitigated by the events of the Famine and he defended Smith O'Brien and Thomas Meagher after the 1848 Young Ireland rising. (He later defended many Fenians in the years 1865–9, foregoing lucrative briefs to do so.) His Unionism never recovered from the economic and humanitarian disaster of the 1840s and as MP for Youghal (1852–65) he began to advocate a federal system of devolved power which was the beginning of agitation for Home Rule, a term he invented. He founded the Home Government Association in 1870 and later the Home Rule League. After seven years as MP for Limerick he was replaced by Parnell* as leader of the Nationalist Parliamentary Party in 1878. Butt remained a reluctant agitator and proved too gentlemanly for the new Irish party. His fiction includes *Chapters of a College Romance*, mainly tragic stories about TCD undergraduates, which first appeared in the *Dublin University Magazine* under the pseudonym 'Edward J. O'Brien', *Irish Life in the Castle, the Court and the Country* (1840), which has as hero a lawyer with Nationalist friends, and *The Gap of Barnesmore* (1848), set in 1688 during the Jacobite War and making a plea for reconciliation between Catholic and Protestant. His socio-economic works include *Land Tenure in Ireland* (1866), *The Irish Querist* (1867) and *The Problem of Irish Education* (1875).

Byrne, Donn (pseudonym of Brian Oswald Donn-Byrne) (1889–1928), novelist, was born in New York but brought up in Armagh and Antrim. He learned Irish at UCD and also attended the Sorbonne and Leipzig, returning to New York in 1911. He wrote many stories for popular magazines and an autobiography, *The Rock Whence I Was Hewn* (1929). Among many sentimental romantic novels about Ireland, the most popular are *Blind Raftery* (1924), *Hangman's House* (1924) and *Destiny Bay* (1928). Two novels stand out for their psychological conviction: *Brother Saul* (1925), a gripping account of the career of St Paul, and *The Power of the Dog* (1929), a sympathetic portrait of Lord Castlereagh, the architect of Pitt's Act of Union and Liverpool's foreign secretary. Byrne lived in Dublin from 1922 to 1925 before moving to County Cork where he died in a car accident in Courtmacsherry.

Byrne, Seamus (1904–68), playwright, was born in Dublin and graduated LLB from UCD. He practised law in Leitrim for nine years until his arrest in 1940 for IRA involvement. Though given a two-year sentence, he was released nine months later after a three-week hunger strike. His play *Design for a Headstone*, about hunger-strikers in Mountjoy Jail was produced in the Abbey* to the accompaniment of right-wing protests.

He was drama critic for the *Catholic Standard* in the 1950s and his play *Little City*, rejected by the Abbey because of its theme – abortion – was staged by the Gate* in 1964 as part of the Dublin Theatre Festival. He died in Dublin.

C

Caddell, Cecilia Mary (1813–77), novelist, was born in County Meath. A lifelong invalid, she contributed to Catholic periodicals and wrote historical novels, notably *Blind Agnes* (1856) and *Nellie Netterville* (1867), which were set in the period of the Cromwellian campaigns in Ireland. The novels, popular in their time, were translated into French and Italian.

Caisleáin Óir (1924), best known novel of Máire* (Séamus Mac Grianna). This often bitter account of Rosses (County Donegal) life describes the young love of Seimí Phádraig Duibh for Babaí Mháirtín, his parting to labour in Scotland and the long years of exile before his return from the Yukon a rich man. The last chapter describes his slow journey home and his meeting with the faithful Babaí, no longer young or beautiful. He leaves, unrecognised, with the words, ostensibly about the weather: *'Is é atá,' arsa Séimí, 'fuar, fuar.'*

Callaghan, Mary Rose (b. 1944), novelist, playwright and biographer, was born in Dublin and graduated from UCD in 1962. She taught in Dublin and England, returning to Dublin to take up a career as journalist, dictionary editor and writer. Her novels include *Mothers* (1982) and *Confessions of a Prodigal Daughter* (1985). *A House for Fools* (1983) is about love and mental illness. Her most recent novel *Emigrant Dreams* (1996) is set in America. She has also written a biography of Kitty O'Shea (1989).

Callanan, Jeremiah Joseph (1795–1829), poet, was born in Ballinahassig, County Cork, and studied for the priesthood at Maynooth. He left in 1816 (before ordination) and attended TCD for two years before poverty drove him to enlist in the British army. Bought out, he joined the staff of Dr Maginn's school. He already had some reputation as a poet, mainly of English versions of Gaelic poems that he had collected, notably 'Droimeann Donn Dílis' and 'Príosún Cluain Meala'. He attempted a Byronic sequence with *The Recluse of Inchidoney* (1830) but is now remembered mainly for 'The Outlaw of Loch Lene' and the lyric 'Gougane Barra'. He fell in love with Alicia Fisher but they parted because she was a Methodist and refused to become a Catholic. He died of a throat infection aggravated by tuberculosis when working as a tutor to a Cork family living in Lisbon.

Call My Brother Back (1939), Michael McLaverty*'s first and best-loved novel, is set partly in Rathlin* and partly in the Belfast of the Anglo-Irish War*, the danger increased by added sectarian freelancers. The McNelis family have had to leave their home on the island after the death of their father and at the urging of Alec, the eldest son, and live in a Belfast slum. The book is mediated through the child Colm whose confusion and sadness the reader shares. Sent as a boarder to a college in Belfast by the local curate, he pines for his family and the life he knew, but his joy at regaining them is marred by the realisation that Rathlin is lost to him forever. The family's grief becomes unbearable when Alec is shot as a Volunteer. McLaverty's pleasure in the bustle and life of what was in normal times a friendly city shines through his account of urban life.

Campbell, Joseph (Seosamh Mac Cathmaoil) (1879–1944), poet and playwright, was born in Belfast and educated at St Malachy's College. He left school at the age of sixteen suffering from a debilitating condition resulting from scarlatina. His enforced idleness was put to good effect so that by the time he was twenty and running his father's construction business with the help of his younger brother John, he had become extremely well-read in poetry and Irish history and heritage. He was naturally drawn to the Ulster Literary Revival* with its periodical *Uladh** and plays presented in the Ulster Hall. He wrote a play, *The Little Cowherd of Slaigne* (1905), and set words to traditional airs that had been collected by the composer Herbert Hughes. These were published as *Songs of Uladh* (1904) as by Seosamh Mac Cathmaoil, with decorations by his brother as Seaghan Mac Cathmaoil. Among the songs was the famous 'My Lagan Love' which has since become a standard concert piece. Other collections of poetry followed: *The Rushlight* (1906), *The Gilly of Christ* (1907) and *The Mountainy Singer* (1908). He settled in Lackendarragh, County Wicklow, with his wife Agnes Maude in 1912. Always of strong Nationalist feelings, he was peripherally involved in the Easter Rising* and as a known republican was interned for eighteen months in the Curragh during the Civil War*. He lived in the United States from 1925, having parted from his wife. He returned to Ireland and lived a reclusive life on a small farm in Glencree until his death.

Campbell, Michael (1924–84), novelist, was born in Dublin and educated at TCD and King's Inns. He became *Irish Times* London correspondent and author of several novels: *Peter Perry* (1956), about Dublin art circles, *Oh Mary, This London* (1961), *Across the Water* (1961) and *The Princess in England* (1964), about the Irish in Britain. His best known work *Lord Dismiss Us* (1967) deals with homosexuality in his old school, St Columba's. He became Fourth Baron Glenavy on the death of his brother Patrick in 1980.

Campbell, Patrick (1913–80), humorist, was born in Dublin, brother of Michael Campbell* and son of the Second Baron Glenavy, acceding to the title in 1963 on the death of his father. He was educated at Oxford, the Sorbonne and in Germany. He served in the Irish Marine Service during the war and was on the staff of *The Irish Times* from 1944 till 1947 under Smyllie*, becoming its wittiest 'Quidnunc' and third-leader writer. He continued as a humorous columnist for the rest of his life, working for London papers, including the *Sunday Dispatch* and *Sunday Times*. A slight speech impediment he turned to advantage, finding copy in the disability and overcoming it sufficiently to become a much-loved personality on television. His articles were reprinted in sixteen volumes, including *The P-p-penguin Patrick Campbell* (1965) and *A Short Trot with a Cultured Mind* (1952), a title which sums up his comic genius. He died in Cannes, his home in later life.

CAMPBELL'S COFFEE HOUSE, meeting place in the 1930s and 1940s of a band of Ulster writers and artists, 'young men consumed with a terrible thirst for culture', as Sam Hanna Bell*, one of their number, described them. The company might include 'Richard Rowley*' (Richard Valentine Williams, 1877–1947) who founded the Mourne Press; John Boyd* (b. 1912), when he could spare the time from teaching; Joseph Tomelty* (1911–95) who had left his trade of decorating to become an actor and playwright and co-founder of the Ulster Group Theatre*; Denis Ireland* (1894–1974) who, like Rowley, retired from a family business and was for many years a freelance journalist; Jack Loudan, the Armagh playwright who was to be Amanda McKittrick Ros*'s biographer. There were also the artists Willie Conor (1881–1968), Gerard Dillon (1916–71) and George Campbell (1917–79), with occasional irruptions from John Hewitt* and the engineer John D. Stewart who wrote stories and plays. Separated brethren who looked in on visits north from Dublin were Lynn Doyle* (Leslie A. Montgomery), Rutherford Mayne* (Samuel Waddell) and Cathal O'Shannon (1889–1969) the trades union activist.

Campion, John Thomas (1814–90), poet and novelist, was born in County Kilkenny, where he practised as a physician. He wrote stories for *The Nation* and the *United Irishman* and published a number of historical novels, including *Alice* (1862), about the fourteenth-century Kilkenny witch, and *The Last Struggles of the Irish Smugglers* (1869), set in Wicklow at the turn of the century.

Cannon, Moya (b. 1956), poet, was born in Dunfanaghy, County Donegal and studied at UCD and Corpus Christi College, Cambridge. Her collections are *Oar* (1990) and *Murdering the Language* (1996). She has given readings in Ireland and abroad and her work has been broadcast and set to music. In 1996 she was editor of *Poetry Ireland Review*.

Carbery, Ethna (pseudonym of Anna MacManus, née Johnson) (1866–1902), poet, was born in Ballymena, County Antrim. She contributed many poems to *The Nation** and the *United Ireland* and with Alice Milligan* founded in 1896 the nationalist paper the *Shan Van Vocht* (orig. the *Northern Patriot*). It was suppressed after three years because of unionist complaint and the existence of a stronger Sinn Féin journal, Arthur Griffith's the *United Irishman*. She married Seumas MacManus* in 1901. Her poetry, mainly patriotic, including the famous ballad 'Roddy McCorley' and 'The Passing of the Gael' (quoted by Joxer in *Juno and the Paycock**) was published in *The Four Winds of Ireland* (1902). Her prose was collected as *The Passionate Hearts* (1903), stories set in the west of Ireland, and *In the Celtic Past* (1904).

Cards of the Gambler, The (1953), Benedict Kiely*'s imaginative novel which mixes folklore and a realistic story, the elements of magic and cleverness, the symbols and significant locations, wonderfully and wittily matched.

Carey, Matthew (1760–1839), journalist, was born in Dublin and emigrated to the United States. He founded the *Pennsylvania Herald* in 1785 and published *Carey's American Atlas* (1795), the first of its kind. His *Vindiciae Hibernicae* (1819), a counterblast against unionist accounts of 1641, was popular with nineteenth-century nationalist historians.

Carleton, William (1794–1869), novelist, was born to a family of Irish-speaking farmers at Prillisk in the Clogher Valley of County Tyrone. He was the youngest of fourteen children and inherited from his mother a store of *béaloideas* which stood him in good stead in his avocation. His memories of youth were entirely idyllic and his account of poor nineteenth-century Irish peasantry is unmatched. His education was the rough and ready but remarkably extensive one of the hedge scholar, and in the largely autobiographical *Traits and Stories of the Irish Peasantry** (1830) he shows acquaintance with experiences as diverse as Lough Derg pilgrimages, faction fights and Ribbonism. At first he fancied that he might become a priest but in Dublin he came under the influence of the fanatical Protestant proselytiser Caesar Otway, who recognised from the conversation of the young travelling tutor that he would be a suitable writer for his journal, the *Christian Examiner*. Carleton's sketches, though suitably anti-papist, took on a life of their own. His work caught the attention of Maria Edgeworth who helped obtain for him a Civil List pension, the acceptance of which was regarded as further proof of his renegadism. His sense of priority was that of the poor peasant survivor and he managed to contain his psychological dissonance by writing for anyone who would pay him and drowning his unease in drink. Though he continued to live in Dublin, he still wrote of the people he knew, and such realistic novels as *Fardorougha the Miser*

(1839), *The Black Prophet: A Tale of the Famine* (1847) and *The Tithe Proctor* (1849) show his genius at its best.

Carnduff, Thomas (1886–1956), poet and playwright, was born in Belfast and, though a committed socialist, was prominent in the Independent Orange Order. He worked in the shipyard, took part in the UVF gun-running (1913) and served in WWI. He wrote proletarian ballads, rather like those of Patrick MacGill* and Robert Service, and had five plays staged in the Abbey* and the Empire Theatre by the Belfast Repertory Company, notably *Workers* (1932). He also contributed to special issues of *The Bell** in 1941 and 1951.

Carney, Frank (1902–?), playwright, was born in Galway, worked for many years as a civil servant in the Old Age Pensions Department and wrote several plays for the Abbey*. *The Righteous Are Bold* (1946), about demonic possession, was very popular and is still revived by amateur companies.

Carney, James (1914–89), Gaelic scholar, was born in Portlaoise and educated at UCD and Bonn. Professor in the Dublin Institute of Advanced Studies, he was an authority on Old and Middle Irish poetry. His published works include *The Problem of St Patrick* (1961) and *Early Irish Poetry* (1965).

Carr, Marina (b. 1964), playwright, was brought up in County Offaly and educated at UCD. She worked for some time as a teacher in New York. Her plays *This Love Thing* (1990), *Ullaloo* (1991) and *The Mai* (1994) were first staged in the Peacock, and she is regarded as a leading young playwright. *Portia Coughlan* (1997) is a more recent work.

Carroll, Paul Vincent (1900–68), playwright, was born in Annagassan near Dundalk and educated at St Patrick's College, Dublin. He taught for sixteen years in Glasgow (1921–37) until the success of *Shadow and Substance* enabled him to live on his earnings as a playwright. In such Ibsenite plays (though with Irish settings) as *The Things That Are Caesar's* (1932), *The White Steed* (1939) and *The Wise Have Not Spoken* (1944) he railed against mercenariness and puritanism, considering them both alien to true Christianity, a stance that had him dubbed anticlerical. *Shadow and Substance*, which had a Broadway success, concerned the intellectual struggle between a priest and a teacher, both of whose lives are affected by an innocent servant girl who has visions of St Brigid (the patron of Carroll's home area). Later works, especially *The Devil Came from Dublin* (1951) and *The Wayward Saint* (1955), were lighter but still effectively satirical. He died in Bromley, Kent, his home since 1945.

Carson, Ciaran (b. 1948), poet, was born in Belfast and educated at QUB. He worked as a teacher and civil servant before becoming Traditional Arts and Literature Officer with the Arts Council of NI, which he joined in 1975. He has published four collections of verse: *The New Estate* (1976), the prizewinning *The Irish for No* (1987), *Belfast Confetti* (1989), and *First Language* (1993). His work, which is informed by his bilingualist command of Irish, is concerned with the diverse cultures of Ulster, the magic capacities of language and the experience of the Troubles, the whole imbued with a straight-faced but gleeful humour. He has also written books on Irish traditional music, including *Last Night's Fun* (1996), and a memoir cum oral history, *The Star Factory* (1997).

Cary, [Arthur] Joyce [Lunel] (1888–1957), novelist, was born in Derry, a member of a family that had held land at Castle Cary near Moville in Inishowen since the reign of Elizabeth I. The family fortunes were then in decline and Cary was reared in London where his father was a civil engineer. Holidays were spent in his grandmother's house in Inishowen and, though most of the novels – notably *Aissa Saved*(1932), *Mr Johnson* (1939) and *The Horse's Mouth* (1944) – which have made him a major figure in English literature are set in England and Nigeria (where he served as district officer from 1917 until 1920), two, *Castle Corner* (1938) and *A House of Children* (1941), draw heavily upon experiences of the summer place and paint a picture of life in a decaying Big House, without Somerville & Ross gothicism, but as half-understood by an intelligent child. Cary lived in Oxford from 1920 until his death of motor neurone disease.

Casey, John Keegan (1846–70), poet, was born near Mullingar, the son of a teacher. He taught school himself and later worked as a clerk until his arrest as a Fenian in 1867. He contracted tuberculosis in prison and, released with generally weakened health, was unable to recover from injuries sustained in a traffic accident on the Dublin quays. His funeral was attended, it is said, by 50,000 people, a tribute to both his politics and his verse. As 'Leo' he was a regular contributor to *The Nation** and his famous ballad 'The Rising of the Moon' was written when he was fifteen. His verse, both pastoral and patriotic, including the love song 'Máire, My Girl', was published in *A Wreath of Shamrocks* (1866) and *The Rising of the Moon* (1869).

Casey, Juanita (b. 1925), novelist, short story writer and poet, was born in England to a family of travellers. Her Irish mother died in childbirth and her English father abandoned her when she was a year old. She was educated by wealthy patrons and later became horsemaster in a circus. Her fiction – a collection of stories, Hath *the Rain a Father?* (1966), and novels *The Horses of Selene* (1971) and *The Circus* (1974) – is characterised by comic, vibrant language, rich prose, a sense of sisterhood and a strong empathy for animals. Her work, including some 'unpoetic' poetry, is often illustrated by her own drawings.

Casey, Kevin (b. 1940), novelist, was born in Kells, County Meath, and educated at Blackrock College, Dublin. The production of *The Living and the Lost* (1962) made him the youngest Abbey* playwright ever. He is best known for his novels, especially *The Sinner's Bell* (1968) which is a bleak account of a blighted marriage and seems to epitomise the repressed Ireland of the 1950s. *A Sense of Survival* (1974) and *Dreams of Revenge* (1977) are about 'ordinary' heroes facing violent situations, the first set in Tangiers, the second involving the IRA in west Belfast. He is married to Eavan Boland*.

Casey, Philip (b. 1950), poet and novelist, was born in London and brought up in Gorey, County Wexford. His poetry collections include *After Thunder* (1985) and *The Year of the Knife: Poems 1980–1990* (1991). His play, *Cardinal*, was performed in Hamburg in 1991 and an award-winning novel, *The Fabulists*, set in Dublin and focusing on the attempts made by a woman and a man to transcend the mundane in their search for a fulfilling sexual relationship, was published in 1994.

Castle Rackrent (1800), Maria Edgeworth*'s first and best novel and a significant key to the understanding of the Ireland of the Act of Union and the decline and fall of the landlord class. The story is narrated by Thady Quirk, an old family retainer, who is a marvellously unreliable witness. His account of the rackety Rackrents, Sir Patrick the lavish sot, Sir Murtagh the litigious miser, Sir Kit the unuxorious gambler and Sir Condy the ineffectual politician, is deliberately comic but not entirely inapplicable to the unabsentee landlord classes of the time. Sir Walter Scott praised it as the first of the 'regional' novels and its Hiberno-English register provided a language for the novelists and playwrights that followed.

CASTLETOWNSHEND, village in County Cork, site of Drishane House, birthplace of Edith Somerville* whose many works of largely comic fiction written with her cousin Violet Martin used a judicious mixture of its topography and that of the wilder scenery of Ross House, Moycullen, Martin's home.

CATHLEEN NÍ HOULIHAN, one of the many personifications of Ireland as a woman. The name appears as the title 'Caitlín Ní Uallacháin' of an aisling* by Liam Dall Ó hIfearnáin*, the heroine waiting for the return of Charles Stuart who would restore her to glory. Others are 'Róisín Dubh', the 'Sean Bhean Bhocht' and 'Granuaile' ('Gráinne Umhaill', based upon the historical character Grace O'Malley, the sixteenth-century Mayo chieftain).

Céitinn, Seathrún (Geoffrey Keating) (*c.* 1580–*c.* 1644), historiographer and poet in Irish, was born at Burges near Cahir, County Tipperary, into a family of Norman extraction and of sufficient prosperity to send him to ecclesiastical colleges at Bordeaux and Salamanca. He returned to Ireland in 1607, a Doctor of Divinity, to serve as a curate for the parish of Tubrid near his birthplace. His

Foras Feasa ar Éirinn*, a groundwork for the history of Ireland written to counter the slanders of Giraldus Cambrensis, Edmund Spenser and other English writers. was completed by about 1634. Céitinn's poetic output was small but impressive. '*Óm Sceol ar Ardmhagh Fáil*' is about the dispersal of the Gaelic aristocracy after Kinsale and the Flight of the Earls, and '*Mo Beannacht Leat, A Scríbhinn*' is a nostalgic letter home from France. His famous poem '*A Bhean Lán de Stuaim*' shows an acquaintance with sensuality unexpected in a priest, especially the author of *Trí Biorghaithe an Bháis* (*The Three Shafts of Death*), a theological tract. Facts about Céitinn's life are obscure. There is a story that a sermon preached by him against a local squireen's mistress caused him to go into hiding, and another that he was murdered by Cromwellian soldiers in Clonmel in 1649. He is buried in Tubrid, County Tipperary

Celtic Twilight, The (1893), originally a book of folk and supernatural writings by Yeats* that claimed a special poetic vision for the residual Celts (which implicitly the Anglo-Saxons had lost). The idea became one of the main elements of the cultural nationalism which characterised the Irish Literary Revival*.

Cent[i]livre, Susannah (?1667–1723), playwright, was probably born in County Tyrone, the daughter of a Cromwellian client called Freeman. Details of her early life are obscure and romantic: co-habiting, dressed as a boy, with one Anthony Hammond at Cambridge, having had two husbands killed in duels, and after some years as a strolling player finally settling down in marriage with the French royal chef who tended both Queen Anne and George I. By then she had overcome anti-feminist prejudice to become a successful playwright. The best known of her nineteen plays are her first, *The Perjur'd Husband* (1700), and *A Bold Stroke for a Wife* (1718) which contains the character, 'the real Simon Pure'. She was assailed in Pope's *Dunciad* because of the perceived anti-Catholic and anti-clerical tone of her plays.

Chaigneau, William (1709–81), novelist, was born in Dublin, of Huguenot extraction, and lived there for the rest of his life, apart from service in the army in Flanders. In 1752 he published *The History of Jack Connor*, the first consciously Irish novel, which has as hero the offspring of a Protestant father and Catholic mother and tells of his picaresque adventures in Ireland and Europe. The picture of Ireland and the hero is sympathetic and implicitly critical of the contemporary stage-Irish stereotype.

Chambers, Anne (b. 1950), biographer, novelist and screenwriter, was born in Castlebar, County Mayo and took an MA in History at UCC. She is the author of four biographies, her subjects including Granuaile (Grace O'Malley), Eleanor, Countess of Desmond and the prima donna Margaret Burke Sheridan. She contributes features to the national and international press and to magazines, and has written documentaries for RTÉ. Her ambitious historical novel, *The Geraldine Conspiracy*, was published in 1994.

Cheasty, James (b. 1928), playwright, was born in County Waterford and is the author of several plays, including *The Lost Years* (1958), a study of strong farmers, and a novel, *The Captive* (1965).

Cherry, Andrew (1762–1812), playwright, was born in Limerick and became a strolling player before graduating to Drury Lane. His opera *The Outcast* (1796) was produced there, as were all of his fourteen plays. *The Soldier's Daughter* (1804) and his one-act opera *Spanish Dollars; or The Priest of the Parish* (1806) were regularly revived until the mid-century. He is the author of the song 'The Green Little Shamrock'. He died in Monmouth.

Cheyney, Peter (1896–1951), crime writer, was born Reginald Evelyn Peter Shorthouse-Cheyney in County Clare, and, after war service and work as a Fleet Street journalist, set up his own detective agency in 1932. Early experience as a law clerk and work in military intelligence gave a superficial authenticity to more than fifty thrillers (featuring either the FBI man Lemmy Caution, the private eye Slim Callaghan or both) written between 1936 and the year of his death. With such titles as *Dames Don't Care* (1937) and *Dark Wanton* (1948), these bestselling books were, in spite of much gore and political incorrectness, really romantic, escapist and very much of their time.

Childers, [Robert] Erskine (1870–1922), novelist and patriot, was born in London but spent much of his youth in Ireland. After education at Haileyborough and Trinity College, Cambridge, he became a clerk in the House of Commons. He fought in the Boer War and used his yacht *Asgard* to bring in guns to Howth for the Irish Volunteers in 1914. He was principal secretary for the Treaty negotiations but took the Republican side in the Civil War*. He was executed by a Free State firing squad in Beggar's Bush Barracks. His son, also called Erskine (1905–74), was Ireland's fourth President. His maritime thriller *The Riddle of the Sands* (1903), set in the Baltic and dealing with German preparations for an invasion of England, is a classic and was written to alert Europe to the reality of the German threat.

Children of the Dead End (1914), Patrick MacGill*'s first and best known novel, is set in the author's native Donegal, in County Tyrone and on construction sites in Scotland. Strongly autobiographical, its searing account of the conditions imposed upon migrant workers and its savage criticism of both employers and the unheeding Church caused it to be widely censured, and even more widely read, in Ireland. The story of Dermod Flynn, the navvy poet, is twinned, so to speak, with *The Rat Pit* (1915), which tells the unhappy story of his sweetheart Norah Ryan.

CIVIL WAR, THE (1922–23), the violent reaction to the Treaty which ended the Anglo-Irish War* and set up the Irish Free State. The terms agreed by the delegation headed by Michael Collins were rejected by Eamon de Valera and others in January 1922. Hostilities, which took the form of ambushes, assassinations and attacks on barracks, were conducted mainly in Munster (though the occupation and destruction of the Four Courts in Dublin effectively began the conflict) and continued until May 1923 when de Valera ordered a cessation. Among the 2,000 casualties were Collins, shot in an ambush in County Cork in August 1922, Rory O'Connor, Liam Mellows and seventy-five other Republicans, executed by the new government in reprisal for the assassination of TDs. A late victim was Kevin O'Higgins who was murdered in July 1927 because he had been a member of the cabinet which ordered the executions. The war left a legacy of deep bitterness which only recently ceased to dominate politics; it also gave the NI state an unexpected chance to establish itself.

CLAIDHEAMH SOLUIS, AN (1899–1930), the main journal of the Gaelic League*, which replaced Fáinne an Lae (begun on 8 January 1898). It was bilingual and popular and when Pearse* became its editor in March 1903 he shaped it to his own ends, educational and propagandist. It published Eoin MacNeill's pamphlet answer to the UVF, The North Began (1913).

Clarke, Austin [Augustine Joseph] (1896–1974), poet and verse-playwright, was born in Ðublin and educated at Belvedere and UCD. He succeeded in 1917 to the lectureship there left vacant by the execution of Thomas MacDonagh* but a mental breakdown and an unhappy and short-lived marriage to the playwright Geraldine Cummins led to a retreat to London in 1922. He supported himself there as a book reviewer for fifteen years, during which time he forged a poetic technique which would reflect in English the assonantal strength of Gaelic prosody. All of his writing is imbued with a sense of the Celtic past, as exemplified in the sagas, and the contrast between its perceived heroic sensuality and the national Catholic piety of the Ireland in which he grew up mirrored his own sexual guilt. In all he published eighteen books of poetry, from The Vengeance of Fionn (1917) to the Collected Poems (1974), the latter giving a map of his poetic progress, including the seventeen-year hiatus between Night and Morning (1938) and Ancient Lights (1955). The later poetry was notably satirical of his country and happily erotic, the Catholic Church's Laocoön-like coils shrugged off. During the 1930s Clarke wrote two of his three prose romances about medieval Ireland and founded the Lyric Theatre (arising out of his Dublin Verse-Speaking Society) for which he wrote eleven plays, published as Collected Plays (1963) and including The Son of Learning (1927) and the satirical Black Fast (1941). He wrote two books of autobiography, *Twice Round the Black Church* (1962) and *A Penny in the Clouds* (1968). Clarke, who stands with Heaney* and Kavanagh* as a leading poet of modern Ireland, died at his home in County Dublin.

Cleeve, Brian (b. 1921), novelist and dictionary compiler, was born in Essex of Irish parents and educated there until he ran away to sea at seventeen. He served in the merchant navy and counter-intelligence during WWII and worked as a journalist, travelling widely. He settled in Ireland in the 1950s and wrote many novels, including thrillers, historical romances and often seedy pictures of modern Dublin. *The Horse Thieves of Ballysaggert* (1966) is an interesting collection of short stories. He compiled a three-volume *Dictionary of Irish Writers* (1967–71) which he later expanded with Anne Brady as *A Biographical Dictionary of Irish Writers* (1985). His most recent book is a novel, *A Woman of Fortune* (1993).

Clifford, Sigerson (1913–85), poet and playwright, was born Edward Bernard Clifford in Cork, the adopted 'Sigerson' being his mother's surname. He spent his childhood in Cahirciveen and, having joined the civil service in 1932, served in Dungloe, Tralee and Dublin, which became his home in 1943. He is best known as the author of the song 'The Boys of Barr na Sráide' and though he wrote eleven plays, including *The Great Pacificator* (produced in the Abbey* in 1947), and published a collection of stories, *The Red-Haired Woman* (1989), the title of his 1955 collection, *Ballads of a Bogman*, sums up his particular genius. He made a version of Gerald Griffin*'s *The Collegians* to accompany William MacLysaght's reconstruction of the murder of Ellen Hanly in *The Tragic Story of the Colleen Bawn* (1953).

Clive, Kitty (1711–85), playwright, was born in Belfast, the daughter of William Rafter, a Kilkenny Jacobite lawyer. They moved to London and by 1731 Kitty was the leading comic actress of the day, having joined Colley Cibber's company in 1728. Her marriage to George Clive in 1731 lasted only a few months but they remained friends and she kept his name for her stage career and the four farces she wrote, including *The Rehearsal* (1753) and *The Faithful Irishwoman* (1765). Her forte was low comedy and burlesque of Italian opera, using a magnificent singing voice that won her a part in the first performance of Handel's *Samson*. She became a lifelong friend of the composer and also counted Dr Johnson, Gay and Horace Walpole among her intimates. When she retired she lived on Walpole's Strawberry Hill estate, in a cottage which became known as Cliveden.

Coady, Michael (b. 1939), poet, was born in Carrick-on-Suir, County Tipperary and still lives and works there as a teacher. He was educated locally, at St Patrick's College of Education, and at UCG and UCC. He has written short stories and the best kind of local journalism and published several collections of poems, including *Two for a Woman, Three for a Man* (1980), *Oven Lane* (1987) and *All Souls* (1998), all rooted in his dear perpetual place.

Cochrane, Ian (b. 1942), novelist, was born in County Antrim and in five disturbing novels emerged as that *rara avis*, a delineator of the feckless Ulster Protestant underclass. *A Streak of Madness* (1973), *Gone in the Head* (1974), *Jesus on a Stick* (1975), *Ladybird in a Loony-Bin* (1978) and *F for Ferg* (1980) – the overtones of lunacy in three of the titles are significant – portray life in housing estates where poverty, madness and violence are so self-centred that the endemic sectarian temper of NI seems to play no part. Cochrane emigrated to England while still a teenager and his later novel, *The Slipstream* (1983), has no particular Irish dimension, except that the main character Ron Connell may have come from Ireland and fits with little trauma into giro-cheque life in Notting Hill squats.

Coffey, Brian (1905–1995), poet, was born in Dublin, son of the Professor of Medicine and first President of UCD. He was educated at Clongowes and in France and studied science in UCD. He was one of Jacques Maritain's students of Philosophy and after taking his doctorate lectured in the subject in the mid-1950s in St Louis, Missouri. His first poems were issued with those of his friend Denis Devlin in 1930 but he wrote little in the next two decades until *Missouri Sequence* (1961–5).

Coffey, Charles (?1700–45), comic opera writer, was born in Dublin and became a schoolmaster. In his spare time he wrote comic opera libretti, both original and in adaptations from English and French. *The Beggar's Wedding* (1729) clearly owes much to John Gay, as does the inclusion of local ballads like 'Lillibulero' and 'Eileen Aroon'. Peg Woffington became the star of Smock Alley* when Coffey insisted that she be given the lead in his play *The Devil to Pay* (1731) which was an equal success in Drury Lane and continued in the repertory until 1800.

Coffey, Thomas (b. 1925), playwright and novelist, was born in Ennis, County Clare. He was educated at St Flannan's and afterwards became a teacher. His first full-length play *Stranger Beware*, set in west Kerry, was produced in the Abbey* in 1958, as was his farce *Anyone Could Rob a Bank* (1959). His best known play *Them* (1962) is about a family coping with a severely retarded child. A morality play *It Would Be Funny If It Wasn't So Bloody Ridiculous* was produced at the Lyric Theatre* , Belfast, in 1974. Since the mid-1960s Coffey has worked in business systems, the source of his satirical novel *Don't Get Mad, Get Even* (1996).

Coghill, Rhoda (b. 1903), poet, was born in Dublin and educated at Alexandra College and TCD. Known mainly as a composer, concert pianist and music teacher, she published two poetry collections, *The Bright Hillside* (1948) and *Time Is a Squirrel* (1956).

Coimín, Mícheál (1688–1760), poet in Irish, was born near Milltown Malbay, County Clare. He is the author of a long poem in traditional metre, *Laoi Oisín ar Thír na n-Óg*, and a prose romance taking its inspiration partly from the Fenian cycle, *Eachtra Thoirdhealbhaigh Mhic Stairn*.

Coláistí Samhraidh, Na, summer schools founded in the Munster (Ballingeary, County Cork, 1904), Connacht (Tourmakeady, County Mayo, 1905) and Ulster (Cloughaneely, 1906) gaeltachts to train Gaelic League* teachers where they might have access to native speakers. By 1910 the number of schools had risen to eight. There were also winter schools in Belfast and Dublin, with a number of native speakers on the staffs. The idea caught on and most gaeltacht areas, from Inishowen to Ring, had summer schools (usually local schools made available by the parish priests). The need for these adult colleges increased with the coming of the new state in 1921 as all teachers were required to have some competence in Irish. Since the 1930s the schools have been used mainly by secondary pupils combining holidays with language learning, though they are also used to meet the needs of undergraduate specialists and vocational groups.

Colgan, John (?1592–1658), hagiographer, was born near Carndonagh, County Donegal, and was ordained as a secular priest in 1618. He joined the Franciscan order in Louvain in 1620 and spent the next fourteen years lecturing in Theology at various colleges in Germany. Returning to Louvain in 1634 he was made Master of Novices and began his monumental work of hagiography, *Acta Sanctorum Hiberniae*, the first volume of which appeared in 1645. *Triadis Thaumaturgae*, which dealt specifically with Patrick*, Brigid and Colum Cille*, was published in 1647. Further volumes were compiled but shortage of funds and Cromwell's depredations in Ireland prevented their publication and the manuscripts were lost at the suppression of the college during the French Revolution. One final work, a study of Duns Scotus, appeared three years before his death. Colgan was the first to apply the title *The Annals of the Four Masters** to the work of his contemporary Franciscan colleagues.

Collegians, The (1829), Gerald Griffin*'s novel, based on events in County Limerick in 1819 when John Scanlon was tried for the murder of his mistress Ellen Hanley, describes how Eily O'Connor is murdered by Danny Mann at the suggestion of his master, her husband Hardress Cregan. Mann and Cregan are finally brought to justice, the perpetrator hanged, the other transported. The novel was dramatised as *The Colleen Bawn* (1860) by Boucicault*, who transferred the action to the more romantic Killarney*, and in turn Sir Julius Benedict (1804–85) made it into an operetta, *The Lily of Killarney* (1862).

Collins, Michael (b. 1964), novelist and short story writer, was born in Limerick and now teaches at Notre Dame University in Indiana. He has published *The Meat Eaters* (1992), a collection of violent short stories, and a novel about schizophrenia, *The Life and Times of a Teaboy* (1994). Another short story collection, *The Feminists Go Swimming*, appeared in 1995. His latest novel is *Emerald Underground* (1998).

Collis, John Stewart (1900–84), his twin **Robert** (1900–75) and **Maurice** (1889–1973), three sons of a Dublin solicitor, who in different ways made an impression on twentieth-century literature. John Stewart, like Maurice educated at Rugby and Oxford, spent the years of WWII working the land and wrote a number of books about man and nature, notably *The Worm Forgives the Plough* (1973). He died at his home in Surrey. Maurice was in the Indian civil service from 1911 till 1934 and on retirement began a second career as a writer, mainly of biography and art history. His best known works are his first, *Siamese White* (1936), about the eighteenth-century traveller Samuel White, and his biography *Somerville and Ross* (1968). Robert was an internationally known pediatrician, author of two successful plays, *Marrowbone Lane* (1939) and *The Barrel Organ* (1941), and a patron of Christy Brown*. He died after a riding accident in County Wicklow.

Colum, Padraic (1881–1972), man of letters, was born Patrick McCormac Colm in Longford, son of the master of the workhouse. The family moved to Sandycove, County Dublin, and Padraic worked for five years as a clerk before a scholarship from a wealthy American allowed him time to study and write. He wrote a number of plays for the Abbey*, including *The Land* (1905) and *Thomas Muskerry* (1910), about a workhouse keeper who ends up as an inmate, establishing a tradition of realism in what had been intended as a heroic or poetic theatre. He emigrated to America in 1914 and spent most of his life there. In *Life and the Dream* (1947), by his wife Mary Maguire whom he married in 1912 while she was still a student at UCD, their acquaintance with all the literary figures of the period is memorialised. Known now mainly for such perennial favourites as 'The Drover', 'The Old Woman of the Roads', 'She Moved through the Fair' and 'Cradle Song', Colum also wrote many books for children and a late novel, *The Flying Swans* (1957).

Colum Cille, St (?521–97), saint and *peregrinus*, was born in Gartan, County Donegal, and educated at Glasnevin and Bangor. He founded monasteries at Durrow, Swords and, perhaps, Derry. After seventeen years of preaching, teaching and copying manuscripts, in 563 he and twelve companions left for Iona to establish a base for the conversion of Pictish Scotland. He returned to Ireland only once, for the convention of Druim Cett in 575 which settled the succession of the Christian kingdom of Dál Riata, which straddled Antrim and southwest Scotland, and regularised the position of the *filid*, the learned class, a pre-Christian survival, who were at odds with the new dispensation. He probably wrote the Latin hymns *'Altus Prosator'* ('Great Progenitor') and *'Noli, Pater'* ('Do Not, Father') but many other poems, prophecies, anecdotes and curses assigned to him are part of the accretion of *seanchas* which naturally adheres to a patron saint. The supposed reasons for his *peregrinatio pro Christo* are equally fabulous, though as a prince of the Cenél Conaill he may have been present at the savage battle of Cúl Dreimhne (561) which is the traditional cause of his exile. He died in Iona and his spiritual life is recorded in *Vita Columbae* by a later abbot of Iona, Adamnán*.

Combar (estd. 1942), a monthly Irish-language journal, concerning itself with literature, culture and politics. Contributors have included the most distinguished writers in Irish of their day, such as Máirtín Ó Díreáin*, Eoghan Ó Tuairisc* and Nuala Ní Dhomhnaill.* Editors, equally distinguished, have included Breandán Ó hEithir* and Tomás Mac Síomóin*.

Concannon, Helena (1878–1952), historian and hagiographer, was born in Maghera, County Derry, the sister of Louis Walsh*. Educated at Loreto Convent, and in Dublin, Rome, Paris and Berlin, she married Thomas Concannon in 1906 and moved to Salthill, Galway. She served as both TD and senator in Dáil Éireann, with a notable feminist agenda. She wrote much female biography and hagiography, including *Women of 'Ninety-Eight* (1919), *Daughters of Banba* (1922) and lives of St Columba (1915), St Paschal Baylon (1930) and many others.

Conlon, Evelyn (b. 1952), short story writer, novelist and critic, was born in County Monaghan and educated at Maynooth University. She is a significant fiction writer, her work addressing in an eloquent and sometimes angry way the emotional and social experiences of women. Her short story collection *My Head Is Opening* (1987) was followed by a novel *Stars in the Daytime* (1989) and a second collection of short stories, *Taking Scarlet as a Real Colour* (1993). *A Glassful of Letters*, her most recent novel, was published in 1998.

Connaughton, Shane (b. 1946), novelist, actor and screenwriter, was born in Kingscourt, County Cavan, and lived in Redhills, the scene of his darkly comic scenario *The Playboys* (1993), until 1957. He was educated locally and at the Bristol Old Vic Theatre School. His novels *A Border Station* (1989) and *The Run of the Country* (1991) both describe life in the remote, lakey border country as observed by a clear-eyed adolescent whose father is a policeman. Connaughton co-wrote the screenplay for the Academy Award-winning film of Christy Brown*'s *My Left Foot*.

Conner, [Patrick] Rearden (1907–91), novelist, was born in Dublin, the son of a head constable in the RIC, and educated at Presentation College, Cork.

He became a landscape gardener and published his first novel *Shake Hands with the Devil* in 1933. It is a realistic account of the Black and Tan War and of the gradual dehumanising of Lenihan, an IRA commander, through violence. It was filmed in 1960 in Ireland with James Cagney as the 'devil'. Conner also wrote *A Plain Tale from the Bogs* (1937), an autobiographical novel of the same period.

CONNRADH NA GAEILGE, see Gaelic League*.

Cooke, Emma (b. 1934), novelist and short story writer, was born in Portarlington, County Laois, and educated at Alexandra College and Mary Immaculate College, Limerick. That city has been her home since her marriage in 1959. *Female Forms* (1982), her collection of short stories, was followed by the novels *A Single Sensation* (1981) and *Eve's Apple* (1985), painting a frank if bleak picture of modern Irish life. *Wedlocked* (1994) is a much lighter entertainment.

COOLE PARK, home of Sir William and Lady Gregory*, near Gort, County Galway, wantonly razed in 1941, was a powerhouse of literary activity, providing hospitality not only for Yeats*, a regular visitor, but also for Synge*, O'Casey*, Shaw*, Violet Martin ('Martin Ross' of the Irish RM* stories), Æ* and others, who were invited to carve their initials on the trunk of an immense copper beech.

Corkery, Daniel (1878–1964), man of letters, was born in Cork and educated locally, at St Patrick's College in Dublin and at the Crawford Municipal School of Art in Cork where he discovered a talent for watercolour. A lifelong bachelor and crippled by poliomyelitis, he was a dedicated not to say obsessive enthusiast for the Irish language. He taught in Cork, eventually being appointed, not without controversy, Professor of English at UCC (1931–47) in place of his former and better-qualified pupil, Sean O'Faolain*. His academic work benefits from his dedication to the Irish language. *The Hidden Ireland**(1924) was followed by *Synge and Anglo-Irish Literatu*re (1931), which is rather more complimentary to Synge than one might have expected. Corkery's short story collections *A Munster Twilight* (1916), *The Hounds of Banba* (1926) and *The Stormy Hills* (1929) are sited in the city and county of Cork, where people earn a living in factory and farm, their grey lives only briefly affected by the shocks of insurrection. He also wrote a bleak novel, *The Threshold of Quiet* (1917), and a number of plays, including *The Yellow Bittern* (1917), about the death of the happily dissolute poet Cathal Buí Mac Giolla Gunna*.

Country Girls, The (1960), Edna O'Brien*'s first novel of a trilogy about Caithleen Brady and her wilder (and richer) friend Baba Brennan, their schooldays in Loughrea, their three apprentice years in Dublin and Caithleen's innocent relationship with the middle-aged 'Mr Gentleman'. The prose was so fresh and the scene where Caithleen and 'Mr Gentleman' showed each other their naked bodies was so lyrical (and cleverly written) that the book was banned. It marked the beginnings, however, of a very significant Irish writer.

Coyle, Kathleen (1886–1952), novelist, was brought up in Derry and Donegal, educated by governesses and 'my father's library', and lived in Paris for many years. She wrote at least fourteen novels but dismissed all of them except *A Flock of Birds* (1930) which describes the effect on a family of the imprisonment and execution of a man for a political murder. She died in Philadelphia, having spent the last ten years of her life in America. Her autobiography *The Magical Realm* (1943) gives little statistical information about her early life. Some of her works have recently been republished and have earned praise from a new generation of critics.

Craig, Maurice [James] (b. 1919), poet and historian, was born in Belfast and educated at Magdalene College, Cambridge, and TCD, graduating PhD. He worked for the British Board of Works Historical Buildings Department until 1970, returning to Ireland to take up a similar position. He published a number of poetry collections, including *Black Swans* (1941), and is justly famous for his squib 'Ballad to a Traditional Refrain' about his less than elegant native city, the anatomy of which he reveals in his memoir, *The Elephant and the Polish Question*

(1990). He has written a life of Lord Charlemont (1728–99), *The Volunteer Earl* (1948), and the fascinating *Dublin 1660–1860* (1952). Much of his other work has dealt with Irish architecture.

Crawford, Julia (1799–1860), poet and composer, was born Louise Matilda Jane Montague in County Cavan, daughter of a British officer. Little is known about her except that she wrote many songs, including the famous 'Kathleen Mavourneen' and 'Dermot Asthore' and probably the music for Moore*'s 'Oft in the Stilly Night'.

Cré na Cille (1948), best known novel of Máirtín Ó Caidhin*. The setting is a Connemara graveyard (the title means the clay of the graveyard) and the voices are those of the dead, from under the clay. The subject of their witty, caustic, excruciatingly honest scrutiny is the life of the recently dead Caitríona Pháidín. Ó Caidhin's book, modernist in style and regarded as one of the finest novels ever written in Irish, aroused controversy at the time of its publication for its frank and unromantic depiction of a gaeltacht community.

Crock of Gold, The (1912), James Stephens*'s fantasy novel in which a philosopher, his wife and a peasant girl undertake quests in which they meet Pan and Angus Óg (the Celtic god of love). The book is a comedy, with talking animals and leprechauns guarding their crocks of gold, but as with all of Stephens's books there are serious philosophical concepts at play.

Croker, Mrs B[ithia] M[ary] (1850–1920), popular novelist, was the daughter of the Rev. William Sheppard, rector of Kilgefin, County Roscommon. She married Lieutenant-Colonel Croker of the Royal Munster Fusiliers and lived in Burma and India for many years before settling in England. The staple of turn-of-the-century lending libraries, her many novels often had an Asian background but some, like *In the Kingdom of Kerry* (1896), *Beyond the Pale* (1897) and *Lismoyle* (1914), have Irish locations and characters. Her characterisations of both Indians and Irish were affectionate and uncondescending.

Croker, T[homas] Crofton (1798–1854), folklorist, was born in Cork and apprenticed to an accountant. He later held an Admiralty clerkship in London. As a boy he became interested in Munster folklore and collected many stories and songs. Though his work was flawed by a scanty knowledge of Irish, books like *Fairy Legends and Traditions of the South of Ireland* (1825) and *Legends of Killarney* (1832) secured an amount of lore that might otherwise have been lost, and it is probably due to him that knowledge of such icons as the Claddagh ring and the Blarney Stone reached a wider public.

Crone, Anne (1915–72), novelist, was born in Dublin and educated at Methodist College, Belfast, and Somerville College, Oxford. She taught in Princess Gardens School in Belfast and published three novels dealing with sectarianism, passionate women and rural Fermanagh, her mother's home: *Bridie Steen* (1948), about the suicide of a Catholic daughter of a mixed marriage caused by religious family pressure, *This Pleasant Lea* (1952), set like Bullock*'s work on Lough Erne, and *My Heart and I* (1955).

Crone, John S[myth] (1858–1945), bibliographer, was born in Belfast and educated at Inst and QUB, qualifying in Medicine and practising for many years in Willesden, London. He founded the *Irish Book Lover* (1909–57) and produced the *Concise Dictionary of Irish Biography* (1928), the first since Webb*.

Cronin, Anthony (b. 1928), poet, critic and novelist, was born in Wexford and educated at UCD. He was a sub-editor of *The Bell** in its final days and then edited the liberal journal *Time and Tide* (1920–77). In 1980 he became cultural adviser to C. J. Haughey and is credited with having helped to establish Aosdána*. His most significant work of poetry is *RMS Titanic* (1964) and his comic novels *The Life of Riley* (1964), and *Identity Papers* (1979) are mordant accounts of Dublin literary and pub life (in so far as they differ). *Dead as Door Nails* (1976) is probably the best account of the Dublin of Behan*, Kavanagh* and Flann O'Brien* that is likely to be written, and *No Laughing Matter* (1989) is a full treatment of the career of O'Brien. His critical works include *Heritage Now* (1982) and a biography of Beckett: *Samuel Beckett: the Last Modernist* (1996).

Cross, Eric (1905–80), biographer and short story writer, was born in Newry and trained as a chemical engineer. He is best known as the Boswell of Tim Buckley, the Tailor of Gougane Barra, and his interrupting wife Ansty, recorded in *The Tailor and Ansty** (1942), though the Tailor first appeared in print in *The Bell** in February 1941. *Silence Is Golden*, a collection of stories and essays, appeared in 1978.

CROW STREET THEATRE (1758–1820), founded by Spranger Barry (1719–79), Harry Woodward (1717–77) and briefly Charles Macklin*, as a rival to the faltering Smock Alley*, becoming the licensed equivalent of the Theatre Royal, Drury Lane, and sharing its plays and actors. Barry's gorgeous productions bankrupted him and he was forced to sell to Henry Mossop (1729–74) of Smock Alley. After the usual story of grandeur, debts and many managers, the theatre building became a hat factory.

Crowe, Eyre Evan (1799–1868), novelist, was born in Southampton of Irish parents and educated at Carlow and TCD but left to become a journalist before taking his degree. He wrote much journalism and many works of history, including one of France in five volumes, but his main Irish writing consists of two books, *Today in Ireland* (1825) and *Yesterday in Ireland* (1829). The first consists of four novellas about the Ireland at the time of agitation for Catholic Emancipation, with the author firmly on the side of the oppressed native Irish. The second book has two tales: 'Corramahon', about post-Stuart Ireland, with a splendid picture of a rapparee in Ulick O'More, and 'The Northerners of Ninety-Eight' which describes the fate of Catholic insurrectionists in Ulster at the hands of the Orange Yeomanry.

Cúirt an Mbeán Oíche, (*The Midnight Court*) (c. 1780), a 1206-line poem, the work for which Brian Merriman* is known, is a brilliant piece of comic literature in Irish. Its Rabelaisian tone and parodic elements show an informed appreciation not only of the Irish poetry of Merriman's predecessors but of the formal European tourneys, the courts of love. The poet-narrator, who is a bachelor, is summoned in a dream to the court of Queen Aoibheall to account for his being unmarried when so many women are longing for love. The women who accompany her and who espouse the values of sensuality and fertility give long diatribes on celibacy and loveless (sexless) marriages. The narrator wakes up as he is being severely chastised by the women. The poem gives an excellent picture of rural Ireland in the late eighteenth century and its feminism and denunciation of celibacy including that of the clergy make it seem contemporary. Although utilising elements of the contemporary aisling* form, the work is predominantly comic and bawdy and was in the past much censored by conservative educationalists. It has been translated by many different writers, notably Frank O'Connor*.

Curran, John Philpot (1750–1817), orator and poet, was born in Newmarket, County Cork, and educated at TCD and the Middle Temple. He was an MP in the Irish Parliament (1783–97) and a strong Emancipationist. He defended the United Irishmen, especially Hamilton Rowan (1751–1834) who got off with two years' imprisonment. His daughter Sarah was the fiancée of Robert Emmet (1778–1803) and Curran's reaction to Emmet's rising was one of disenchantment and depression. He moved to London in 1814 and was an intimate of Tom Moore*, Byron and Sheridan*. His best known poem is 'The Deserter's Lament' with the refrain 'Let us be merry before we go!'

Curtayne, Alice (1901–81), novelist and biographer, was born in Tralee, County Kerry, and educated in England and Italy. Her biographies include *Catherine of Siena* (1929), *Oliver Plunkett* (1953), *Patrick Sarsfield* (1934) and *Francis Ledwidge* (1972). Her novel *House of Cards* (1940) is a spare account of an Irish girl's discovery that home is best. Curtayne was married to Stephen Rynne (1901–80), the philosopher farmer whose book *Green Fields* (1938) is a bucolic classic.

D

D'Alton, Louis (1900–51), playwright and novelist, was born in Dublin, the son of Charles A. D'Alton, a touring actor-manager. He worked as a civil servant before forming his own company. His first dramatic success was *The Man in the Cloak* (1937), a play about the life of Mangan* set against a cholera epidemic in the Dublin slums. This was followed by *Tomorrow Never Comes* (1939), about a murderer's moral collapse, and *The Spanish Soldier* (1940), which deals with the return to civilian life of an Irish Brigade volunteer in Franco's army. Of eight other plays the most significant were *Lover's Meeting* (1941), a stark family tragedy of made-marriages, the popular comedy *They Got What They Wanted* (1947) (filmed in 1951 as *Talk of a Million*), *The Devil a Saint Would Be* (1951), a comedy about piety, and *This Other Eden* (1953), about the oppressive dullness of the immediate postwar years in Ireland. D'Alton's novels *Death Is So Fair* (1936), about the struggle for Irish freedom, and *Rags and Sticks* (1938), about the last years of a 'fit-up' touring company, have largely been ignored. He died in London.

Daly, Ita (b. 1944), novelist and short story writer, was born in Drumshanbo, County Leitrim, moving to Dublin in 1957. She graduated from UCD with an MA and taught for some years. She contributed stories to David Marcus's 'New Irish Writing' page in the Irish Press, two of which won the Hennessy Award. She married Marcus in 1972 and they have one daughter. Her stories were collected as *The Lady with the Red Shoes* (1980) and four novels, *Ellen* (1986), *A Singular Attraction* (1987), *Dangerous Fictions* (1989) and *Unholy Ghosts* (1996), show her to be a subtle delineator, in apparently effortless prose, of thoughtful, not very successful women. *All Fall Down* (1992), something of a departure, shows a fine satirical talent. She has also written two books for children.

Danaher, Kevin (b. 1913), folklorist, was born in Athea, County Limerick, and, after service as a captain in the Irish army, became a full-time ethnologist for the Irish Folklore Commission* in 1945. When the Commission moved to the Belfield campus of UCD he became lecturer in folk life. He was as fine a writer as he was a folklorist and his many works include *In Ireland Long Ago* (1962), *The Year in Ireland* (1972), *Ireland's Vernacular Architecture* (1975) and *A Bibliography of Irish Ethnology and Folk Tradition* (1978). He was editor of *The Irish Sword*, the journal of military history, from 1960 to 1970.

Dancing at Lughnasa (1990), Brian Friel*'s extremely successful play about the five unmarried Mundy sisters and their brother Jack, a retired missionary priest, who live near Ballybeg, Friel's Irish Everytown. The festival of Lughnasa, dedicated to Lugh, the Celtic god of light, at which first fruits were celebrated by fire, feasting and dancing, is re-enacted in their country kitchen. Father Jack's memories of similar festivals in Uganda combine with modern (1936) ballroom steps and local folk memory to provide a marvellous dance sequence full of manic joy, courage and stoic acceptance before the family disintegrates.

Dark, The (1965), John McGahern*'s second novel, based partly on boyhood memories. The unnamed central character is the only child of a widower. Living in his home in the west midlands, he has to face the stress of sexual frustration, the unhappiness of his father and the need to win a university scholarship. (The book, which describes in some detail the character's regular masturbation and features a homosexual priest, was banned.) At the end the character finds sufficient maturity to make a gesture of reconciliation with his father and to decide not to accept the scholarship.

Darley, George (1795–1846), poet, was born in Dublin and educated at TCD. He moved to London in 1820 intending to become a writer. He wrote drama criticism and published monographs on mathematics. His poetry was admired by other poets but it is too ethereal for the modern taste. His lyric 'It Is Not Beauty I Demand', with the lines 'A crystal brow, the moon's despair/Nor the snow's daughter, a white hand,/Nor mermaid's yellow pride of hair', was printed by Palgrave as a genuine anonymous Caroline lyric.

Davis, Thomas (1814–45), poet, journalist and patriot, was born in Mallow, the posthumous son of an English army surgeon, educated at TCD and called to the bar in 1838. At TCD he was the leader of a group of Protestant intellectuals who tried to direct their fellows to Irishness, proclaiming in his inaugural speech as auditor of the Historical Society, 'Gentlemen, you have a country!' With Charles Gavan Duffy (1816–1903) and John Blake Dillon (1816–66) he founded *The Nation**, the organ of their Young Ireland movement. In a series of stirring essays about language and nationhood, and even more stirring ballads, including 'A Nation Once Again', 'Lament for Owen Roe O'Neill', 'Clare's Dragoons' and 'The West's Awake', he provided the literary correlative to O'Connell's Repeal Association. He disagreed with O'Connell about non-denominational education, an issue brought to a head by the Queen's Colleges proposals, and about his subservience to the Church and the Whig party, but if he had not died of scarlatina he might well have dissuaded Smith O'Brien (1803–64) from his inept rising in 1848.

Davison, Philip (b. 1957), novelist, scriptwriter and playwright, published his first novel *The Book Thief's Heartbeat* (1977) at the age of twenty. His other novels include *The Private Citizen* (1985) and *The Crooked Man* (1997). His first play, *The Invisible Mending Company*, was performed at the Peacock Theatre in 1996.

Davitt, Michael (b. 1950), poet in Irish, was born in Cork and educated at UCC. At university he was influenced by the work of Seán Ó Tuama* and Seán Ó Ríordáin* and became active in poetry circles (which included his co-eval Corkman Liam Ó Muirthile*), founding the journal *Innti* in 1970. He subsequently became a producer in RTÉ. His collections include *Gleann ar Ghleann* (1982), *Bligeard Sráide* (1983) and *An Tost á Scagadh* (1993); his poetry is lively, witty and engagé, and influenced by popular culture. It has attracted translators of the calibre of Paul Muldoon*. A *Selected Poems* with translations in English was published in 1987.

Dawe, Gerald (b. 1952), poet and critic, was born in Belfast and educated at NUU and UCG. He lived in the west of Ireland from 1974–92 and now lives in Dublin, where he is a lecturer in TCD. His poetry, which addresses personal subjects but also issues to do with community and culture, is collected in *Sheltering Places* (1978), *The Lundys Letter* (1985), *Sunday School* (1991) and most recently *Heart of Hearts* (1995). *Against Piety* is a volume of critical essays and *The Rest is History* (1998) is a partly autobiographical look at cultural roots and cultural icons in the divided society of Northern Ireland.

Deane, John F. (b. 1943), poet, prose writer and publisher, was born in Achill and educated at Mungret and UCD, graduating with an MA. After some years training for the priesthood and teaching in Dublin he resigned to become a full-time writer and to found *Poetry Ireland* and Daedalus Press. His poetry, published in such collections as *High Sacrifice* (1981), *The Stylised City* (1991), *Walking on Water* (1994) and *Stalking after Time* (1997), beautifully reflects the dilemmas of modern man in regard to religion, nationality and love. *Free Range* (1994) is a collection of often violent short stories and Deane's novel about post-Treaty Ireland, *One Man's Place* (1994), confronts the dilemma of morality and violence for the patriot.

Deane, Raymond (b. 1953), composer and novelist, was born in Achill in 1953 and is a member of Aosdána* as a classical composer. His *Death of a Medium* (1991), a pastiche Irish Gothic novel, is influenced by Poe, Lewis, and our own home-grown Maturin*, Stoker* and the great Le Fanu*, but with an ironic eroticism that is all its own.

Deane, Seamus (b. 1940), poet, critic and novelist, was born in Derry and educated at St Columb's College (along with Seamus Heaney*), QUB and Cambridge, where he took his PhD. He was Professor of Modern English and

American Literature at UCD before moving to Notre Dame, Indiana, in August 1993 as Keough Professor of Irish Studies. His critical works, mainly about Irish literature, include *Celtic Revivals: Essays in Modern Irish literature 1880–1980* (1985), *A Short History of Irish Literature* (1986) *The French Revolution and Enlightenment in England, 1789–1832* (1988) and *Strange Country: Modernity and Nationhood in Irish Writing since 1790* (1997). He was also general editor of the *Field Day Anthology of Irish Writing* (1991). His collections of poetry, *Gradual Wars* (1972), *Rumours* (1977) and *History Lessons* (1983), are passionately intellectual, concerned among other things with nationality, culture and the sectarian division in the North. A *Selected Poems* appeared in 1988. *Reading in the Dark* (1996) is a searingly beautiful semi-autobiographical novel of childhood and youth in a troubled republican family in Derry in the 1940s and 1950s.

Death and Nightingales (1992), novel by Eugene McCabe*, set in the marches of Fermanagh and Monaghan where the county borders are as complicated as the politico-religious persuasions of the people. Elizabeth is the Catholic daughter of the dead wife of Protestant Billy Winters. It is the time of the Phoenix Park murders by the Invincibles (1882). Elizabeth becomes pregnant by Liam Ward, a renegade Fenian, who intends to kill her after getting her stepfather's money, and escape to America. Elizabeth finally overcomes her disbelief and drowns Ward in one of the many local lakes. A symbolic rapprochement between Elizabeth and Winters suggests the only hope for the benighted province.

De Bhaldraithe, Tomás (1916–1996), scholar, lexicographer and editor in Irish, was born in Limerick and educated at UCD and in Paris. He became Professor of Modern Irish Language and Literature at UCD in 1960. Arising from his doctoral research he published several books on the Irish spoken in Cois Fharraige in the Connemara gaeltacht. His *English-Irish Dictionary*, published in 1959, was a lasting contribution to the modernisation of vocabulary in the Irish language. He also collaborated with Niall Ó Donáill* on the latter's *Foclóir Gaeilge-Béarla* (1977). Among other works, he edited the ground-breaking *Nuascéaláíocht* (1952), the stories of Padraic Ó Conaire* and *Cinn Lae Amhlaoibh Uí Shúilleabháin* (1970), the diary of a County Kilkenny hedge schoolmaster.

De Blácam, Aodh (1890–1951), journalist and critic, was born Hugh Blacam in London, son of the MP for Newry. He learned Irish from Robert Lynd* before coming to Ireland to work as a journalist and Sinn Féin activist when he began using an Irish form of his name. He wrote stories and novels, most significantly *Holy Romans* (1920), a largely autobiographical novel about an Ulster Protestant brought up in London and converted to Catholicism and Irish Nationalism. He was for many years 'Roddy the Rover' of the *Irish Press* and his most significant work was *Gaelic Literature Surveyed* (1921). He wrote biographies of Tone and Colum Cille* and an account of his father's native Ulster, *The Black North* (1939). The title, his own coinage, has become proverbial. He died in Dublin.

de Blaghd, Earnán, see Ernest Blythe*

De Brún, Monsignor Pádraig (1889–1960), poet in Irish, scholar and translator, was born in County Tipperary and educated at UCD, Paris and Rome. He was ordained a priest in 1913 and was Professor of Mathematics at Maynooth from 1914–45, then became President of UCG. He is remembered now for his translations from the classics into Irish, notably Sophocles's *Antigone* and *Oedipus Rex* and Homer's *Odyssey* (*Odaise*) and for lyrics like 'Tháinig long ó Valparaiso'. His niece Máire Mhac an tSaoi* edited his own long poem *Miserere* (1971).

December Bride (1951), Sam Hanna Bell*'s first and finest novel, set at the turn of the century and based upon the true story of a *ménage-à-trois* in a Protestant area on the shores of Strangford Lough in County Down, where the canker of sectarian dissension is only a distant threat. Sarah Gomartin is 'that woman at Rathard', a servant who becomes the mistress of two brothers who work an isolated farm. She refuses to name the father of her child until in middle age she agrees to marry the elder brother for her daughter's sake. With its spare beauty of language, sense

of the country year and celebration of the Presbyterian virtues of industry, efficiency and independence of mind, it is one of the finest Irish novels of this century, and its dialogue makes it a linguistic resource for the rapidly vanishing Ulster-Scots dialect.

Deevy, Teresa (1894–1963), playwright, was born in Waterford and exchanged UCD for UCC to be nearer home because of an attack of Ménière's disease which left her totally deaf before graduation. She studied lip-reading in London and became so proficient that she could enjoy the theatre, which became her passion. Her plays are distinguished by the excellence of the dialogue. Her best known works are *The King of Spain's Daughter* (1935) and *Katie Roche* (1936), which involve unlikely romantic heroines and their reconciliations in not-so-loveless marriages. The Abbey*, where her plays were produced, was during her most fertile period a pretty fustian place; in other decades there might have been greater encouragement for her to continue with theatrical work. As it was, her later work was done mainly for radio. She died at home in Waterford.

De Híde, Dúghlas, see Douglas Hyde*

Delaney, Frank (b. 1942), broadcaster and novelist, was born in Tipperary and after some years as a banker joined the staff of RTÉ. Since then he has moved to London. He has written a number of well crafted, readable novels, including a projected five-book sequence of which *The Sins of the Mothers* (1992), *Telling the Pictures* (1993), *A Stranger in Their Midst* (1995) and *Desire and Pursuit* (1998) are the first four. A novel, *The Amethysts*, was published in 1998. His book programmes, a series for television about the Celts, and an account of his retracing of Boswell's *Journal of a Tour of the Hebrides* (1785) seem particularly appropriate to his affable bookish talents.

Delanty, Greg (b. 1958), poet, was born in Cork (which figures significantly in his work) and educated at UCC, later lecturing at St Michael's College, Vermont. His first collection was *Cast in the Fire* (1986). Then came *Southward* (1992) and *American Wake* (1994). His most recent collection, *The Hellbox* (1998), is informed by the poet's experience of growing up in a family of printers.

De Vere, Aubrey (1814–1902), poet, son of Sir Aubrey de Vere (1788–1846) of Curragh Chase, County Limerick (also a poet and a responsible landlord), was educated at TCD and, through his father, was friendly with most of the mid-Victorian poetic establishment. He assisted his elder brother Stephen in relief schemes during the Famine and afterwards wrote *English Misrule and Irish Misdeeds* (1848). He became a Catholic in 1851 and wrote much religious poetry. His main Irish work is *Inisfail* (1861) and he also managed a sanitised version of *Táin Bó Cuailgne* as *The Foray of Queen Maev*. His ballad 'The Death of Conor Mac Neasa' used to

figure in school anthologies and 'The Little Black Rose' still finds its place. He lectured in English Literature to the students of Newman's Catholic University.

Dicuil (?765–*c*. 825), astronomer, grammarian, mathematician and geographer, of Irish birth, was for some time a monk of Iona. He left for the continent *c*. 806, probably to escape the Viking attacks, and became a teacher at the palace school of Charlemagne at Aachen. His great work *Liber de Mensura Orbis Terrae* (*The Book of Measurement of the Earth*) was presented shortly before his death.

Dillon, Eilís (1920–94), novelist and children's author, was born in Galway and educated at the Ursuline Convent in Sligo. Sister of the Gaelic scholar Myles Dillon and mother of the poet Eiléan Ní Chuilleanáin*, she married Cormac Ó Cuilleanáin, Professor of Irish at UCC, and on his death the critic Vivian Mercier. Her output included novels, plays, works in Irish and three classical whodunnits. Her best known works of adult fiction, *Across the Bitter Sea* (1973) and *Blood Relations* (1977), are family chronicles with a background of Irish republican politics. She began writing children's stories with *The Lost Island* (1952) and continued to provide excellent literate yarns with Irish and historical backgrounds until a few years before her death.

DOLMEN PRESS, THE, was founded by Liam Miller (1923–87) and his wife Josephine in 1951 as a small hand-press to publish particular works of Irish authors and became famous as the originator of some of the world's best-designed books. The press produced works by most Irish writers of any significance, often beautifully and expensively illustrated, so that profit eluded the company and it went into liquidation in 1987 after Miller's death.

DONERAILE, village fourteen miles from Mitchelstown, County Cork, part of Edmund Spenser's estate. Tadhg Ó Duinnín, the last hereditary poet of the MacCarthys of Blarney, died as parish priest there in 1726 and Canon Sheehan*, a later holder of the office (1895–1913), wrote his ten novels there. Here also was situated Bowen Court, ancestral home of novelist Elizabeth Bowen*.

Donoghue, Emma (b. 1969), novelist and playwright, was born in Dublin and educated at UCD and Cambridge. Her play, *I Know My Own Heart: A Lesbian Regency Romance*, was performed in Dublin in 1993. She has also published *Passions Between Women: British Lesbian Culture 1668–1801* (1993) and two novels, *Stir Fry* (1994), a story of student lesbian love, and *Hood* (1995). A collection of short stories, *Kissing the Witch,* appeared in 1997.

Donovan, Katie (b. 1962), poet, was born in Dublin. She has published two lively, sensual collections of poetry, *Watermelon Man* (1993) and *Entering the Mare* (1997). She is also the author of *Irish Women Writers: Marginalised by Whom?*, and co-edited *Ireland's Women: Writings Past and Present* (1994) and *Dublines* (1996). She works as a journalist and critic with *The Irish Times.*

Dorcey, Mary (b. 1950), poet and fiction writer, was born in Dublin. As a young woman she travelled extensively and worked at a variety of occupations. She joined the Irish women's movement in 1972 and was a founder member of Irish Women United. *Kindling* (1982) was her first poetry collection. *A Noise from the Woodshed* (1989), a book of short stories, was admired for its strength and the honesty of her depiction of relationships. Her poetry is sensitive and often deeply emotional. She has published two further collections, *Moving into the Space Cleared by Our Mothers* (1991) and *The River That Carries Me* (1995). Her début novel, *Biography of Desire* (1997), has as its subject a doomed lesbian relationship.

Dorgan, Theo (b. 1953), poet and arts administrator, was born in Cork and educated at UCC. He has been, inter alia, literature officer with Triskel Arts Centre and Director of Cork Film Festival and he is at present Director of Poetry Ireland. With Gene Lambert he edited *The Great Book of Ireland.* His published works include *The Ordinary House of Love* (1991), *Rosa Mundi* (1995) and *Sappho's Daughter* (1998).

Doyle, Lynn (pseudonym of Leslie A. Montgomery) (1873–1961), humorous writer, was born in Downpatrick,

County Down, the 'Ballygullion' of his many comic stories written between 1908 and 1951, which feature the omniscient narrator Mr Pat Murphy, a character who owes something to Flurry Knox of the Irish RM* stories of Somerville & Ross*. Montgomery's account of small-town Ulster life and of the misadventures of the staid Protestant solicitor Mr Anthony touches gently on sectarian differences – one of his books is called *Green Oranges* (1947) – but is too genial to go very deep. The use of a pseudonym, originally 'Lynn C. Doyle' (linseed oil), was considered necessary for a bank official in 1914 when Montgomery's play *Love and Land* was put on by the Ulster Literary Theatre* in the Grand Opera House in Belfast.

Doyle, Roddy (b. 1958), novelist and playwright, was born in Dublin and educated at Sutton CBS and UCD. He taught in Kilbarrack (the 'Barrytown' of his comic and dark fiction) and this contact with young north Dublin undoubtedly contributed to the demotic accuracy of the dialogue in his novels and in the stark and violent four-part teleplay *Family* (1994). The novels of his Barrytown trilogy, *The Commitments* (1989), *The Snapper* (1990) and *The Van* (1991), a funny and scabrous account of contemporary working-class Dublin, were all successfully filmed. *Paddy Clarke Ha Ha Ha* (winner of the Booker Prize in 1993) deals with a bright middle-class lad's response to parental separation and *The Woman Who Walked into Doors* (1996) is a prose version of *Family*.

Drennan, William (1754–1820), United Irishman and poet, was born in Belfast and qualified as a physician at Edinburgh in 1778. He was arrested for treason in 1794 and successfully defended by John Philpot Curran*. He did not take part in the '98 rising but wrote the ballad 'The Wake of William Orr' (1797). His poem 'When Erin First Rose' contains the lines: 'Let no feeling of vengeance presume to defile/The cause of, the men of, the Emerald Isle'; he was the first so to describe Ireland. He was one of the founders of the Belfast Academy (later 'Inst').

Dracula (1897), Bram Stoker*'s famous vampire novel of the Transylvanian Count Dracula, has spawned more films than those of any other character with the exception of Sherlock Holmes and has been elevated thereby to the level of modern myth. Based on the Wallachian tyrant Vlad the Impaler and on folk belief in the 'Undead' who, infected through another vampire's bite, require ever more human blood to survive in their twilight world, the character also owes something to the appearance, temperament and relentless demands of Sir Henry Irving, whose business manager Stoker was. The book is quite sedate in its documentary use of diaries, letters and newspaper cuttings, and as an example of its genre owes much to its superior Irish precursor, Le Fanu*'s 'Carmilla' (1872).

Drama at Inish (1933), frequently revived comedy by Lennox Robinson* about the hilarious effects on a small Munster seaside resort of a summer season of sombre drama staged by the Hector de la Mare Repertory Company. The normally placid populace become morbid and suicidal and a hitherto silent TD brings down the government after a dose of Ibsen.

DRUID THEATRE, theatrical company founded in Galway in 1975 by Garry Hynes, Mick Lally and Marie Mullen, noted for an adventurous repertoire of new plays and fresh appraisals of both standard and neglected works of Irish theatre. Garry Hynes's Druid production of *The Beauty Queen of Leenane* by leading young playwright Martin McDonagh was a spectacular Broadway success in 1998.

DRUMCLIFFE, village in County Sligo where Yeats*'s remains were reinterred in 1947 according to his poetic instruction: 'Under bare Ben Bulben's head/In Drumcliffe churchyard Yeats is laid.'

DUBLIN MAGAZINE, THE (1923–25; 1926–58), a literary magazine edited by Seumas O'Sullivan* which until *The Bell** began tolling in 1941 was the main literary magazine in Ireland, publishing work from the leading Irish writers of the period, from Joseph Campbell* to Yeats*.

Duffaud, Briege (b. 1941), novelist and short story writer, was born in south Armagh, where her novel *A Wreath upon the Dead* (1993) is set,

and she now lives in Brittany. The novel gives the history of Claghan (a deliberately non-specific name which means simply 'village') from the time just before the Famine up to the present day. It is a long work and uses many different modes of narration, including letters, playlets, diaries, newspaper stories and several first-person narrators (as well as the authorial third-person mode), as it tells the story of two families, one low-level Ascendancy, the other native, proud Irish. The result is a literary *tour de force* with skilful pastiche of the many narrative forms used and an uncompromising view of the origin and nature of the Northern Troubles. She has also published a collection of short stories, *Nothing like Beirut* (1994), and a novel set in France, *The Long Stem Rose* (1995).

Dufferin, Lady (Helen Sheridan Blackwood) (1807–67), poet, novelist and playwright, sister of Caroline Norton* and granddaughter of Richard Brinsley Sheridan*, was born in England and brought up in Hampton Court. She wrote the song lyrics 'The Exile's Lament', 'The Bay of Dublin' and 'Terence's Farewell'.

Dunne, Seán (1956–95), poet and anthologist, was born in Waterford and educated at Mount Sion CBS and UCC. He worked as a journalist in Cork, becoming literary editor of the *Cork Examiner*. He published two collections of poetry, *Against the Storm* (1985) and *The Sheltered Nest* (1992), and an autobiographical memoir *In My Father's*

House. (1991). His anthologies include *Poets of Munster* (1985), *Something Understood: A Spiritual Anthology* (1995) and the posthumous *The Ireland Anthology* (1998).

Durcan, Paul (b. 1944), poet, was born in Dublin in 1944 and educated at Gonzaga College and UCC. One of Ireland's best known and most widely enjoyed poets, his strikingly individual collections include *The Berlin Wall Café* (1985), *Daddy, Daddy* (1990), winner of the Whitbread Poetry Prize, *Crazy about Women* (1995) and *Give Me Your Hand* (1994), the latter two comprising poems inspired by pictures in the National Gallery of Ireland and the National Gallery in London. His work is satirical and deeply concerned with unnecessary stupidity and cruelty at a personal and national level, and he celebrates women as few others. His most recent collections are *A Snail in My Prime* (1993) and *Christmas Day* (1996).

E

Easter Rising, The, occurred between 24 and 29 April 1916. The Irish Volunteers and the Irish Citizen Army occupied various public buildings, including the GPO and City Hall in Dublin, on Easter Monday while many of the population were at the races. The 1916 Proclamation was read and most of the action consisted in the insurgents defending their positions. The capitulation 'to prevent the further slaughter of Dublin citizens' followed the shelling of the GPO by the gunboat Helga. The signatories to the Proclamation, including Pearse*, MacDonagh* and the labour leader James Connolly, were executed by firing squad. Though public reaction was initially lukewarm, the executions and the general harshness of the British authorities' handling of the matter achieved the Rising's intention and it was taken as the beginning of the modern independent state of Ireland.

Edgeworth, Maria (1767–1849), novelist, was born in the family mansion Edgeworthstown, County Longford. Her father Richard Lovell Edgesworth (whose record as a landlord preserved his life during the '98 rising) married four times and Maria spent much of her early life educating her many step-siblings. She and her father wrote *Practical Education* (1798) and she illustrated her lessons with moral tales so skilfully that she was encouraged to write novels. Her finest novel *Castle Rackrent* (1800) deals with a decaying Big House and the relationship between Protestant landlords and Catholic tenants. It influenced Sir Walter Scott and is taken not only as the first regional, but also the first Anglo-Irish novel. Though she spoke for the enlightened members of her class, her treatment of the Irish is sympathetic. Of the eighteen volumes which constitute her complete works, the other most significant books are *The Absentee* (1812) and *Ormond* (1817), which implicitly criticise the English for their lack of responsibility towards the Irish. Her strictures are leavened, though, by humour and a fine sense of plotting. She just outlasted the worst of the Famine, during which she cared efficiently for her tenants.

Egan, Desmond (b. 1936), poet and publisher, was born in Athlone, County Westmeath in 1936 and educated at Maynooth. He was classics master at Newbridge College in County Kildare until 1987. He founded the Goldsmith Press in 1972 and edited *Era* an occasional literary magazine. His poetry collections include *Midland* (1972), *Leaves* (1974), *Siege!* (1976), *Athlone?*

(1980), *Seeing Double* (1983), *Collected Poems* (1983), *Poems for Peace* (1986), *A Song for My Father* (1989) *Selected Poems* (1991) and *Peninsula* (1992). He has also published a collection of essays, *The Death of Metaphor* (1990).

ÉIRE-IRELAND (estd. 1966), journal of Irish Studies, published by the Irish-American Cultural Institute at St Paul, Minnesota, founded by Eóin McKiernan, who was the journal's editor for nearly thirty years.

Enright, Anne (b. 1962), novelist and short story writer, was born in Dublin and educated at TCD and the University of East Anglia. Her first collection of short stories, *The Portable Virgin* (1991), was much praised for its sharpness of observation, striking originality and surreal humour. A novel, *The Wig My Father Wore*, followed in 1995. She works as a television producer with RTÉ.

Eriugena, John Scottus (?810–?77), theologian, was born in Ireland (his name indicates this twice) and was at the court of Charles the Bald (823–77), grandson of Charlemagne. He was a teacher of Greek (among other subjects) at the palace at Laon where he wrote *De Predestinatione* (851), a work condemned as *pultes Scotorum* ('Irish porridge') by the Council of Valence. His great work *Peri Pheusis* (in Latin *De Divisione Naturae*), written in 867, attempts to reconcile Christianity with Neo-Platonism and stayed on the *Index Librorum Prohibitorum* until modern

times. It and his translation of the *Pseudo-Dionysius* had a profound effect on medieval thought and prepared the way for modern metaphysics. There is a story that he was stabbed to death by the pens of his pupils at Oxford in 880 when abbot of Malmesbury in Wiltshire, but it is likely that he died in France shortly after the death of his royal patron.

Ervine, St John (1883–1971), playwright, novelist, biographer and critic, was born John Irvine, the son of deaf-mutes, in east Belfast and worked as an insurance clerk before joining the Fabian Society in London out of admiration for Shaw*. His first play *Mixed Marriage* (1911) dealt with Ulster bigotry and *John Ferguson* (1915), about Presbyterian rectitude, was produced during his time as manager of the Abbey*, a post he left after conflict with the company over the Easter Rising*, to join the Dublin Fusiliers. He lost a leg in France and settled in Devon to become a trenchant but readable drama critic for several papers, including the *Observer*. Through the 1920s he wrote such light West End comedies as *Anthony and Anna* (1926) and *The First Mrs Frazer* (1929), the latter a box-office success about a man who divorces to marry his first wife, but it is likely that he will be remembered for such Ulster comedies as *Boyd's Shop* (1936) and *Friends and Relations* (1941). He wrote several realistic novels of Belfast life, and uncritical biographies of Edward Carson and James Craig, the founders of the NI state, but these were muted compared with his huge adulatory life of Shaw (1956). He was an offshore defender of Unionism and often crossed swords in friendly journalistic struggle with the nationalist Robert Lynd*.

Evans, E[myr] Estyn (1905–89), geographer, was born in Shrewsbury and educated at Aberystwyth. Appointed to the Geography Department of QUB in 1928, he became the laureate of the east Ulster landscape and encouraged a new folk-in-environment approach to his subject. His books, including Irish Heritage (1942), *Mourne Country* (1951) *Irish Folkways* (1957), *Prehistory and Early Christian Ireland* (1966) and *The Personality of Ireland* (1973), are important contributions to the cultural history of Ireland. He helped to found the Ulster Folk and Transport Museum at Cultra and became the first Director of the Institute of Irish Studies at QUB in 1968.

Evans, John (b. 1966), was born in Wexford. He spent some years working in Germany, an exile that inspired his well-regarded first novel, *Pilgrims*, (1998), about a man who uses his expatriate existence as one of many means of evading his emotional responsibilities.

F

Fahy, Francis A[rthur] (1854–1935), songwriter, was born in Kinvara, County Galway, and after education in the local national school joined the English civil service in London in 1876. A native speaker, he became President of the London Gaelic League* and founder of the Irish Literary Society which played its part in the Irish Literary Revival*. He is famous as the author of such songs as 'The Ould Plaid Shawl', 'The Queen of Connemara', 'The Donovans', 'Little Mary Cassidy' and 'Haste to the Wedding' which first appeared in *Irish Songs and Poems* (1887).

Faith Healer (1979), Brian Friel*'s play about Frank Hardy, who is cursed with an occasional gift of healing and whose life consists of travels throughout Ireland and the UK with his 'show'. The action consists of four monologues spoken by Hardy, his wife Grace and Teddy their Cockney manager, with a coda by the now dead Hardy. The accounts differ in substantial detail – a typical Friel reminder – but all are clear about Hardy's been beaten to death by the disappointed brothers and friends of one of his failures in Ballybeg. With the experimental nature of the writing, its mantra of placenames visited and the thematic link with the nature of artistic genius, the play is a powerful piece of theatre.

Fallon, Padraic (1906–74), poet, was born in Athenry, County Galway, and after education in Roscrea joined the Customs and Excise Department, being appointed to Wexford in 1939 where he lived until retirement in 1970. He lived thereafter in Kinsale. His poetry was relatively unknown because no collection was published in his lifetime. His work is strongly sensual and yet devotional, evidencing a mind steeped in classics and Irish literature, patriotic yet clear-eyed. His verse drama based on Irish sagas made successful radio plays in the 1950s, and the teleplay *The Fenians* (1966) told the story of Stephens, Rossa, Kickham* and the rest as part of the fiftieth anniversary celebrations of the Easter Rising*.

Fallon, Peter (b. 1951), poet and publisher, was born in Germany and came home to County Meath when he was six. Educated at Glenstal and TCD, in 1970 he founded Gallery Press which became Ireland's premier poetry house, though he also publishes other literary material, the plays and short stories of Brian Friel*, for example. His own work appeared in volume form from 1971.

Early work such as *Coincidence of Flesh* (1973) dealt with love, sex and such things, but as the poet grows older he looks outward to the world of work and nature. His most recent collection, *News of the World: New and Selected Poems*, was published in 1998.

Farquhar, George (?1677–1707), the last and most decorous of the Restoration playwrights, was born in Derry, son of the curate of Liscooley near Castlefinn, County Donegal, and had his education at the Derry Free School interrupted by the famous Siege (1688–9). He may have been at the Battle of the Boyne in 1690 and certainly left TCD without a degree to join the Smock Alley company in 1696. His stage career was cut short after the accidental stabbing of a fellow actor and it was as a playwright that he went to London with the script of *Love in a Bottle* (1698), the successful production of which at Drury Lane was followed by the equally successful *The Constant Couple* (1670). Other important works were *The Twin Rivals* (1700) and the ultimate breeches-part play *The Recruiting Sergeant* (1704). He married a widow, Margaret Pennell, ten years his senior, in the belief that she was rich, but all she brought to the marriage was three children by her former husband. He bore her no ill-will and she bore him two daughters. Though ill with tuberculosis, he worked steadily at his best and last work *The Beaux' Stratagem* (1707) which was presented with great success as he died. Farquhar's work, especially the three last-named plays, are part of the standard repertoire of British classical theatre, and his stage-Irish characters, though fashionably anti-Catholic, are, like Macklin*'s, rather wittier and cleverer than their social betters.

Farrell, Bernard (b. 1941), playwright, was born in Sandycove, County Dublin. He was educated at Monkstown CBS and worked as a shipping clerk until the success of his first play, *I Do Not Like Thee, Dr Fell* (1979), about the dynamics of an encounter group, allowed him to become a full-time writer. He has had ten plays produced, mainly in the Abbey*, which deal with serious social topics in a comic way. His characters are usually Dubliners, comfortably off, and uneasily learning how to live in the new, sophisticated Ireland. The plays are extremely funny, with underlying violence and an inevitable puncturing of pretension. His most recent play is *Kevin's Bed* (1998). He has also written plays for radio and television.

Farrell, M. J., see Molly Keane*.

Farrell, Michael (1899–1962), novelist, was born in Carlow, the son of well-to-do parents. His medical studies in UCD were interrupted by a spell in prison for possession of illegal documents during the War of Independence. He gave up medicine to run his wife's business. When Sean O'Faolain* started *The Bell** he was its amateur drama correspondent and, as 'Lemuel Gulliver', ran 'The Open Window', its literary causerie, from 1943 till 1954. His autobiographical novel *Thy Tears Might Cease**(1963), which was one of the myths of literary Dublin, was not published until after his death in an edited, workable form by Monk Gibbon*.

Father Ralph (1913), first and best novel of Gerald O'Donovan*, about the career of Ralph O'Brien who, though doubtful of his vocation and being ordained mainly to please his overpowering mother, strives to be a worthy cleric. The novel is largely autobiographical and the description of Maynooth, a majority of priests and the life of small Irish towns at the turn of the century is extremely harsh. Some of the bitterness may be explained by O'Donovan's own treatment by his bishop but the novel gives a largely accurate account of the Church politics of the time.

Feiritéar, Piaras (*c*. 1600–1653), poet in Irish, was chieftain of the Dingle peninsula in County Kerry and a writer who, politics aside, would have fitted very comfortably with his Jacobean and Caroline contemporaries in England. His work bears strong resemblances to theirs and he may also have written in English. He is now best known for love poetry such as 'Léig Díot Th'airm'. In 1641 he supported the anti-English rising for religious rather than for political motives. He continued the struggle for twelve years but although granted safe-conduct at the fall of Ross Castle was treacherously hanged in Killarney in 1653. A 'poet's poet', he was highly trained in the traditional bardic techniques of syllabic poetry. He is one of the 'Four Kerry Poets', to whom a monument stands in Killarney.

Ferguson, Sir Samuel (1810–86), poet and scholar, was born in Belfast and educated at Inst (where he learned Irish), Lincoln's Inn and TCD, which he left without taking a degree. Stimulated by the friendship of Petrie*, O'Donovan and O'Curry*, he became interested in Gaelic literature, and his versions have some of the power of the originals. His rather tepid love affair with Irish Nationalism reached its height with his successful defence of Richard D'Alton Williams* in 1848 on a charge of treason-felony after the Smith O'Brien rising. Thereafter his Liberal Unionism reasserted itself. His poems, including translations from the Irish, published in the volume *Lays of the Western Gael* (1864), are still frequently anthologised and were an early stimulus for the Irish Literary Revival*. He became a QC in 1859, Deputy Keeper of Public Records in 1867 and was knighted in 1878. He was tireless in his work for Irish antiquities and was in favour of some form of limited self-government. He is buried in Dunegore churchyard in County Antrim, the home of his ancestors.

Fiacc, Padraig (b. 1924), poet, was born in Belfast and brought up in Manhattan. In 1946 he returned to live in Belfast. He is author of five collections of poetry, *By the Black Stream* (1969) *Odour Of Blood* (1973) *Nights in the Bad Place* (1977) *Missa Terrablis* (1994) and most recently *Red Earth* (1996). He is a member of Aosdána*.

Fiche Blian ag Fás (*Twenty Years a-Growing*) (1933), autobiographical account of life on the Great Blasket* island by Muiris Ó Súilleabháin*. Unlike Tomás Ó Criomhthain* and Peig Sayers*, Ó Súilleabháin left the island as a young man of twenty to train as a Gárda Síochána (policeman) in Dublin; his memoir conveys the freshness and vitality of youth as well as the age-old traditions of the island.

Field, The (1965), John B. Keane*'s strongest play, first presented in the Olympia Theatre, Dublin. Based on an actual incident, it tells of the murder by 'the Bull' McCabe, a Kerry farmer, of a rival who bids for a field which McCabe has with gargantuan efforts made fertile during his leasehold. In spite of all the efforts of police and Church, the locals refuse to denounce the culprit. The play was successfully filmed with Richard Harris in the part of the Bull McCabe.

FIELD DAY (estd. 1980), theatrical company founded by Brian Friel* and the actor Stephen Rea, and having on its committee Seamus Deane*, David Hammond (the film-maker and folk-music specialist), Seamus Heaney* and Tom Paulin*. Its purpose was to redefine Ireland's cultural identity through drama, pamphlets and the 4,000-page *Field Day Anthology* (1991). The plays written by Friel, Derek Mahon*, Paulin, Heaney, Tom Kilroy*, Stewart Parker* and others gave Derry, the scene of the first productions, a dozen years of political drama and theatrical fame, the pamphlets produced sufficient controversy to justify their writing and the *Anthology* (edited in chief by Deane), though attacked by revisionists (as being too nationalist) and feminists (because of its under-representation of women), is a remarkable achievement which generally lives up to its brief of reappraisal.

Fire in the Dust, The (1942), Francis MacManus's finest novel, about the pernicious lack of charity that was often a feature of the Ireland of the 1930s and 1940s. Set in Kilkenny, it describes the effect of the significantly named Golden family who come to live in the small city and offend its ultra-conservative and uncopious citizens with their sophistication and unaffected hedonism. The forces of reaction are led by Minnie Dreelin, who deals in religious objects, and her mania is such that she is the cause of young Stephen Golden's death by drowning in the Nore. MacManus's spare poetic style elegantly puts the case for real Catholicism against the blight of small-town Jansenism.

Fitzmaurice, Gabriel (b. 1952), poet in Irish and English and translator, was born in Moyvane, County Kerry. He was educated at Mary Immaculate Training College, Limerick and is now a teacher in Moyvane. He is a prolific and consistently interesting poet and translator, with many published works to his credit. Among these are six collections of poetry in English, including *Rainsong* (1984) and *The Space Between: New and Selected Poems 1984–92* (1983); three collections in Irish, *Nocht* (1989), *Ag Síobshúil Chun an Rince*

(1995) and *Giolla na nAmhrán: Dánta 1988–98* (1998), and several collections of poetry in English and Irish for children. He has translated from the Irish the work of poets like Michael Hartnett* (*The Purge/An Phurgóid*, 1993) and Cathal Ó Searcaigh* (*Homecoming/An Bealach 'na Bhaile*, 1993), published critical essays (including *Kerry of the Mind*, 1998), and edited bilingual anthologies: *An Crann Faoi Bhláth/The Flowering Tree* (1991, with Declan Kiberd*) and *Poems I Wish I'd Written* (1996, his own translations).

Fitzmaurice, George (1877–1963), playwright, was born near Listowel, County Kerry. He worked in a bank and in the Land Commission, and served in the army during WWI. His later life was spent in reclusion in Dublin. His plays, seventeen in number, were compared with those of Lady Gregory* and Synge* but, except for the naturalistic *The Country Dressmaker* (1907) and *'Twixt the Giltinans and the Carmodys* (1923), never received the attention they deserved. Many of them, like *The Pie-Dish* (1908), about obsessive craftsmanship, *The Magic Glasses* (1913), through which the owner can see marvellous sights, and *The Dandy Dolls* (1913), about puppets and the world of the fairies, were too fantastic for the audiences of the time. Fitzmaurice's closest friend was Seumas O'Sullivan* and most of his later work appeared in print in the *Dublin Magazine*.

Foras Feasa ar Éirinn (1618–34), comprehensive history of Ireland by Seathrún Céitinn* and drawing on the ancient historical and mythological cycles as well as the annals* and other earlier works of Gaelic scholarship. Céitinn had as his avowed aim to justify and explain Gaelic society in all its complexity and nobility to the unenlightened English and the Nua-Ghaill ('new foreigners': planter stock) who thought Gaelic Ireland barbaric. Some scholars see in this work evidence of postcolonialism *avant la lettre*.

Foster, Roy (b. 1949), historian, was born in Waterford and educated at TCD. His doctoral thesis on Parnell in his family setting was published in book form in 1976. He lectured in Birkbeck College, London University, becoming Professor of Modern British History in 1983 and Carroll Professor of Irish History at Oxford in 1991. His published work includes *Lord Randolph Churchill* (1982), the magisterial *Modern Ireland* (1989), *Paddy and Mr Punch* (1993) and the first volume of the authorised biography of Yeats* (1997). His work is brilliantly written and approaches the troubled Irish history with such fresh, though soundly based, opinions that his work has been called 'revisionist'. True, he has reconsidered some aspects of the Irish past which had been deemed settled for good, but in general his revisionism is merely the application of modern scholarship to the past.

French, Percy (1854–1920), entertainer, was born in Cloonyquin, County Roscommon, and after a leisurely career as an undergraduate at TCD finally emerged as an engineer to become 'Inspector of Drains', as one of his songs recalls, in County Cavan. Even as a student he had begun to write the mainly comic songs for which he is famous, including the often miscredited 'Abdul the Bulbul Ameer'. When his work as an engineer finished in 1887, he edited (and largely wrote) the comic paper *The Jarvey*, and on its demise a year later he collaborated with Houston Collisson (1864–1920) in a musical comedy, *The Knights of the Road* (1888). Its success launched him on his career as a touring performer of his own material: songs (sometimes to his own accompaniment on the banjo and usually with music by Collisson), monologues and sketches. He was a talented watercolourist and lightning paintings became part of his act, including the extra trick of doing 'double' pictures, turning the canvas on his easel upside-down to reveal a different picture. His songs are as popular now as when he wrote them. 'Come Back, Paddy Reilly', 'Phil the Fluter's Ball', 'The Mountains of Mourne', 'Are Ye Right There, Michael' and 'Slattery's Mounted Fut' are still sung widely. French died in Formby, Lancashire, after a short illness. Collisson, who had taken orders in 1899 and officiated at his friend's funeral, died a week later.

Friel, Brian (b. 1929), short story writer and playwright, was born in Omagh and educated in his father's primary schools and at St Columb's College, Derry, and Maynooth. He taught for ten years in Derry and then became a full-time writer, scoring a notable success with the play *Philadelphia, Here I Come!* (1964) which had a successful Broadway run. He had already published a volumes of short stories, *The Saucer of Larks* (1962) and went on to publish *The Gold in the Sea* (1966). The stories, many of which had appeared in the *New Yorker*, deal with childhood, loss, the consolation of admitted illusion (a characteristic of some of his plays) and the individual's sense of fitness. The plays since *Philadelphia* (excluding versions of Chekhov, Turgenev and Macklin*) amount to eighteen, all noted for their humour, irony, the simple brilliance of the dialogue and a sense of the tears of things kept at bay by a belief in the possibility of dreams some day coming true. Friel is a restless experimenter in dramatic form, seeming to push the idea of the play to its furthest definition. He uses music, dance, time rearrangement, extrusive characters and individual monologue rather than dialogue in such plays as *Faith Healer** (1979) and *Mollie Sweeney* (1994), but his work is verbally precise and perfectly logical. The occasional (and illusory) sense of formlessness upsets some critics but his plays continue to affect the attentive theatregoer long after the final curtain. His work, though of universal appeal, is undoubtedly Irish; his Everytown is Ballybeg, and Irish history and politics are his primary material, either specifically as in *The Freedom of the City* (1973), *Volunteers* (1975), *Translations* (1980) and the ambivalently titled *Making History* (1988), or as part of the consciousness of the vocal and fragmenting families that often form the dramatis personae of his plays. Perhaps *Dancing at Lughnasa** (1990), with its use of a narrator who is also one of the characters grown up, dance, ritual, clash of cultures, the existential nature of memory, compassion and Ballybeggary, might crudely be taken as a representative play.

G

Gaelic League, The (*Connradh na Gaeilge*) was the last and most successful of nineteenth-century attempts at the restoring of Irish as a spoken language. It was founded on 31 July 1893 by a committee led by Eoin MacNeill and Douglas Hyde*. Its method was the simple one of using native speakers to teach adults at evening classes and encouraging the teaching of Irish in schools, where it was already acceptable as a subject in the Leaving Certificate examination. The organisers, known as *timirí* ('messengers'), arranged for *múinteorí taistil* (travelling teachers) to visit classes in particular areas, usually several in one night, travelling mainly by bicycle, as the tributary poem 'The Man on the Bicycle' by Alice Milligan* makes clear. Other measures sponsored by the League were the establishment of *Coláistí Samhraidh** ('summer colleges'), the setting up of a newspaper, *An Claidheamh Soluis**, and the founding of feiseanna, which in turn encouraged original material written in Irish by offering prizes. Under the influence of Pearse* and MacNeill the League became heavily politicised and Hyde resigned in 1915. The League's thinking shaped the educational policy of the new state and the primacy granted Irish in the 1937 Constitution was in keeping with its ideals.

Gallagher, Patrick (Paddy the Cope) (1871–1964), autobiographer, was born in Cleendra near Dungloe, in the Rosses of Donegal. His claim to literary fame is *My Story* (1939), a gripping account of his life and work in the cooperative movement. Born on Christmas Day, the eldest of a family of nine children who lived on a poor holding of reclaimed bogland, he had barely three years' schooling and was hired out each year from 1881 till 1896 when he went to work in Scotland as farm hand, building labourer and coal miner. It was there that he learned the principles of co-operation, and his eventual establishment, in spite of great opposition, of the Templecrone 'Cope' in his own area broke the power of the local gombeen men. He also set up a large store and a glove factory, and provided Dungloe with a public lighting system. His book is often funny and is a piece of matchless social history.

Galvin, Patrick (b. 1927), poet and playwright, was born in Cork and educated by the Presentation Brothers. His plays *And Him Stretched* (1963) and *Cry the Believers* (1965) were staged at the Dublin Theatre Festival. Galvin's most productive period was when he was Leverhulme Fellow at the Lyric Theatre* in Belfast, with *Nightfall to*

Belfast (1973), about the Catholic working class in the Protestant city, *We Do It for Love* (1975), his greatest success (20,000 people saw it), which in song and story recorded life at the height of the Northern conflict, and *The Last Burning* (1974), overtly about witchcraft but generally about racial prejudice. His work is marked by interpolated ballads, written by himself, and he has published four volumes of poetry. *Song for a Poor Boy* (1990) and *Song for a Raggy Boy* (1991) describe youth and early manhood in his native city. A *Selected Poems* was published in 1996.

Ganly, Andrew (1908–82), playwright and novelist, was born in Dublin. He was educated at TCD and became a dentist, an early patient being his classmate Samuel Beckett*. His one-act play *The Dear Queen* (1938), about memories of nineteenth-century Ascendancy life, is a small comic classic, and his novel *The Desolate Sky* (1967) develops the theme of Anglo-Irish Big House decay and dissolution.

GATE THEATRE, THE (estd. 1930), Dublin's second 'literary' theatre, converted from the supper-rooms of the old Assembly Buildings (1785) in Parnell Square. It was founded by Hilton Edwards and his partner Mícheál Mac Liammóir* to present international drama and experimental theatre, complementary to the Abbey* with its mainly Irish offerings. The partners maintained a creditable array of classical and modern drama, with lighting and production mainly by Edwards, acting and design (and new plays) by Mac Liammóir. Chronically insecure financially, the Gate Theatre company alternated semesters with Longford Productions from 1936, touring when not in Dublin, but continued to provide a choice of theatre fare unavailable even in London at the time. From time to time the theatre was leased to independent companies, especially after Mac Liammóir's death in 1978, but with government subsidy and an outstanding new director, Michael Colgan, the theatre continued to present a programme of commercial and critical successes in enlarged premises from 1993.

Gébler, Carlo (b. 1954), novelist and short story writer, was born in Dublin, reared in Dublin and London and educated at the University of York. His novels include *The Eleventh Summer*(1995), *The Cure (1994),* with a historic/folkloric theme, *and How to Murder a Man (1998),* a historical work. He is also the author of a travel book, *Driving Through Cuba*, published in 1988 and an interesting work of non-fiction/reportage, *The Glass Curtain: Inside an Ulster Community.* He lives in Enniskillen, County Fermanagh.

Gentleman, Francis (1728–84), playwright and critic, was born in Dublin, the son of an army officer. His own military career was abandoned for acting and, like Farquhar*, he turned his hand to dramaturgy in London, producing a politer version of Ben Jonson's *The Alchemist* (1612) called *The*

Tobacconist (1771). *The Modish Wife* (1773) is regarded as his best play but his most useful writings are to be found in *The Dramatic Censor* (1770), which gives an account of the theatre of his time. He died in penury in Dublin.

Geoghegan, Arthur Gerald (1810–89), poet, was born in Dublin and became Collector of Revenue in 1857, moving to London in 1869. He published *The Monks of Kilcrea*, a long narrative poem, anonymously in 1853 and contributed regularly to *The Nation**, the *Dublin Penny Journal** and the *Irish Monthly* . His poem 'After Aughrim' is still anthologised. He died in London.

Gibbon, Monk (1896–1987), poet, was born in Dublin and educated at St Columba's and Keble College, Oxford. He was invalided out of the army in 1918 having spent four years in France and after the war he became a teacher. His well-made and happily unmodern poems are collected in *For Daws to Pick At* (1929), *This Insubstantial Pageant* (1951) and *The Velvet Bow* (1972). He also wrote autobiographical and travel works – *The Seals* (1935), *Mount Ida* (1948) and *The Pupil* (1981) – and he quarried a workable novel, *Thy Tears Might Cease** (1963), out of Michael Farrell**'s drift of papers.

Gigli Concert, The (1983), play by Thomas Murphy, about King, an unqualified counsellor, who claims to be able to be help people reach their potential. He is visited by a rich, self-made property developer who wants to sing like the Italian tenor Beniamino Gigli (1890–1957). It is in fact King who in enabled, out of 'the audacity of despair' at the loss of his lover through cancer, to sing like the tenor.

Gilbert, Stephen (b. 1912), novelist, was born in Newcastle, County Down, the son of a Belfast merchant whose firm he joined after a period as a journalist with the *Northern Whig*. His fantasy novels *The Landslide* (1943), set in a boy's world of talking dragons, and *Monkeyface* (1948), about a jungle boy brought to Belfast, were influenced by Forrest Reid*, whose protégé he was. *The Burnaby Experiments* (1952) and *The Ratman's Notebook* (1968) have fantasy elements but also describe the Ulster mercantile class in decay. *Bombardier* (1944), his account of an anti-aircraft battery during WWII, shows him an effective naturalistic writer.

Gogarty, Oliver St John (1878–1957), man of letters, was born in Dublin and educated at a variety of Jesuit institutions (including the Royal University) and TCD where he qualified in Medicine. He later became a leading practitioner in ENT surgery with a house in Ely Place. As a postgraduate student he shared accommodation at the Martello tower at Sandycove with James Joyce* and R. S. Chenevix Trench and was immortalised as 'stately plump Buck Mulligan' in *Ulysses**. The 'plump' was more euphonious than accurate since he was known for his athleticism. In Ireland he was a 'buck' in his Rolls

Royce (a butter-coloured one). His poetry, in spite of over-inclusion in Yeats*'s *Oxford Book of Modern Verse* (1936), is too well made for modern taste, but the temper of the man lives in *As I Was Going Down Sackville Street* (1937) and *It Isn't This Time of Year At All* (1954). He was a strong supporter of Arthur Griffith and the Treaty and, finding he could no longer live in the Ireland of de Valera, moved in 1939 first to England and then to America where he died.

Goldsmith, Oliver (1728–74), man of letters, was born in Pallas, County Longford, the son of an Anglican curate whom he immortalised as Dr Primrose in *The Vicar of Wakefield* (1766). He was educated in Athlone and attended TCD as a sizar. After a rackety career he graduated in 1749, being refused ordination. He studied Medicine in Edinburgh and at Leyden in Holland and, after a *petit tour*, became a teacher and hack in London in 1756. His plays *The Good-Natured Man* (1768) and *She Stoops to Conquer* (1773) show him outstripping his master Farquhar*, and 'The Deserted Village', though ostensibly set in England in a place called Auburn, owes much of its inspiration to Lissoy*, County Westmeath, where he spent nearly all his childhood, and which was devastated by a grasping landlord and the Penal Laws. His *Manners and Customs of the Native Irish* (1759) show him as kindly but conservative towards his fellow countrymen. Though rather the butt of Dr Johnson's Club, he was loved for his sweet nature, valued for the excellence of his essays ('he wrote like an angel and talked like poor Poll') and infamous for his fecklessness.

Good Behaviour (1981), Molly Keane*'s first novel under her own name, written when she was in her mid-seventies. It is a black comedy about the slow decline of the Big House of the St Charles family. The narrator is the middle-aged daughter Aroon who, on the occasion of her widowed mother's death, recalls her childhood and adolescence and betrays an arrogant unawareness of what actually happened, failing to understand that the governess who committed suicide was her father's mistress or that her adversary, the remaining servant Rose, was also his sexual partner.

Gore-Booth, Eva (1870–1926), poet, was born in Lissadell, County Sligo, and was one of the 'two girls in silk kimonos' of Yeats*'s poem. She moved to Manchester in 1892 and with her partner Esther Roper started a lifetime commitment to feminism and pacifism, changing some of the belligerence of the originals in her versions of Irish myth. She wrote much poetry and unstageable drama and is chiefly remembered now for such lyrics as 'The Little Waves of Breffny'. She died in Hampstead, London.

Grace Notes (1997), novel by Bernard MacLaverty* with the theme of artistic inspiration, delineating the life and work of Catherine Anne McKenna, a young Northern Ireland composer. It is structurally a diptych, the first part depicting Catherine's trip home from Glasgow for the funeral of her father, a small-town publican. The second half describes the (earlier) composition and performance of Catherine's percussive work *Vernicle* (a pilgrim's badge), and, almost as part of the process, the birth of her daughter Anna, severe post-natal depression and the sloughing off of her alcoholic partner, Anna's father.

Graves, A[lfred] P[erceval] (1846–1931), poet and balladeer, was born in Dublin to Charles Graves who was chaplain to Dublin Castle and later bishop of Limerick. He graduated from TCD in 1871 but spent most of his life in England where he was for some time assistant editor of *Punch*, a Home Office clerk and inspector of schools. He was the father by his second wife of the romantic poet and gadfly critic Robert Graves, whose book of WWI experiences, *Goodbye to All That* (1929), spurred A. P. to write a most entertaining book of reminiscences, *To Return to All That* (1932). He is remembered as an anthologist and collector of Irish songs and as the author of such lyrics as 'Father O'Flynn' and 'Trotting to the Fair'. He died in Harlech, Wales.

Graves, Clotilde (pseudonym 'Richard Dehan') (1864–1932), playwright and novelist, and cousin of A. P. Graves*, was born in Buttevant, County Cork. She was a popular playwright at the turn of the century and a serious but popular novelist with one bestseller,

The Dop Doctor (1911), set in South Africa.

Greacen, Robert (b. 1920), poet, was born in Derry and educated at Methody, Belfast, and TCD. He was part of the remarkably active literary scene in Belfast during and immediately after WWII, contributing to *The Bell** and *Lagan* and editing two anthologies of Ulster writing. He left for London in 1948 and worked there for many years as a teacher. He returned to poetry in 1975 with *A Garland for Captain Fox*, after having 'ditched' it in the mid-1950s ('Or did poetry ditch me?'). Now resident in Dublin, he continues to publish verse and memoirs. These have included *Even without Irene* (1969), *Brief Encounters* (1991) and *The Sash My Father Wore* (1997). *Collected Poems 1944–1994* was published in 1995.

Great Hunger, The (1942), poem by Patrick Kavanagh* describing the sterile life of his representative figure Patrick Maguire as he works to make a small County Monaghan farm pay, while tending to an aged mother who 'praised the man who has made a field his bride'. The poem's title looks back to the Famine of the 1840s and the change in the Irish psyche whereby a narrow parsimony and puritanism, sedulously taught by a narrow-minded Church, replaced the gaiety of earlier times. The spiritual hunger of such as Maguire in the 1940s is taken to be as devastating as the earlier cataclysm.

Gregory, Lady (née Augusta Persse) (1852–1932), playwright and folklorist, was born to an Ascendancy family in Roxborough, County Galway. She married Sir William Gregory of Coole Park, a former governor of Ceylon, in 1880 and on his death in 1892, under the influence of Yeats*, rekindled an earlier interest in the Irish language and the folklore of Connacht. Her relationship with Yeats was one of mutual literary creativity. Together with Edward Martyn, a local Catholic landlord, they conceived the idea of a National Theatre, which found its fullest expression in the Abbey*. She wrote plays, notably *Spreading the News* (1904), *Hyacinth Halvey* (1906), *The Gaol Gate* (1906), *The Rising of the Moon**(1907), *The Workhouse Ward* (1908) and versions of Molière written in 'Kiltartanese', the Hiberno-English mode that reflected the local speech and in which she wrote her translations of the Celtic sagas, *Cuchulain of Muirthemne* (1902) and *Gods and Fighting Men* (1904). She was a vigorous defender of her theatre and of Irish nationalism, which she had espoused with vigour before the turn of the century.

Gregory, Padraic (1886–1962), poet, was born in Belfast and became a well known ecclesiastical architect, designing among other churches the Catholic cathedral in Johannesburg. He published a number of books of ballads, simple, singable pieces such as such as 'Padric the Fidiler', which were often set as pieces for *feiseanna*.

Grennan, Eamon (b.1941), was born in Dublin and studied at UCD and Harvard University. He has published four collections of poetry, *Wildly Days*, (1983), *What Light There Is* (1987) *As If It Matters* (1991) and *So It Goes* (1995). He has also produced a volume of translations, *Leopardi: Selected Poems* (1995). He currently teaches at Vassar College, Poughkeepsie, New York.

Griffin, Gerald (1803–40), poet and novelist, was born and educated in Limerick and went to England to become a playwright but failed because of 'the fickleness of public literary taste'. He tried to make a living by hack work in London and at home, supported by a Quaker patron, Mrs Lydia Fisher, as all the while his religious fervour increased. In 1836 he became a Christian Brother in Dublin and he died in the monastery in Cork. He is famous as the author of *The Collegians**(1829), a novel of passion and murder based upon an actual case, which became very popular and provided Boucicault* with his first success as *The Colleen Bawn*. (1860). He also wrote the lyrics 'My Mary of the Curling Hair', 'Hy-Breasail' and 'Eileen Aroon'.

Gulliver's Travels (1726), Swift*'s political satire in which Lemuel Gulliver, a ship's surgeon, visits various fantastic countries where mores are thinly disguised versions of attitudes in Ireland and Britain. In Lilliput the people are tiny, with factional minds, in Brobdingnag they are gigantic and physically repellent, and in the Land of the

Houyhnhnms the vertical bipeds are savage animals called Yahoos (one of several of Swift's coinages that have become current) while the equine philosophers represent reason. The Swiftian scatological elements removed, the book has become a children's classic.

Gúm, An (estd. 1925), government publishing agency set up by then Minister for Finance Ernest Blythe* to produce textbooks and literature in Irish – a prerequisite for the desired revival of the language – and still in existence. Much of its work has involved producing Irish translations of works written in English and other languages but it has also published some of the finest writers in Irish, such as Seosamh Mac Grianna* and Máirtín Ó Cadhain*.

Gwynn, Aubrey (1892–1983), historian, was born in Dublin and educated at Clongowes, UCD (the first student to sign its register), Queen's College, Oxford, and Louvain. He was ordained a Jesuit priest in 1924 and later became Professor of Medieval History at UCD (1949–62) and the leading authority on the medieval Irish Church.

Gwynn, Stephen (1864–1950), poet and man of letters, was born at St Columba's College, Rathfarnham, where his father, later Professor of Divinity at TCD, was Anglican warden. Almost immediately the family left for Ramelton, County Donegal, his father's new living, and it was there that Gwynn spent a happy boyhood. He was educated at Brasenose, Oxford, and became Nationalist MP for Galway City. He was grandson of the revolutionary Smith O'Brien, father of Aubrey Gwynn* and a follower of John Redmond. He joined the army as a private and rose to the rank of captain in the Connaught Rangers, becoming a chevalier in the Legion of Honour. He was the quintessential Protestant Nationalist, loving and serving Ireland but appreciating British culture, writing excellent biographies of Swift*, Moore*, Scott of the Antarctic, Sir Walter Scott and Robert Louis Stevenson. He also wrote verse, evocative travel books – notably *Highways and Byways in Donegal and Antrim* (1903), *The Fair Hills of Ireland* (1906) and *Beautiful Ireland* (1911) – and entertaining memoirs, *Experiences of a Literary Man* (1926).

H

Hackett, Francis (1883–1962), novelist, was born in Kilkenny and educated at Clongowes. He emigrated to America in 1901 and became literary editor of the *New Republic*. He returned to Ireland in 1927 but, when his semi-autobiographical novel *The Green Lion* (1936) was banned, went to live in Denmark, which he later celebrated in *I Chose Denmark* (1940). The tenor of all his work afterwards was critical of de Valera's Ireland. He wrote much history, including studies of Henry VIII and François I, and died in Denmark, to which he had returned after the Nazi occupation.

Haicéad, Pádraigín (c. 1600–c. 1654), poet in Irish, was born in the Cashel area of Tipperary. He was educated at Louvain and became a Dominican monk. He was prior of Cashel in 1624 and from then until his death was deeply involved in the politics of the time, attempting to act as a peacemaker during the troubled 1640s. He was, however, not a natural pacificier: much of his life was taken up with conflict and polemic, and his poetry shows signs of personal animus. His poem, 'Múscail do Mhisneach, a Bhanba', written when the Confederation of Kilkenny split in 1646, is both a patriotic battle-cry and an attack on those whom he saw as

betraying their country. In 1651 he returned to Louvain, the better to carry on a pugnacious correspondence with Rinuccini, the controversial Papal Nuncio to Ireland. In 1654 his differences with the head of his order in Ireland led to his being admonished. He died shortly afterwards.

Hall, A[nna] M[aria] (1800–81) and **S[amuel] C[arter]** (1880–89), travellers. Anna Fielding was born in Dublin and married Samuel Hall, the Waterford-born son of an English army officer, in 1824. Their most important work was *Ireland, Its Scenery, Character &c* (1842) which gives a sympathetic but clear-eyed account of pre-Famine Ireland. Their purpose was to make British readers understand the true nature of their neglected colony. Anna also wrote nine novels and four successful plays, including *The Groves of Blarney* (1838).

Halpine, Charles Graham (pseudonym 'Private Myles O'Reilly') (1829–68), journalist, comic poet and Young Irelander, was born in County Meath, the son of a clergyman, N. J. Halpine. He emigrated to America in 1851 and became a journalist in New York. He joined the Federal army in 1861 and rose to the rank of brigadier-general in the famous

'Fighting 69th', having as a colonel commanded the first Afro-American regiment. He wrote two historical novels and many songs and comic poems, including 'Irish Astronomy', which includes the anastronomical lines: 'You'll see O'Ryan any night/Amid the constellations'. He died from an accidental overdose of chloral taken for insomnia.

Hamilton, Hugo (b. 1953), novelist and short story writer, was born in Dublin of an Irish father and a German mother. His first novel *Surrogate City* (1990) is a love story set in West Berlin before the fall of the Berlin Wall. Hamilton has published three other novels, most recently *Headbanger* (1997), and a short story collection *Dublin Where The Palm Trees Grow* (1996), all of which feature probing examinations of contemporary Ireland, although frequently against an international backdrop.

Hanley, Gerald (b. 1916), novelist and travel writer, was born in Cork, brother of James Hanley*, and went to work in East Africa in 1935. He joined the army in 1939 and used his experiences in Burma in his first published novel *Monsoon Victory* (1946). His best known and first-written book *The Consul at Sunset* (1951) describes the twilight of empire in a manner reminiscent of Graham Greene. Other works set in Africa are *The Year of the Lion* (1953) and *Drinkers of Darkness* (1955). *Noble Descents* (1982) is set in post-Independence India.

Hanley, James (1901–85), novelist, playwright and short story writer, brother of Gerald Hanley*, was born in poverty in Dublin and, like the brutalised and shortlived hero of his banned novel *Boy* (1931), went to sea at thirteen, serving in the Canadian navy during WWI and later as a merchant seaman. His literary output was prodigious, comprising nearly thirty novels, sixteen volumes of short stories (one originally published in *The Bell**), numerous scripts for radio and television and seven volumes of other writings, including an autobiography, *Broken Waters* (1937). His sea stories have an unmistakable air of authenticity, but a series of novels about a Liverpool-Irish family – *The Furys* (1935), *The Secret Journey* (1936), *Our Time is Gone* (1940), *Winter Journey* (1950) and *An End and Beginning* (1958) – is his finest achievement.

Harbinson, Robert (b. 1928), short story writer, autobiographer and travel writer, was born Robin Bryans (a name he still uses for many travel books) in Ballymacarret, east Belfast, and educated there and in Fermanagh, to which he was evacuated during WWII. He left Ireland to study Theology at a Bible College in South Wales in 1944 and subsequently taught in England, Canada and Venezuela. He has published a collection of Ulster stories, *Tattoo Lily* (1961), but his best work consists of his four-volume autobiography: *No Surrender* (1960), *Song of Erne* (1960), *Up Spake the Cabin Boy* (1961) and *The Protégé* (1963), possibly the finest and funniest account of the making of an Ulster working-class Protestant, his informal education along the Erne and his years as an evangelical preacher. He now lives in west London.

Harte, Jack (b. 1944), poet and fiction writer, was born at Easkey in County Sligo in 1944.. He has published a book of poetry, *Poems of Alienation*, a collection of short stories *Murphy in the Underworld* and a novel *Homage*. (1992). In 1986 he founded the Irish Writer's Union and in 1991 helped to establish the Irish Writers' Centre. His most recent work is *Birds and Other Tails* (1996).

Hartnett, Michael (b. 1941), poet in Irish and English and translator, was born in Croom, County Limerick. From his first published work his was regarded as a fresh and noteworthy new voice. He published poetry in English and translations from Irish and Spanish until in 1975, with *A Farewell to English*, he announced his intention thereafter to write in Irish – although he returned to English with *Inchicore Haiku* (1985). Collections in Irish include *Adharca Broic* (1978) and *An Lia Nocht* (1985). His most recent collection, *Selected and New Poems*, was published in 1994. Hartnett continues to translate from Irish – including versions of his own Irish poems – and from other languages into Irish. He now lives in Dublin and writes in Irish and English.

Haverty, Anne, novelist, poet and biographer, was born in County Tipperary and educated at TCD. *One Day as a Tiger* (1997), a skilful first novel about a genetically engineered sheep, Missy, a farming community and an illicit love affair, was highly praised. She has also published a biography, *Constance Markievicz: an Independent Life* (1988) and her poetry has appeared in journals and magazines.

Hayes, Richard (1902–76), bibliographer, was born in Abbeyfeale, County Limerick, and graduated with unique triple honours in Celtic, Modern Languages and Philosophy from TCD, where he later graduated LLD. He joined the staff of the National Library in 1923, and when made Director in 1940 he was the youngest to hold such a post anywhere in the world. He garnered much important material for the library. His great bibliographical contribution was his compilation of guides to manuscript sources for the 'history of Irish civilisation', both in English and in Irish, in a total of twenty-three volumes with more than 300,000 entries, assembled between 1938 and 1970. He died in Dublin after much varied service to Irish culture.

Healy, Dermot (b. 1947), poet and novelist, was born in Finea, County Westmeath, and educated in Cavan, where he afterwards edited the journals *Drumlin* and *Force 10*. His short story collection *Banished Misfortune* was published in 1982. The novel *A Goat's Song* (1993) is the story of the misalliance between a Donegal Catholic and a Protestant policeman and *The Bend for Home* (1996) is part memoir and part fictional contrivance. He has written plays and the scenario for the film *Our Boys* (1980).

Healy, Gerard (1918–63), actor and playwright, was born in Dublin and educated at Synge Street CBS. He joined the Gate Theatre* and wrote *Thy Dear Father* (1943), a study in fanatic piety, and *The Black Stranger* (1945), one of the best of the plays about the Great Famine. He was married to the actress Eithne Dunne and died in London while playing the Jesuit preacher in Hugh Leonard*'s *Stephen D*.

Heaney, Seamus (b. 1939), poet, was born in Mossbawn near Castledawson, County Derry, and educated at St Columb's College, Derry (where he was a classmate of Seamus Deane*), and QUB. He taught for some time in a Belfast school where the principal, Michael McLaverty*, encouraged his writing. He later lectured in English at St Joseph's College of Education and QUB (1966). He has published nearly a score of books of poetry and associated work (including *The Cure at Troy*, a version of the *Philoctetes* of Sophocles, *Sweeney Astray*, a rendering of the medieval poem *Buile Shuibhne*, and *The Midnight Verdict*, a translation of parts of Merriman*'s *Cúirt an Mhéan-Oíche*) and, as the award of the Nobel Prize for Literature (the culmination of many other awards) in 1995 proclaimed, he is one of the foremost

poets writing in English and Yeats*'s true successor as the Irish poet of the twentieth century. His early works, *Death of a Naturalist* (1966) and *Door into the Dark* (1969), reflect his precise observation of the country and the farm year he knew as a child, but already his artisans are becoming archetypes and the land that is worked is clearly the partitioned Ireland that had begun to show its sectarian sickness in the Civil Rights marches and the Protestant response, themes prominent in *Wintering Out* (1972) and especially *North** (1975). Heaney, a Catholic nationalist, has always resisted either the temptation or the pressure to 'speak' for any cause, maintaining the rooted stance 'Ich am of Irlaunde' and preferring polite put-downs to thunder, as when in one of the pamphlets of Field Day* (of which he is a director) he refused the description of British poet. Later work shows even deeper digging into Irishness but with worldwide referents, as *The Haw Lantern* (1987) indicates. *Station Island* (1984) calls to his table such significant figures as Joyce* and Carleton*, and *The Spirit Level* (1996), his first collection since his Nobel accolade, might be summed up by the title of one of its poems, 'Keeping Going'. Heaney moved to Wicklow in 1972 and now lives mainly in Dublin when his responsibilities as Boylston Professor of Rhetoric in Harvard permit. His lectures as Professor of Poetry at Oxford (1989–94) appeared as *The Redress of Poetry* in 1995 and he has also published three volumes of excellent literary essays.

Hearn, Lafcadio (1850–1904), orientalist, was born on the island of Levkas (for which he was named) to an Irish navy surgeon and his illiterate Greek wife. He was reared by puritanical Dublin aunts and sent by the one who was Catholic to Ushaw. He emigrated to America and later to Japan, changed his name to Yakumo Koizumi and married a Japanese wife. His writings reflect his approval of the integration of all aspects of life into Japanese philosophy and he is the foremost interpreter of his adopted country to the West. His most accessible work for Western readers is *Kwaidan* (1904), a book of legends and ghostly tales. He died at Okubo.

Heartbreak House: *A fantasia in the Russian manner on English themes* (1920), play by Shaw* attempting to write after the manner of Chekhov's *The Cherry Orchard*. It describes the visit to the house (built in the shape of a ship) of the eighty-eight-year-old mysterious eccentric Captain Shotover by a young, idealistic woman, Ellie Dunn. The household consists mainly of charming, romantic, kind but irresponsible people, including Shotover's two daughters, Hesione (whose husband has been wooing Ellie) and Ariadne, Lady Utterwood and Boss Mangan, an anti-romantic, anti-English Irishman who is the sole casualty when the house narrowly misses destruction during an air-raid. It is part satire on Bloomsbury, part reaction to WWI, and in its extensive, witty debate on capitalism, colonial exploitation and decadence, though oddly moving, it is obstinately Shavian and hardly Chekhovian at all.

Hewitt, John (1907–87), poet, was born in Belfast and educated at Methody and QUB. He joined the staff of the Belfast Museum and Art Gallery in 1930, and during the next three decades, like his friends E. Estyn Evans*, John Boyd* and Sam Hanna Bell*, was an active socialist and associate editor of *Lagan*. He left to become Director of the Herbert Art Gallery and Museum, Coventry, in 1957, believing that his radicalism was preventing his advancement in a unionist-dominated institution. He returned to Belfast on retirement in 1972 and continued writing poetry and interesting himself in the arts. He was poet-in-residence at NUU (1973–6) and at QUB (1976–9). His MA thesis was 'Ulster Poets (1800–1870)' and among several anthologies edited by him are *The Poems of William Allingham* (1967) and *Rhyming Weavers* (1974). His own work has the recurring theme of the honourable separateness of his forebears ('Once Alien Here') and the natives who were displaced to make room for them. In 1970 he and John Montague* collaborated in the significantly named *The Planter and the Gael*. His volume of *Collected Poems* (1991), edited by Frank Ormsby, contains over 700 poems. He has written monographs on Ulster artists and was co-editor with Bell and Nesca Robb of *The Arts in Ulster* (1951). He is honoured in the John Hewitt International Summer School held each year at Garron Tower on the Antrim coast.

Hickey, Christine Dwyer (b. 1958), novelist and short story writer, was born in Dublin. She has won several awards for her stories, and two volumes of a family trilogy, *The Dancer* (1995) and *The Gambler* (1997), show her to be a writer of mature skill.

Hidden Ireland, The (1924), influential work of historical criticism by writer and scholar Daniel Corkery*, which from a viewpoint unequivocally nationalistic evokes the lives and society of many of the great Irish poets of the eighteenth century, including Aogán Ó Rathaile* and Eoghan Rua Ó Súilleabháin*. Although taking little account of scholarly research into the actual social conditions of eighteenth-century Ireland, it is still a fascinating and emotionally accurate account of the Gaelic poets of the period.

Higgins, Aidan (b. 1927), novelist and short story writer, was born in Celbridge, County Kildare, and educated at Clongowes. He had a number of temporary jobs, including touring with a marionette company in Europe and Africa. His collection *Felo de Se* (1960) contains, along with stories set in Europe, the novella 'Killachter Meadow' which was later developed into the novel *Langrishe, Go Down**(1966). Other novels include *Balcony of Europe* (1972), set in Andalusia, *Scenes from a Receding Past* (1977), which shows if nothing else the

unreliability of memory, *Bornholm Night Ferry* (1983), a tale of a love affair between an Irish writer and a Danish poet told in letters, and *Lions of the Grünewald* (1995) with the usual Higgins relationship of Irish man and European woman. He has also published two volumes of autobiography, *Donkey's Years* (1996) and *Dog Days* (1998)

Higgins, F[rederick] R[obert] (1896–1941), poet, was born in Foxford, County Mayo, and brought up in Dublin. His father, an engineer from County Meath, was a strict unionist, but the son was strongly radical and, influenced by the Irish Literary Revival*, became a close friend of Yeats* and Austin Clarke*. (This apparently caused no rift since several of his poems are about his father, especially 'Father and Son' and 'The Boyne Walk'.) He lost his job as a clerk when he founded a clerical workers' union and he later became editor of the first Irish women's magazine. It was a shortlived venture, the first edition being called *Welfare* and the second (and last) *Farewell*. His early poetry was influenced by the life of the Connacht people he admired, and he and Clarke endeavoured to strengthen their verse with Gaelic assonance and metres. Higgins became business manager and a director of the Abbey*. He published in all five collections of poetry, notably *The Dark Breed* (1927) and *The Gap of Brightness* (1941).

Higgins, Rita Ann (b. 1955), poet and playwright, was born in Galway and 'self-educated' while convalescing from tuberculosis. She has published five collections of bright, sardonic, angry poetry about women, children, poverty, politics and the business of living in Ireland: *Goddess on the Mervue Bus* (1986), *Witch in the Bushes* (1988), *Goddess and Witch* (1991), *Philomena's Revenge* (1992) and Higher Purchase (1998). *Sunny Side Plucked*, a *New and Selected Poems*, appeared in 1995. Her plays, which include *Face-Licker Come Home* (1991) and *God-of-the-Hatch Man* (1993) are dramatic extensions of her poems.

Hogan, Desmond (b. 1950), short story writer and novelist, was born in Ballinasloe, County Galway, and educated at Garbally and UCD. While still a schoolboy he had stories published in David Marcus*'s 'New Irish Writing' page in the *Irish Press*. Most of his work is dark and heavy with metaphor, with cruelty, oddity and deviation the norm. In his stories plot takes second place to atmosphere. His first novel *The Ikon Maker* (1976), a promising tale about a mother-son relationship, loses itself in tingling symbols. Hogan has written plays for stage and television and four other novels, but his most enduring work is likely to be his stories, of which *Lebanon Lodge* (1988) is the best collection.

Holloway, Joseph (1861–1944), diarist and architect, was born in Dublin and educated at Castleknock and the Metropolitan School of Art. He was the architect who converted the Mechanics Institute into the Abbey* and he became its most relentless attender; it was said that he missed no theatrical event in Dublin for fifty years and was therefore the appropriate person to edit the theatre section of Stephen Brown*'s *A Guide to Books of Ireland*.* (1912) He recorded his impressions in a diary which ran to 200 volumes, from which were hewed *Joseph Holloway's Abbey Theatre* (1967) and *Joseph Holloway's Irish Theatre* (three vols. 1968–70). They reveal a crusty but kindly, opinionated, narrow-minded, totally besotted theatregoer.

Horniman, Annie E[lizabeth] (1860–1937), theatre founder, was born in London, the daughter and heir of a wealthy Quaker tea merchant. She studied art at the Slade and developed a passion for the theatre and later for Yeats*, for whom she provided the Abbey*. They eventually quarrelled, ostensibly about the Nationalism of some of the theatre's plays and the popular prices, with a final clash over the theatre's staying open during the period of mourning for the death of Edward VII, but the real reason may have been Yeats's lack of romantic interest. She continued her patronage of theatre in Britain, buying and supporting the Gaiety Theatre as the home of 'the Manchester School' between 1908 and 1917, and 'discovering' such realistic English classics as *Hindle Wakes* (1912) by Stanley Houghton (1881–1913) and *Hobson's Choice* (1916) by Harold Brighouse (1882–1958). Her initiative laid the roots of the repertory movement, which had such a profound effect on modern British theatre and its acting tradition.

How Many Miles to Babylon? (1974), Jennifer Johnston*'s third and most successful novel, about Irish soldiers in the trenches of WWI. Alex Moore, the son of a Big House, and Jerry Crowe, a stable-boy who works on the estate, grow up as friends with a shared interest in horses and the romantic Irish past, in spite of the disapproval of Alex's mother Alicia. The friendship continues in France against the instructions of their commanding officer, Major Glendinning. Jerry, the realist, has joined up to learn to fight for Ireland in the coming times, and is sentenced to death for going AWOL to settle a family problem. When Glendinning, in Blimpish fashion, puts Alex in charge of the firing-squad he shoots Jerry himself and tells their story as he awaits execution.

Hutchinson, Pearse (b. 1927), poet in Irish and English and translator, was born in Glasgow but brought back to Dublin by his Irish parents while still a child and educated at Synge Street CBS and UCD. He published some early poems in *The Bell** and in *Combar**, and, after a period spent in Spain, a volume of translation from Catalan. He has continued to translate from the Iberian languages and from Irish, including his own work in *The Soul That Kissed the Body* (1990). His English-language collections include *Climbing*

the Light (1985). He has contributed a column in Irish to the *RTE Guide* for the last ten years and is co-editor of *Cyphers* magazine and a member of Aósdana.

Hyde, Douglas (1860–1949), (Dúghlas de Híde), Gaelic revivalist and first President of Ireland, was born the son of the Anglican rector of Frenchpark, County Roscommon, and educated at home because of childhood illness. He learned Irish as a child and later studied it as part of the Divinity course at TCD. There he joined the Society for the Preservation of the Irish Language and became one of the main players in the Irish Literary Revival* and in the wave of cultural Nationalism generated by the old Fenian John O'Leary and involving such people as T. W. Rolleston*, Katharine Tynan*, George Sigerson* and Yeats*, whom Hyde had already met. Though he graduated LLD in 1886, his principal concern was language. Proficient in Latin, Greek, Hebrew, German and French (he served as Professor of Modern Languages in the University of New Brunswick for the academic year 1891–2), his main interest was in Irish, which according to Yeats he had learned 'from the company of old countrymen'. He published poems in Irish and English, often using the pseudonym '*An Craoibhin Aoibhinn*' ('the pleasant little branch'). His first book *Leabhar Sgeulaigheachta* (1889), a collection of tales, rhymes and riddles that he had gathered in Connacht, was followed by *Beside the Fire* (1890), a trailblazing, scholarly collection of Irish folktales, which had an obvious effect on the works of Gregory*, Yeats and Synge*. Collaboration with Yeats led to the writing and production of *Casadh an tSúgáin* (*The Twisting of the Rope*) (1901), the first play of any merit in modern Irish, to be followed by nine others. *Love Songs of Connacht* appeared in 1893, and two important works of Gaelic scholarship, *The Story of Early Gaelic Literature* (1895) and *A Literary History of Ireland* (1899) effectively refuted the slurs of Mahaffy and others bent upon belittling the language revival, and made Hyde the obvious choice for the Chair of Modern Irish at UCD in 1905. In 1892 he became President of the National Literary Society and his inaugural lecture 'The Necessity for De-Anglicising Ireland' paved the way for the founding of the Gaelic League* the following year. He remained its President until 1915 when, under the influence of such IRB members as Eoin MacNeill* and Patrick Pearse*, it ceased to be the non-sectarian, non-political organisation that Hyde had intended at its foundation. He served as a Free State senator (1925–6) and retired from his university chair in 1932. He was persuaded out of his retirement at 'Ratra' (the house presented to him by the Gaelic League) to serve as the country's first President, from 1938 until his death as a semi-invalid in Aras an Uachtaráin.

I

Importance of Being Earnest, The (1895), the fourth and most famous of Oscar Wilde*'s 'trivial comedies for serious people', written in the few years before his imprisonment. It describes the wooing by Jack Worthing and Algy Moncrieff, two witty young men with private incomes, of Gwendolen Fairfax, daughter of the dragonish Lady Bracknell, and Cecily Cardew, Worthing's ward. The wooing is complicated by the fact that Jack is a foundling who claims his name is Ernest (and thus *non grata* to both mother and daughter) and refuses permission for his ward's marriage to the 'dissolute' Algy. The complications are satisfactorily resolved in dialogue of surpassing brilliance. The play has been deconstructed both as a gay and as a Nationalistic text.

Importance of Being Oscar, The (1960), the one-man entertainment written and performed by Mícheál Mac Liammóir* and directed by his partner Hilton Edwards, about the life and works of Oscar Wilde*, in which biography is interlaced with commentary and excerpts acted by the performer. His Wilde is the public one that his subject would have approved, even to the extent of a somewhat vulgar Lady Bracknell.

In a Glass Darkly (1872), a collection of five stories by Le Fanu*, linked as cases of the German psychicist Martin Hesselius and dealing with hauntings and drug-induced hallucinations. 'Carmilla', the final tale, is a powerful combination of vampirism and lesbian attraction, remarkable for its specificity and for its influence on many modern films and on its inferior successor, Stoker*'s *Dracula**.

Informer, The (1925), Liam O'Flaherty*'s most famous novel, set in the Dublin of the War of Independence. It tells the story of Gypo Nolan, the eponymous outcast who, for what seems to his slow brain sufficient reason, betrays a member of the 'organisation' to the British authorities. Its analysis of the hunted man, his motivation and inevitable execution, is rendered with marvellously nightmarish effect and the book was a natural for its successful filming by John Ford in 1935.

Inglis, Brian (1919–91), journalist, was born a 'West Briton' (the title of his first, unapologetic autobiography, published in 1962) in Malahide, County Dublin, and educated at Shrewsbury, Magdalen College, Oxford, and TCD. He served in the RAF during WWII and later became London correspondent of The *Irish Times* and editor of the *Spectator*

(1954–9). He presented the television programmes *What the Papers Say* and *All Our Yesterdays* and wrote much about alternative medicine and the paranormal. *The Story of Ireland* (1956) was a useful short history at the time of writing and *Downstart* (1990), an extended version of *West Briton*, gives a witty and fascinating account of a surviving Protestant enclave in Free State Dublin.

Ingram, John Kells (1823–1907), balladeer, was born near Pettigo, County Donegal, and educated in Newry and TCD, where he eventually held the Chair of Greek. He published the famous 'Who Fears to Speak . . .' ballad 'The Memory of the Dead' in *The Nation** in 1843. He was the founding editor of *Hermathena*, the TCD journal (1874), and became President of the Royal Irish Academy (1892) and Vice-Provost of TCD (1898). He was a noted sociologist and, in spite of his fiery ballad, whose authorship he never denied, a unionist in politics.

Inventing Ireland (1995), work of historical criticism by Declan Kiberd*, is a wide-ranging and penetrating study of Irish literature in the light of post-colonial theory. Agree or disagree, the work provides a lively critical framework for an understanding of how Ireland's identity was shaped and how this is reflected in the literature of the nation. Kiberd is particularly strong on Synge and on the ethos of Free State Ireland, and *Inventing Ireland* has been read and admired far beyond academe.

IONA, island of the Inner Hebrides in the kingdom of Dál Riata, properly called *I*, lying about eighty miles from Ireland (but not visible from it) where Colum Cille* established the monastery of his self-imposed exile. From there he and his monks christianised most of Pictish Scotland and northern Britain. Later abbots included Adamnán* (the founder's biographer) and at least part of the *Book of Kells* was written there. The monastic life of the community ended with a massacre by Vikings in 825, the last of a series of raids which had begun in 795.

Ireland, Denis (1894–1974), journalist and polemicist, was born in Belfast into a prosperous linen-manufacturing family and educated at Inst and QUB, his medical studies abandoned in 1914 when he joined the army. After service in France and Mesopotamia he worked for the family business in America and Canada until early retirement in 1930. He worked as a journalist and broadcaster for forty years, having become an ardent nationalist, finding Unionism a tragic aberration. His main autobiographical writings are contained in *An Ulster Protestant Looks at His World* (1931), *From the Irish Shore* (1935), *Statues round the City Hall* (1939) and *From the Jungle of Belfast* (1973). *Patriot Adventurer* (1936) is an edition of some of Wolfe Tone's writings with Ireland's own commentaries and biographical sketch. He took an active part in the Campbell's Coffee House* coterie of writers, broadcasters, artists, etc. of the 1930s and 1940s.

Iremonger, Valentin (1918–91), poet and translator, was born in Dublin and educated at Synge Street and Coláiste Mhuire. He joined the Abbey* acting school and was with the company from 1942 to 1944 and with the Gate* from 1944 to 1946. In 1947 he took part in the famous audience protest with Roger McHugh about the decline in Abbey standards. Having joined the Department of Foreign Affairs in 1946, he served as ambassador to the Scandinavian countries, Luxembourg, Portugal and India, retiring in 1980. He was co-editor with Robert Greacen* of *Contemporary Irish Poetry* (1949) and poetry editor of *Envoy*. His own work won the Æ Memorial Award in 1945 and is published in *Reservations* (1950), *Horan's Field and Other Reservations* (1972) and *Sandymount, Dublin* (1988). He is known to a wide readership as the translator of Mící Mac Gabhann*'s *Rotha Mór an tSaoil* (1959) as *The Hard Road to Klondike* (1962) and Dónal Mac Amhlaigh's *Dialann Deoraí* (1960) as *An Irish Navvy* (1964).

IRISH FOLKLORE COMMISSION, THE, was established on a shoestring government budget in 1935 by Séamus Ó Duilearga (Delargy) and accumulated a magnificent archive of material (reaching, by 1964, 1.5 million pages) garnered under the direction of Seán Ó Súilleabháin* and Kevin Danaher*. Bríd Mahon*'s *While Green Grass Grows* (1998) is an entertaining informal history of the Commission by one of its former employees.

Irish RM, The, comic stories by Somerville & Ross*, originally intended as hunting sketches, but blossoming into useful social documents of turn-of-the-century Irish rural life. Published as *Some Experiences of an Irish RM* (1899), *Further Experiences of an Irish RM* (1908) and *In Mr Knox's Country* (1908), they recount the misadventures of the naïve Major Yeates RM, his Anglo-Irish friendly adversary Flurry Knox, Slipper the wily drunken horse-coper and many other characters both peasant and half-mounted. They were disowned as stage-Irish by Sinn Féin and by the National Literary Movement as unpoetic but, in their precise and sympathetic observation of Irish life as it was lived with decaying 'gintry', nationalist petite bourgeoisie and clear-eyed surviving peasantry, they give a remarkably true picture of post-Parnellite Ireland. Edith Somerville was firmly nationalist but it was Violet Martin (of Catholic ancestry and unionist inclination) whose dark imagination supplied the Gothic elements in some otherwise light-hearted stories.

Irish Sketch Book, The (1843), genial, generally sympathetic but astute account by William Thackeray* (1811–63) of a tour, as by Michael Angelo Titmarsh, in pre-Famine Ireland (1842). The book is decorated by excellent drawings (though one of Daniel O'Connell could have come from the anti-Paddy *Punch*, established a year earlier). The admission of the complicated nature of Irish society, with sectarian attitudes bristling on both sides, and Thackeray's anticlericalism made the book unpopular with Young Ireland but it is one of the best of its kind and provided the author with excellent background material for *The Luck of Barry Lyndon* (1844).

IRISH WRITING (1946–57), quarterly literary magazine edited by David Marcus* and Terence Smith until 1954, and for its remaining life by Sean J. White. The list of its contributors is a kind of literary *Who's Who* of the period, with pieces by O'Casey*, O'Faolain*, MacNeice*, Lavin* and many others.

Irvine, Alexander (1862–1941), evangelist and biographer, was born in Pogue's Entry in Antrim town and shared the terrible poverty of his mother Anna Gilmore, whom he made famous as *My Lady of the Chimney Corner* (1913). He became a coal miner in Scotland and later served in the Royal Marines. Missionary work among the derelicts in the Bowery of New York led to his serving as a padre in WWI. He had an active career in labour relations, being asked to mediate in the British general strike of 1926. He began writing with the encouragement of Jack London. *The Souls of Poor Folk* (1921) and *Anna's Wishing Chair* (1937) were further books about his charismatic mother. He wrote three volumes of memoirs – *From the Bottom Up* (1910), *God and Tommy Atkins* (1918) and *The Fighting Parson* (1930) – and a book of short stories, *The Man from the World's End* (1926).

Irwin, T[homas] Caulfield (1823–92), poet, was born in Warrenpoint, County Down, to wealthy parents who had him educated privately. His fortunes declined and he moved to Dublin where he supported himself with journalism, fiction and verse, much of it written for *The Nation**. His poetry was greatly regarded by his contemporaries, and certain pieces, 'The Faerie's Child' and some sonnets, still find and deserve their place in anthologies. He died in Rathmines, regarded by his neighbours as 'the mad poet'.

J

Jenkinson, Biddy (b. 1949), poet in Irish, writes under a pesudonym and eschews personal publicity. Her work has been published in magazines like *Combar** and *Innti* and is highly regarded. Her collections include *Baisteadh Gintlí* (1987), *Uiscí Beatha* (1988) and *Dán na hUidhre* (1991). She writes with emotional intensity and strenuous lyricism about subjects such as femaleness and motherhood. Although she normally resists the translation of her work into English, some of her poems appear in *An Crann Faoi Bhláth* (1991), a bilingual anthology edited by Gabriel Fitzmaurice* and Declan Kiberd*.

John Bull's Other Island (1904), Shaw*'s brilliant, topsy-turvy play about an Ireland he knew better than most of his countrymen, probably because he had not lived there for twenty-eight years. He Wildlely reverses the stereotypes, making the Irishman Larry Doyle clear-eyed and hard-headed, a product of the Ireland of fact, and Broadbent the Englishman the dreamy, romantic one. In an authentic, bitter finish, it is the colonial master, however benign, who wins in the end, taking the girl, the seat in Parliament and the tourist business venture as his right.

Johnston, Denis (1901–84), playwright and war correspondent, was born in Dublin, the son of a judge of the Supreme Court, educated in Edinburgh, Cambridge and Harvard and called to the English (1925) and Irish (1926) bars. He became very interested in theatre, married the actress Shelagh Richards and wrote *The Old Lady Says 'No!'** finally produced in the Gate* in 1929. *The Moon in the Yellow River* followed in 1931. Both were experimental plays reflecting disenchantment with the Free State after the glory days of 1916 and the War of Independence. Work as a pioneer television producer was interrupted by WWII when he became a war correspondent, being one of the first to discover the horrors of Buchenwald, which he first wrote about in *The Bell** in March 1951 and further described in his war autobiography *Nine Rivers to Jordan* (1953). He was Director of Programmes for the BBC from 1946 till 1948 when he resigned to become a freelance writer and teacher. He wrote several books and plays about Swift* and in 1976 published *The Brazen Horn* (1976), a philosophical treatise on time and theology. *The Scythe and Sunset* (1958), about the Easter Rising*, is a sardonic companion piece to O'Casey*'s *The Plough and the Stars**.

Johnston, Jennifer (b. 1930), novelist, was born in Dublin, the daughter of Denis Johnston* and the actress Shelagh Richards, and educated at Park House School and TCD. She has been recognised as a significant Irish writer since the achronological publication of her first two novels, *The Captains and the Kings* (1972) and *The Gates* (1973), both of which deal with the isolation of relicts of former Irish Big House families. In *How Many Miles to Babylon?* (1974), set mainly in the trenches of WWI, the last hurrah of the Big House feels the urgency of the new Ireland. The most distressful country is the background of most of her ten novels, although she manages to bleed it to the margins in more personal work such as *The Christmas Tree* (1981), about a patient dying from leukaemia, *The Illusionist* (1995), a case of who (*precisely*) is your father and *Two Moons* (1998), a story of three generations of women. Her characterisation is universally faultless, her style lyrically spare and her humour blessedly relieving.

Jordan, Neil (b. 1950), short story writer, novelist, screenwriter, film director, was born in Sligo and educated at UCD. After a collection of short stories, *Night in Tunisia* (1976), he published three novels, *The Past* (1980), *The Dream of a Beast* (1983), and *Sunrise with Seamonster* (1994), the last being a vivid sensual tale set in the climate of betrayal of wartime Ireland and the Spanish Civil War. Jordan is now much better known as a screenwriter and film director. His films include *Mona Lisa, Interview with a Vampire,* *Michael Collins, The Butcher Boy* and the insightful drama, *The Crying Game*, for which he won an Oscar for best screenplay in 1993.

Joyce, James (1882–1941), novelist and short story writer, was born in Dublin and educated at Clongowes, Belvedere and the Royal University. The family was middle-class but on the slide, due to the egotism and fecklessness of the Cork father, who tended to be, according to his sharp-tongued and witty eldest son, 'a praiser of his own past'. Joyce's literary destiny, descried in early life, was 'to forge in the smithy of [his] soul the uncreated conscience of [his] race' and the means were to be 'silence, exile and cunning'. (Oddly for such an accomplished linguist, Gaelic was to play little part in Joyce's work; an early disagreement with his evening-class teacher, Patrick Pearse, may have been partly to blame.) His first published prose work *Dubliners* (1914), a collection of stories about the city that he imposed upon the geographical Dublin (so that accounts of it are actually autobiographical), is written on the theme of middle-class, post-Parnellite paralysis. Stylistically the stories are of their time, often with a lushness of imagery that is at variance with the spare nature of tales written 'with scrupulous meanness'. More obvious autobiography is to be found in *A Portrait of the Artist as a Young Man* (1916), a shorter, refined version of the rejected *Stephen Hero* (1914). Joyce uses events and thinly disguised characters from the first twenty years of his own life to paint a picture of intellectual and spiritual development, illuminated by the 'epiphanies' of the quasi-sacerdotal subject Stephen Dedalus, who is a literary extension but not a doppelganger of the author. By the time of its publication Joyce had been a far from silent exile for twelve years and, though there were visits home, the rest of the artist's life was spent in Paris, Trieste and Zurich, with his constant companion Nora Barnacle, the maidservant from Galway whom he finally married in 1931. *Ulysses**(1922), Joyce's greatest work, a Homeric account of a single day's life in Dublin, 16 June 1904 (the day of his first date with Nora), became and has remained a work of great critical and textual contention. His last book *Finnegans Wake* was not completed until two years before his death, though work had begun on it in 1922. It was to be the synthesis of the literature of the West, the dreaming of all Irish history and myth, a kind of gargantuan, comic *Encyclopaedia Hibernica*, and, in its polylingual punning, its auditory rather than visual imagery (Joyce's sight was weak for most of his adult life) and its impenetrability to all but the most resolute, the great unread book of Irish literature. Joyce died and was buried in Zurich, survived by Nora for ten years.

Joyce, P[atrick] W[eston] (1827–1914), Gaelic scholar, was born in Ballyorgan, County Limerick, and, after teaching and obtaining qualifications from TCD, worked for the Commissioners of National Education in various capacities from 1845 until his appointment as principal of the Marlborough Street Teachers' Training College in 1874. His anthology of old airs, *Ancient Irish Music* (1873), *Grammar of the Irish Language* (1878) and translations of saga tales as *Old Celtic Romances* (1879) were all of extreme importance in different aspects of the recovery of Irish culture, and his work on *dinnseanchas*, *The Origin and History of Irish Names of Place* (1869–70), has only recently been superseded.

Joyce, R[obert] D[wyer] (1830–83), poet, was born in Glensheen, County Limerick, the younger brother of P. W. Joyce*, and after some years as a teacher studied Medicine at Queen's College, Cork, graduating in 1865. As a student he supported himself by writing, contributing poems and stories to *The Nation** (including the famous '98 ballad 'The Boys of Wexford' and 'The Leprahaun') and publishing *Ballads, Romances and Songs* in 1861. He served for some time as Professor of English Literature at Newman's Catholic University but left hastily for America in 1866 because of his known support of Fenianism. He practised medicine in Boston, lectured in the Harvard Medical School and continued to publish stories and poems until his return to Ireland a month before his death.

Juno and the Paycock (1924), play by Sean O'Casey* set in a Dublin tenement during the Civil War*. It describes the fortunes (or misfortunes) of the Boyle family: the neurotic son Johnny who lost an arm in the Easter Rising* and is hunted by Republicans as an informer; Mary, the daughter, who is made pregnant and deserted by the incompetent Charley Bentham, the source of their false hopes of a substantial legacy; 'Captain' Jack Boyle, the 'paycock', who, drawing upon an imaginary nautical past, manages to avoid work in the company of his ingratiating and ultimately treacherous friend Joxer Daly; and Juno, the wearily faithful and long-suffering wife. The melodramatic plot and a pause in Act II for a singsong aside, the play is rich in language, atmosphere and characterisation and is O'Casey's most popular work.

K

Kavanagh, Patrick (1904–67), poet and novelist, was born (as he frequently reminded people) in Mucker, in the parish of Inniskeen, County Monaghan, the son of a small farmer and cobbler. He left school at thirteen but began to 'dabble in verse', soon displaying an unsentimental awareness of his farm and parish and an intellectual aware-ness of the wide world beyond. His work was published by Æ* in the *Irish Statesman* and by 1936 there was enough for a collection, *Ploughman and Other Poems*. This was followed, at Helen Waddell*'s insistence, by *The Green Fool** (1938), a prose account of his childhood and young manhood, which was withdrawn because of a libel case brought by Gogarty* over a clearly innocent remark. (The book was re-published in 1967.) His extended poem *The Great Hunger** (1942), the poetry collection *Soul for Sale* (1947) and *Tarry Flynn** (1948), an autobio-graphical and inevitably banned novel, marked Kavanagh as a significant Irish writer and perhaps the finest native poet since Yeats*. Living in Dublin from 1939, often in poor health and poverty, he scraped a living by casual journalism. In 1952 he and his brother Peter double-handedly produced the thirteen issues of the polemical *Kavanagh's Weekly*, thereby decreasing their already diminishing store of goodwill. Defeat in a famous libel case over a profile in the *Leader* magazine in 1954 left him ill and penniless but a post as lecturer in the Extra-Mural Department of UCD was arranged by John Costello (taoiseach 1948–51; 1954–7), the all-too-success-ful defence lawyer in the case. Surgery for cancer in 1955 did much to allay his endemic abrasiveness, and subsequent work, *Come Dance with Kitty Stobling* (1960) and *Collected Poems* (1964), is happier, more personal and less ideo-logical. He died in Dublin seven months after his marriage to Katherine Maloney.

Kavanagh, Rose (1859–91), poet, was born in Killadroy, County Tyrone, not far from the birthplace of Carleton*, and educated at Loreto Convent, Omagh, and the Dublin Metropolitan School of Art. She wrote much patriotic poetry and ran the children's section of the *Irish Fireside* and the *Weekly Free-man*. She became a close friend of Kickham* and nursed him when blind and dying. She died of tuberculosis at her home in Knockmany near her birth-place.

Keane, John B[rendan] (b. 1928), playwright and fiction writer, was born in Listowel and has lived there most of his life. His first play *Sive* (1959) was written for the local drama society and made a tremendous impact at the All-Ireland drama finals in Athlone. It deals with the clash of youth and age, greed and idealism, and, with the highly-flavoured speech of north Kerry and a mixture of Brechtian and folk elements, it effectively regenerated the peasant play. Most of his work was first presented by the Southern Theatre group in Cork rather than by the Abbey* and *Sharon's Grave* (1960), *The Highest House on the Mountain* (1960) and *Many Young Men of Twenty* (1961), with its effective title song, its humour and genuine feeling for the wastefulness of emigration, all confirmed his position as the best known Irish playwright of the period. His finest play *The Field** (1965) has a universality which lifts it out of purely regional appeal and it was successfully filmed in 1990. Other successful plays are *The Year of the Hiker* (1963), about a 'shuiler' who comes home to die, and *Big Maggie* (1969), about a hyper-effective matriarch. Keane has written much prose in the form of novels, short stories and epistolary fictions. His most enduring novels are likely to be *The Contractors* and *Durango*.

Keane, Molly (1905–96), novelist and playwright, was born in County Kildare, the daughter of 'Moira O'Neill*', into a huntin', shootin', fishin' family of the kind that features in most of her fiction, both light and serious. Between 1928 and 1952 as 'M. J. Farrell' (a name borrowed from a publican's fascia and meant to hide her artistic talent from her sporting friends) she wrote ten humorous novels, mostly dealing in a latter-day Somerville & Ross* fashion with the life of the steadily diminishing Anglo-Irish and their often uneasy relations with the native Irish. Her first three plays, *Spring Meeting* (1938), *Ducks and Drakes* (1942), *Treasure Hunt* (1949), drawing-room comedies directed by John Gielgud, were popular West End successes, but an adverse critical reaction to *Dazzling Prospect* (1961) in the period of the Royal Court 'angry' revolution ended her career as a playwright. A lacuna of twenty years ended with *Good Behaviour** (1981), the first book published under her own name. Its picture of the Anglo-Irish in greater decay changed the light-hearted books of M. J. Farrell to searing comedies with barely merciful analyses of an Ascendancy in detritus. *Time after Time* (1983) describes the disarray of the Swifts of Durraghglass, as the three sisters and their one-eyed gay brother are nearly destroyed by a malicious cousin. *Loving and Giving* (1988), about revenge for a childhood cruelty, and her last novel, *Conversation Piece* (1991), complete a fine quartet of late-flowering, black but beautifully written comedies.

Kearney, Peadar (1883–1942), songwriter, was born in Dublin and educated at the CBS, Marino. He became a house-painter (as did his famous nephew Brendan Behan*), joined the Gaelic League* and the IRB and worked backstage at the Abbey*. In 1911 he published 'The Soldier's Song' in *Irish*

Freedom and it was adopted as a war song by the IRB and eventually as the national anthem for the new state. After the Civil War* he returned to private life and his first occupation. Among his other songs were 'Down by the Glenside', 'The Tri-Coloured Ribbon' and the satirical 'Whack Fol the Diddle'.

Kearney, Richard (b. 1954), philosopher and novelist, was born in Cork and educated at Glenstal Abbey and UCD, where he is Professor of Philosophy. A prolific author on philosophy, as well as literature, culture and questions of nationality, he has written and edited twenty books, including *States of Mind* and *Poetics of Modernity*. He has also published two novels, *Sam's Fall* (1995) and *Walking at Sea Level* (1997), and a volume of poetry, *Angel of Patrick's Hill* (1991).

Keating, Geoffrey, *see* Seathrún Céitinn*

Keegan, John (1809–49), poet, was born in Queen's County and educated at a hedge school. For such periodicals as *The Nation** he wrote many poems, some of which, especially 'Bouchalleen Bawn' and the famous 'Caoch the Piper', are still recited. He died in Dublin of cholera and was buried in a common grave in Glasnevin.

Kelly, Éamon (b. 1914), actor, seanchaí and writer, was born near Rathmore in County Kerry. He worked as a woodwork teacher before moving to Dublin to become an actor with RTÉ radio and later with the Abbey*. He has had a varied and successful career on the stage, acting in many of the classic plays of his era, including the works of Brian Friel*, Tom Murphy* and Sebastian Barry*. He produced a series of books based on his one-man storytelling shows, including *In My Father's Time* and *English That for Me*, and two finely wrought volumes of memoir, *The Apprentice* (1995) and *The Journeyman* (1998).

Kelly, John (b. 1965), novelist, journalist and broadcaster, was born in Eniskillen, County Fermanagh and educated at QUB, where he took a degree in Law. He has published a novel, *Grace Notes and Bad Thoughts* (1994), strongly influenced by Irish traditional music and mythology, and an autobiographical volume, *Cool About the Ankles* (1996).

Kelly, Maeve (b. 1930), novelist, short story writer and poet, was born in Dundalk and trained as a nurse in England. Her early stories were published in David Marcus*'s 'New Irish Writing' page in the *Irish Press* and 'A Life of Her Own' – later the title story of her first collection (1976) – won a Hennessy Award. Some of these stories were reprinted in a later collection, *Orange Horses* (1991). Her main characters are women put upon by men, life and their own expectations, though her experiences as a farmer's wife in County Limerick provided the themes for some telling stories. *Necessary Treasons* (1985) is about the moral education of a young woman in feminism, while

Florrie's Girls (1991) is based upon her career as a student nurse. A book of poetry, *Resolution*, was published in 1986. Though she is deeply interested in equality and fair treatment for women, her writing is not doctrinaire and humour can leaven an often bleak vision.

Kelly, Mary (1825–1910), poet, born in Headford, County Galway, was one of the leading woman contributors to patriotic papers, becoming known as 'Eva of *The Nation*'. She became engaged to Kevin Izod O'Doherty (1823–1905) who was transported after imprisonment for his part in the Smith O'Brien rising of 1848. They finally married in 1854 and lived for most of the rest of their lives in Brisbane, where they both died.

Kennelly, Brendan (b. 1936), poet, was born in Ballylongford, County Kerry, and educated at St Ita's College, Tarbert, and TCD, to which he returned in 1973 as Professor of Modern English. *The Crooked Cross* (1963), linked sketches of life in the eponymous village, was followed by *The Florentines* (1967), a novel about student life and drinking. Both showed a verbal fluency that was put to better use in a collection of poetry, *My Dark Fathers* (1964), about the wounds of history, especially those inflicted by the Famine and the conditions that caused it. Later work is more buoyant, more ribald, as if the absolute blackness had been exorcised; his Everyman Maloney is truly 'up and at it' (1965, 1985) and the title of the

collection of *Poetry My Arse* (1995) is self-explanatory. But there is room for tenderness and commitment and a continuing worship of women. The Northern Troubles and the recurring nightmare of history produced two long poetry sequences about hate figures, *Cromwell* (1983) and *The Book of Judas* (1991). Kennelly is a positive critic and a genuinely entertaining media personality. His most recent collection *The Man Made of Rain* (1998), is a series of meditations on life and mortality inspired by his experience of serious heart surgery.

Kettle, Thomas (1880–1916), politician and belle-lettrist, was born in Artane, County Dublin, the son of Parnell's lieutenant, Andrew Kettle, and educated at Clongowes and UCD, graduating with a hardly used degree in Law. He was Nationalist MP for East Tyrone (1906–9) and Professor of Economics at UCD (1909–16). He was active in trying to settle the lock-out of 1913 and regarded the Easter Rising* as a betrayal of the Sinn Féin movement, which, with Robert Lynd*, he regarded as the only effective means of achieving Home Rule for all Ireland. He joined the Royal Dublin Fusiliers and was an active recruiter for the war 'for the freedom of small nations', and after the Rising he volunteered for service in Belgium. His essays, witty and profound, were published in *The Day's Burden* (1910) and his famous sonnet 'To My Daughter Betty, the Gift of God' was written shortly before his death at Ginchy on the Somme.

Kiberd, Declan (b. 1951), critic and academic, was born in Dublin and educated at St Paul's Raheny and TCD. He has had a varied career as an academic: lecturer in English and American Literature in Kent, lecturer in Irish at TCD and most recently Professor of Anglo-Irish Literature and Drama at UCD. His combined English and Gaelic scholarship, which informs such books as *Synge and the Irish Language* (1979), *An Crann faoi Bhláth* (1991; co-edited with Gabriel Fitzmaurice*), an anthology of Gaelic poetry and translations, and *Idir Dhá Chultúr* (1993), shows most effectively in his magisterial *Inventing Ireland** (1995).

Kickham, Charles J[oseph] (1828–82), novelist, poet and rebel, was born in Cnoceenagaw near Mullinahone, County Tipperary, and was deaf from the age of thirteen after an accident with gunpowder. He was a strong supporter of Young Ireland and became a Fenian in 1860, editing the movement's newspaper, the *Irish People*. He was arrested in 1865 after the shortlived Fenian Rising and served only four years of his fourteen year sentence because of his health. He survived nearly blind and totally deaf for a further dozen years, writing his famous romance *Knocknagow; or the Homes of Tipperary**, in 1879. This achieved countrywide fame not because of any intrinsic merit but for its Irishness, its politics and its fulfilment of the subtitle. *Sally Kavanagh* (1869), a novel about rural hardship written in prison, also lived up to its grim subtitle 'The Tenantless Grave'.

Kickham wrote lyrics for many still current songs, including 'Slievenamon', 'My Love's an Arbutus' and 'Rory of the Hill'.

Kiely, Benedict (b. 1919), novelist, short story writer and critic, was born in Dromore, County Tyrone, but brought up in Omagh, where he was educated by the Christian Brothers. In 1937 he entered a Jesuit novitiate in Laois but left because of tuberculosis and, after convalescence, took a BA from UCD. He was for many years one of the *personae* of the *Irish Press* diarist 'Patrick Lagan', and his traverse of mainly the northern half of the country increased his wide store of *seanchas*. His first books were non-fiction: *Counties of Contention* (1945), a study of Partition, and *Poor Scholar* (1947), a lyric evocation of the career of his fellow-countryman William Carleton*. His first novel *Land without Stars* (1946) was strongly autobiographical in topography, and its successor *In a Harbour Green* (1949), also set in Omagh, is one of the finest evocations of small-town Irish life. This was followed by *Modern Irish Fiction – A Critique* (1950), a remarkably astute and comprehensive survey of the writers of the period. Between 1950 and 1960 Kiely wrote five further novels – *Call for a Miracle* (1950), *Honey Seems Bitter* (1954), *There Was an Ancient House* (1955), *The Cards of the Gambler** (1953) and *The Captain with the Whiskers* (1960) – all wonderfully digressive and richly entertaining, and based upon the different backgrounds of the author's wide experience. *A Journey to the Seven Streams* (1963) and *A Ball of Malt and Madame Butterfly* (1973), collections of stories, seem to suggest that his real forte as a writer is as a kind of latter-day literary *seanchaí* who holds the reader with an eye as glittering as any ancient mariner. Kiely, who taught creative writing at American colleges, is also a superb radio broadcaster with a compelling voice.

Kilroy, Thomas (b. 1934), novelist and playwright, was born in Callan, County Kilkenny, and educated at St Kieran's College and UCD. He has held many academic posts in Ireland and America, relinquishing the Chair of English at UCG in 1989 after ten years. He has written one novel, *The Big Chapel* (1972), based upon the same historical incident of 1870s clerical politics as that which inspired *The Greatest of These* (1943) by fellow-Kilkennian Francis MacManus*. His first successful play was *The Death and Resurrection of Mr Roche* (1969), about the seedy life of Dublin flat-dwellers. This was followed by *The O'Neill* (1969), Kilroy's account of a character also brought to life by his Field Day colleague Brien Friel*, *Tea, Sex and Shakespeare* (1976), about the writing life, and the very popular *Talbot's Box* (1977), about the Dublin lay saint Matt Talbot (1856–1925), which moved from the Peacock to the Royal Court. Plays for Field Day were *Double Cross* (1986) – in which the same actor played two peripheral characters from WWII, Brendan Bracken, Churchill's mysterious protégé, and William Joyce,

the Nazi collaborator known as 'Lord Haw-Haw'– and *Madam MacAdam's Travelling Theatre* (1991), an uneasy attempt at social comment (on Ireland during the Emergency) using farce. Kilroy has also written versions of Chekhov's The *Seagull* (1981) and Ibsen's *Ghosts* (1989) set in Ireland.

KILLARNEY, justly acclaimed lacustrine beauty spot in County Kerry, which inspired Falconer to call it 'heaven's reflex' and Tennyson to write a much better lyric, 'Blow, Bugle, Blow'. Boucicault* transferred the action of Griffin*'s *The Collegians* to the lakes for his dramatic version, *The Colleen Bawn*, (1860) and Julius Benedict (1804–85) called his opera on the theme *The Lily of Killarney*. Aogán Ó Rathaile* (?1670–1729) and Eoghan Rua Ó Súilleabháin* (1748–84), the great Sliabh Luachra poets, are buried close by in Muckross Abbey.

King of Friday's Men, The (1948), play by M. J. Molloy* about shillelagh fighting and the assumed rights of some eighteenth-century Irish landlords over the daughters of some of their tenants. Bartley Dowd, a giant of a man and champion fighter, falls in love with Una Brehony, the latest 'tally woman' of the landlord Caesar French, and finally kills him, leaving her free to marry her own lover. It is written with great gusto and slightly artificial sub-Syngean language.

Kinsella, Thomas (b. 1928), poet, was born in Dublin and educated at the Model School at Inchicore, O'Connell

School and UCD, his degree completed as an evening student while he worked as civil servant. He published Poems (1956), *Another September* (1958) and *Downstream* (1962), wry looks at his country balanced by celebration of the wonder and danger of loving. He left the civil service in 1965 to serve as poet-in-residence at Southern Illinois University and in 1970 became a professor in the English Department at Temple University, Philadelphia, a college of which he opened in Dublin in 1976. His translation of the Old Irish Ulster epic *Táin Bó Cuailgne* ('The Cattle Spoil of Cooley') as *The Táin* (1969), with illustrations by Louis le Brocquy, was hugely popular, as was *An Duanaire: Poems of the Dispossessed* (1981), an anthology of translations of Gaelic poems (with Sean Ó Tuama*). In 1972 he published *Butcher's Dozen*, a visceral reaction to Bloody Sunday in Derry and the white-wash of the Widgery Tribunal, as the first of his own Peppercanister pamphlets (called after the popular name for St Stephen's Church on Upper Mount Street, close to his home in Percy Place). Later collections of poems are *St Catherine's Clock* (1987), *Poems from Centre City* (1990) and *Madonna and Other Poems* (1991). Now retired from teaching, he lives in County Wicklow.

Knight, Susan (b. 1947), novelist, was born in England but has lived in Dublin since 1977. She has written radio plays and two novels: *The Invisible Woman* (1993), memories of a more or less unhappy past, and the more ambitious *Grimaldi's Garden* (1995), a novel of contemporary Irish life, with a gloss on the career of the great, depressive Italian clown as a kind of counterpoint to the confusion of her characters' lives.

Knocknagow, or the Homes of Tipperary (1879), Kickham*'s sentimental romance of nineteenth-century Irish life. It is strongly Nationalistic, disinclined to see much good in the current land system and justly severe on cruel and avaricious landlords. Such characters as Mat the Thresher and Father Hannigan became as well known to a vast Irish readership as David Copperfield or Little Nell in Britain.

Knowles, J[ames] S[heridan] (1784–1862), playwright, was born in Cork, second cousin of Richard Brinsley Sheridan*. He gave up the study of medicine to join Andrew Cherry*'s company, who eventually produced Knowles's only Irish play, *Brian Boroimhe* (1811), full of 'Danes' and heroic Claremen. He settled in London and became part of a literary life that included Dickens, Coleridge, Lamb and Hazlitt, and his melodramas provided excellent parts for his friends Kean and Macready. He died at Torquay having earlier been granted a pension from the Civil List.

L

Land of Cokaigne, The (14th century), Middle English fantasy poem, written in Ireland, about a land of plenty where the lusts of the belly and other bodily parts are happily satisfied, but which is reached only by a seven-year journey through swine dung. In the edible monasteries the nuns swim naked and the monks are called to food by the sound of the manual slapping of a girl's bottom.

Land of Spices (1941), novel by Kate O'Brien* set in the Irish convent of a French order and based on the author's own experiences of her schooldays in Laurel Hill in Limerick, where she was sent as a very young child after the death of her mother. There are two protagonists. The first is the Reverend Mother, Belgian-born English intellectual Mère Marie Hélène Archer who in the course of the novel hears of her beloved father's death and has to come to terms with the fact that she entered the religious life as a reaction to finding him with his student Etienne 'in the embrace of love' (the phrase for which the novel was banned in Ireland). The second is her pupil, Anna, in whom Marie Hélène sees her talented and idealistic young self. Anna comes under her care at the age of six and she oversees her development through family upheaval and tragedy, managing finally to ensure that she takes up a scholarship to study in UCD rather than a job in a bank as her domineering grandmother would have it. Anna is the first person Marie Hélène has truly loved since entering the religious life and through her she manages to become somewhat reconciled with the changing Ireland in which she has served her order, the nationalism and cultural complacency of which she has hitherto found repellent. Though there are moments of melodrama, the novel is a brilliant and moving study of the mind and character of Marie Hélène especially, a veritable portrait of a lady.

Lane, Denny (1818–95), poet and Young Irelander, was born and lived most of his life in Cork. His father owned a distillery and he was trained as an engineer. He was briefly in prison after the Smith O'Brien rising in 1848 but he continued his professional and business career, eventually owning a railway and serving as President of the Institute of Gas Engineers of Great Britain. Some of his lyrics, originally published in The Nation*, are still sung, including 'Kate of Araglen' and 'Carrighdoun' (a song which with doubled notes gave Percy French* the tune for 'The Mountains of Mourne').

Lane, Temple (pseudonym of Mary Isabel Leslie) (1899–1978), novelist and poet, was born in Dublin, daughter of the future Dean of Lismore. Reared in Tipperary, she was educated in England and graduated PhD from TCD. She wrote much light women's fiction as 'Jean Herbert' but she is remembered as the author of the song-lyric 'The Fairy Tree' and the wartime bestseller *Friday's Well* (1943), about two sisters, one of whom is killed in a railway accident trying to warn an American airman whom they have concealed in their cellar that the guards are coming for him. The story is told with remarkable ironic control.

Langrishe, Go Down (1966), novel by Aidan Higgins* set in the 1930s, about the relationships between the three Langrishe sisters, remnants of an Ascendancy family, and Otto Beck, the mature German student who lives in their ancestral home, Springfield House. The sexual affair between Imogen and Beck, which leaves her shattered, is subtly described and its symbolic relationship to the international situation of the period neatly pointed.

Larminie, William (1849–1900), poet, was born in Castlebar, County Mayo, and educated at TCD before joining the India Office in London. He had some knowledge of Irish and tried to incorporate Gaelic assonance into his own poetry, especially in *Fand* [the wife of

Manannán Mac Lir and mistress of Cúchulainn] *and Other Poems* (1892), which contains the very moving 'Consolation'. This and his interest in folklore collected in Connacht and Donegal and published as *West Irish Folk-Tales and Romances* (1893) make him a kind of forerunner of the Literary Revival*. His poem 'The Nameless Doon' (earlier 'Ruin') about a *dún* in Lough Doon, Donegal, was admired by Yeats*.

L'Attaque (1962), novel in Irish by Eoghan Ó Tuairisc*, recounts the part played by a small group of United Irishmen from County Leitrim in the military revolt which was sparked by the landing of French General Humbert in Killala, County Mayo in 1798. The central character, Mayoman Máirtín Dubh Caomhánach, is content at the beginning of the novel to eke out a peasant existence with his new wife Saidhbhín. When news arrives that the French have landed (*'Tá do cháirde i gCill Ala!'*), Máirtín, like the mythical heroes of old, feels under compulsion (*faoi geasa*) to join the revolt. Through the character of Máirtín, Ó Tuairisc's novel charts the effect of revolutionary fighting on peasant life, the conflicting ideals of the comrades-at-arms and the disorganisation that afflicts their army. Strongly influenced by Tolstoy's *War and Peace*, the novel portrays the inhumanity of war, making ironic use of Irish heroic myths that glorify conflict.

Laurence Bloomfield in Ireland (1964), Allingham*'s long poem about land agitation in mid-nineteenth-century Ireland. As with Trollope*, his distaste for anti-landlord tactics almost overcomes his admission of great wrongs done an inevitably violent peasantry, and his hope for an honourable solution in the persons of enlightened landlords like his eponymous hero seems with hindsight naïvely vain. The verse is excellent in its vigour and wit, as are the poem's characterisation, sociological description and narrative.

Laverty, Maura (1907–67), novelist and playwright, was born in Rathangan, County Kildare, and brought up by her grandmother in Ballyderrig (the 'Derrymore House' of her first novel *Never No More*, published in 1942) on whose death she trained as a teacher. She went to Spain at seventeen and her banned novel *No More than Human* (1944) describes her adventures there as governess, scandalous foreigner, secretary and journalist. She returned to Ireland in 1928 having added Spanish cooking to her extensive culinary expertise. She wrote several popular cookery books and even incorporated recipes in her novels. Her novel of Dublin slum life *Lift up Your Gates* (1946) became a successful play, *Liffey Lane* (1951), for the Edwards-Mac Liammóir company, and its successor *Tolka Row* (1952) became the basis of RTÉ's highly successful first soap. She died suddenly at her home in Rathfarnham.

Lavin, Mary (1912–96), short story writer and novelist, was born in Massachusetts, where her Irish father was a land bailiff. Her mother returned to Ireland in 1920, taking Mary with her, and the family eventually settled in Bective, County Meath, where the father continued his work as estate manager. She was educated in Loreto, Stephen's Green, and UCD; her MA dissertation was on Jane Austen. She married William Walsh, a family friend, and on her father's death in 1945 bought Abbey Farm, also in Bective. Her husband died in 1954 and she supported her three daughters, her writing supplementing the uncertain farm income. She married Michael Scott, a laicised Jesuit, in 1969. Her short stories, meticulously crafted but registering the inconsequentiality of life, place her in the highest rank of such fiction writers. She can make a drama out of the smallest domestic incident and is excellent in the portrayal of children, bereavement and women with women. Her stories (written between 1938 and 1985 and published in fourteen separate books) were collected into three volumes. She also wrote two novels: *The House in Clewe Street* (1945) and *Mary O'Grady* (1950). A new selection of stories, *In a Café*, was published in 1995, shortly before her death.

Lawless, Hon. Emily (1845–1913), poet and novelist, was born in County Kildare, the daughter of Lord Cloncurry, but spent most of her youth in County Galway. She became one of the foremost of Irish writers, sympathetic to the people but regarding hopes of Home Rule as chimerical. Her chief novels are *Hurrish** (1886), about the Land War,

Grania (1892), showing life in the Aran Islands, and two Elizabethan romances, *Maelcho* (1894) and *With Essex in Ireland* (1902). Her verse collection *With the Wild Geese* (1902) contains her justly anthologised pieces 'After Aughrim' and 'Clare Coast'. She moved to England for health reasons but also because of the anti-unionist campaign of Sinn Féin.

Leamy, Edmund (1848–1904), writer of fairytales, was born in Waterford and trained as a barrister before becoming a Parnellite MP and later a Redmondite. His stories, published as *Irish Fairy Tales* (1890), *By the Barrow River* (1907) and *The Golden Spears* (1911), were meant for children and approved by Cardinal Logue.

Lecky, W[illiam] E[dward] H[artpole] (1838–1903), historian, was born in County Dublin and educated at TCD, which he represented at Westminster from 1895 as a Liberal Unionist. His work *A History of European Morals* (1869) established his reputation, and his magisterial eight-volume *History of England in the Eighteenth Century* (1878–90) did much to refute the anti-Irish writings of the English historian J. A. Froude (1818–94). The Irish sections of this work were republished as *The History of Ireland in the Eighteenth-Century* (5 vols., 1892–6) and they remain a necessary work for future historians. He was a very liberal unionist, favouring the release of Fenian prisoners and the establishment of a Catholic University, though he set his face against Home Rule. He was

awarded the OM in 1902. Though he had lived in London since 1871, he was buried in Mount Jerome.

Ledwidge, Francis (1887–1917), poet, was born near Slane, County Meath, and worked as a miner, road mender and shop assistant. He was an active and effective trades unionist and a member of the Gaelic League*. His poetry began to appear in the *Drogheda Independent* and he made himself known to Lord Dunsany, his neighbour, who arranged for the publication of *Songs of the Fields* (1915) and encouraged him to join the Inniskillings (Dunsany's own regiment) in 1914. Ledwidge was a Sinn Féin supporter and no Redmondite but he felt that Germany was an enemy. He survived Gallipoli to be killed at Ypres, having brooded for a year and a half on the significance of the Easter Rising*, as his poems 'Thomas MacDonagh' and 'Lament for the Poets: 1916' indicate. *The Complete Poems*, edited by Dunsany, was published in 1919 and re-edited by Alice Curtayne* for publication at the same time as her biography, *Francis Ledwidge: A Life of the Poet* (1972).

Lee, J[oseph] J. (Joe) (b. 1942), historian, was born in County Kerry and educated at Gormanstown, County Meath, and UCD. He was a fellow of Peterhouse, Cambridge, where he lectured in German history, becoming Professor of Modern History at UCC in 1973. Patriotic rather than anti-revisionist, his view of modern Ireland is that of a country ill-led, both north and south, yet still capable of achieving the goals of its revolutionary ideals. His major work *Ireland 1912–1985: Politics and Society* (1989) is brilliantly entertaining, forceful and sound.

Le Fanu, [Joseph] Sheridan (1814–73), novelist and short story writer, was born in Dublin, the son of an Anglican clergyman (who later moved to Abingdon, County Limerick) and grandnephew of Richard Brinsley Sheridan*. He was educated at home and at TCD, where he read Classics before being called to the bar in 1839. He had already begun writing stories and over the next thirty years he edited and contributed to many periodicals, including the Ascendancy *Dublin University Magazine* (1833–77), which he edited from 1861 till 1869. His wife Susan Bennett died in 1858 after fourteen years of marriage and Le Fanu became a virtual recluse in his Merrion Square house until his death. His best stories of mystery and obsession are to be found in *In a Glass Darkly** (1872), which includes 'Green Tea', 'Mr Justice Harbottle' and the vampire tale 'Carmilla'. He wrote many novels, including *The Cock and Anchor* (1845), *The House by the Churchyard* (1863), *Wylder's Hand* (1864) and the book for which he is most famous, *Uncle Silas* (1864). Some are set in the Ireland of the previous century but all use umbrous Irish topography to establish the menacing scene. His understanding of greed, terror and mental fixation is remarkably modern. The ballads 'Shamus O'Brien' and 'Phadrig Crohore' (1850) show a more rollicking side to his nature.

Leitch, Maurice (b. 1933), novelist, was born in the mill village of Muckamore, County Antrim, became a teacher and worked afterwards as a BBC producer in Belfast and London. Most of his novels, including *The Liberty Lad** (1965), *Poor Lazarus* (1969), *Stamping Ground* (1975), *Silver's City* (1981) and the novella *Chinese Whispers* (1987), are set in the south Antrim of his youth or in Belfast, the city of fascination and danger. Life in the North, even in 'peacetime', even for the educated young, is edged with the blackness of sectarian bitterness, diverting the working class from its appropriate support of radicalism. Only *Silver's City* directly confronts the Belfast of the high Troubles, as the eponymous Protestant icon, an early killer of a 'Fenian', finds his city utterly changed. His latest novel *The Smoke King* (1998) deals with the investigation by an alcoholic Catholic RUC sergeant of the murder in a small Ulster town in 1942 of Mrs Jelley, a bar owner, by a black GI. The mix of two separate sectarian hatreds makes it as powerful and gloomy a book as any in the canon. *Burning Bridges* (1989) charts the rackety career of a country-and-western singer from Ulster, *Gilchrist* (1995) that of a randy hot-gospeller and *The Hands of Cheryl Boyd* (1987) is a collection of grim short stories. Leitch's bleak view of life, especially in his native province, is sometimes highlighted by dark humour and his writing certainly does not lack brio.

Leland, Mary (b. 1941), journalist, novelist and short story writer, was born in Cork. Her novel *The Killeen* (1985) was followed by a collection of short stories, *The Galloway Girls* (1997) and a second novel *Approaching Priests* (1991).

Leonard, Hugh (pseudonym of John Keyes Byrne) (b. 1926), playwright, was born in Dublin and brought up by adoptive parents in Dalkey, where he was educated. From 1945 he worked as a clerk in the Land Commission, the while adding to an encyclopedic knowledge of cinema, becoming heavily involved in amateur theatre and writing his first pieces. By the time he achieved his first local theatrical success *Madigan's Lock* (1958) he had adopted the name of one of his own characters and left Ireland to work with Granada Television, dramatising the works of authors as diverse as Dickens, Saki and Friel*. (He continues to be a brilliant adapter of books for television, combining a deep knowledge of the work and the medium.) *A Walk on the Water* (1960), about a returned Irishman (a recurrent theme), was staged at the Dublin Theatre Festival, the first of a very fruitful relationship, and *Stephen D* (1962), mined from James Joyce*'s *Stephen Hero* and *A Portrait*, was such a success that it transferred to London, as did its author. He wrote many (often extremely funny) plays over the next two decades, usually set in and premièred in Ireland, turning a cold eye on his country and its murderous sentimentality about Republicanism, its *nouveaux*

riches, its attitude to its expatriates and its political corruption. This is especially true of *The Patrick Pearse Motel* (1971), *Suburb of Babylon* (1975) and *Kill* (1982), where satire bubbles over into spleen. His greatest success was with *Da* (1973), a slice of authentic dramatic autobiography, as the prose works *Home before Night* (1979) and *Out after Dark* (1989) confirm. Later came *A Life* (1980), which tells the elegaic story of Drumm, a minor civil servant character in *Da*. Leonard is a master technician of the theatre and writes, as if to order, thrillers, fantasies, Chekhovian threnodies and brilliant pastiche, as in *Time Was* (1980) and *The Mask of Moriarty* (1987).

Leslie, Sir Shane (1885–1971), man of letters, was born John Randolph, a kinsman of Winston Churchill, at his ancestral home, Castle Leslie, Glaslough, County Monaghan, and educated at Eton, Paris and Cambridge. He became a Catholic in 1908, changed his name to an Irish form, interested himself in the Literary Revival*, stood twice as a Nationalist in Derry and conceived the impossible ambition of explaining the Irish to the English. He wrote verse, fiction, biography and history and became a world authority on Lough Derg* and its pilgrimage, the main approaches to which were over his family's lands. His thinly veiled autobiographical novels *The Oppidan* (1922), *The Cantab* (1926) and *The Anglo-Catholic* (1929), are much more revealing than his discreet autobiographies *The Passing Chapter* (1934) and *The Film of*

Memory (1938). He was a connoisseur of ghost stories and no mean practitioner himself, publishing *The Shane Leslie Ghost Book* in 1955.

Letts, Winifred M[abel] (1882–1972), poet, was born in Wexford, the daughter of the rector of Newton Heath, Manchester, and educated at Alexandra College, Dublin. Though she wrote for the theatre, achieving some success with *Hamilton and Jones* (1941) at the Gate*, she is best remembered as a poet with such memorable lyrics as 'A Soft Day'.

Lever, Charles (1806–72), novelist, was born in Dublin and educated at TCD and the Royal College of Surgeons. After some years of travel in Europe, America and Canada, he returned to Ireland in 1832 and lent his medical skills to succouring cholera victims in Kilrush, County Clare. He was appointed dispensary doctor at Portstewart, County Derry, a north coast fishing village and watering place near Coleraine, where Lever House on the promenade still commemorates him. His first 'military' novel *The Confessions of Harry Lorrequer* (1839) was influenced by Maxwell*'s *Wild Sports of the West* (the author of which he met in Portstewart) and established a genre of popular comic fiction describing the (mainly romantic) adventures of young subalterns in an Ireland which, though contemporary with Carleton*'s, bears little resemblance to that dark realism. The literary archetype of the rollicking, devil-may-care, eloquent young Irishman

is his creation. Lever wrote to supplement his professional earnings and to pay for whatever high life Coleraine and trips to Dublin could supply. He left Ireland in 1839 to practise medicine in Brussels, and returned to edit the Dublin *University Magazine*, in which his novel *Charles O'Malley* (1841) was serialised from 1842–5. Thereafter he lived in Europe, settling in Florence in 1847 and serving as consul in Trieste from 1867 until his death. He wrote thirty books in all, of which *Charles O'Malley* and *The Martins of Cro' Martin* (1856) are regarded as his best survivors. The success of his work, particularly in the increasingly serious treatment of politics, undoubtedly stimulated his friend Trollope* to write *The Macdermots of Ballycloran*   (1847) and *The Kellys and the O'Kellys* (1848).

Lewis, C[live] S[taples] (1898–1963), scholar and man of letters, was born in Belfast, the son of a police-court solicitor. His mother's death of cancer when he was nine profoundly affected him and the problem of pain for the Christian exercised him for the rest of his life. He and his older brother 'Warnie' were sent to an English preparatory school and, apart from school holidays when they mocked their father's Belfast accent, never lived in Ireland again. He was educated at Magdalen College, Oxford, interrupting his studies to serve in the army in WWI. He was a fellow and tutor at his old college (1925–54) and Professor of Medieval and Renaissance Literature at Cambridge until his death. His *Allegory of Love* (1936), a study of courtly poetry and its balance of the sensual and spiritual, won the Hawthornden Prize, and *The Problem of Pain* (1940) and *The Screwtape Letters* (1942) established him as an effective champion of Christianity in an increasingly secular world, the latter, an account of the training of a young devil by an older one, becoming a bestseller. He wrote science fiction which was implicitly Christian in its values and his *Chronicles of Narnia* (1950–56) are children's classics. His spiritual autobiography *Surprised by Joy* (1955), which describes his conversion to Anglo-Catholicism, has a retrospective pun in its title since his marriage to Joy Davidman brought him great joy, and grief at her death from cancer in 1960. He died, on the same day as President Kennedy and Aldous Huxley, of osteoporosis.

Liberty Lad, The (1965), first novel by Maurice Leitch*, describing the slow maturing of Frank Glass, a young teacher from a mill village much like the author's own birthplace Muckamore. He is impatient with his father's reverential attitude to the mill owners and his refusal to join a trades union. He objects, too, to the father's religious paranoia, though his own understanding of Catholics is necessarily limited. Though essentially an account of the moral growth of its hero, the nature of the NI state, with its establishment-nurtured sectarian hatred, its artificial air of peace and prosperity and its public propriety, is not balked.

LISSOY, a County Westmeath hamlet on the Ballymahon-Athlone road, the model for the 'Sweet Auburn' of Goldsmith*'s 'The Deserted Village' and the location of the original incident that generated *She Stoops to Conquer*. It also provided the nightmarish topography for that play. The poet first went to school there while his father was rector and it was the scene of many of the funnier incidents of *The Vicar of Wakefield*.

LITERARY REVIVAL, THE, the general term applied to the movement lasting from c. 1890 to the founding of the Free State which involved, among many others, Yeats*, Lady Gregory*, Edward Martyn and Synge*. Its remoter origins are to be found in the renewed interest in the Irish language generated by Charlotte Brooke*'s publication of *Reliques of Irish Poetry* (1789), by the work of Petrie*, O'Curry* and others of the Ordnance Survey and by the poets of *The Nation**. There was also a steadily increasing interest in Celtic mythology. The work of Hyde* and the Gaelic League* in encouraging the resurgence of the Irish language must be accounted a significant part of the Revival's inspiration.

Lonely Passion of Judith Hearne, The (1955), first literary novel of Brian Moore*, written in Canada after the author's long apprenticeship to his craft, in the form of journalism and pulp fiction. Originally published as *Judith Hearne*, the novel received an ecstatic critical reception on both sides of the Atlantic (and was banned in Ireland). In it Moore attempted to recreate the crisis of his own loss of faith and to convey his anger at the political and religious narrowness of Belfast society but took as the model for his protagonist an elderly spinster who used to visit his parents' home. Judith Hearne is middle-aged, genteel, impoverished and bibulous, surviving on an annuity bequeathed her by an aunt to whom she has devoted her life. She loses her few remaining piano pupils, moves from cheap digs to cheaper and pins her last hopes for romance on a crude and exploitative returned Yank, James Madden, her landlady's brother. When he shatters her illusions – he too had illusions, that she was a wealthy woman – she suffers a crisis of faith in which the crawthumping priest of the parish fails her utterly, and then a complete nervous breakdown. The novel, which is bleak and deterministic, is complex and ambitious technically, combining many different narrative modes, including the free indirect style which became Moore's trademark – as did his remarkable insight into the psyche of a female protagonist.

Longley, Michael (b. 1939), poet, was born in Belfast and educated at Inst and TCD, graduating with a degree in Classics. After some years teaching he joined the Arts Council of NI, retiring as Director of Combined Arts in 1991. He has been linked with Seamus Heaney* and Derek Mahon* as a member of a supposed 'Ulster School' originally associated with Philip Hobsbaum of QUB, but like each of them has gone on to be a distinctive voice. His published verse includes *No Continuing City* (1969), *An Exploded View* (1973), *The Echo Gate* (1979) *Gorse Fires* (1991)and *The Ghost Orchid* (1995). His work has neither ignored the Northern Troubles (and other greater evils of the century, like the Holocaust) nor been obsessed by them, but a clever, quietly defiant voice speaks for the personal and the private. His latest book, *Broken Dishes* (1998) is a slim collection of beautiful and heart-rending elegies, including one, of profound simplicity and only four lines long, for his father: 'He would have been a hundred today, my father,/So I write to him in the trenches and describe/How he lifts with tongs from the brazier an ember/And in its glow reads my words and sets them aside.'

Lough Derg, small lake in County Donegal, five miles from Pettigo, and a place of austere pilgrimage since the twelfth century. The scene of St Patrick's Purgatory, it has figured in the work of such Irish writers as Carleton*, Yeats*, Sir Shane Leslie* (whose family owned the approaches), Sean O'Faolain*, Patrick Kavanagh* and Seamus Heaney*. It also provided Hamlet with a worthy oath: 'Yes by Saint Patrick but there is, Horatio,/And much offence too' (I, i, 142–3).

Love à la Mode (1759), most popular play of Charles Macklin*, first performed in Drury Lane. Charlotte Goodchild is courted by four national types: Squire Groom, Archy MacSarcasm, Beau Mordecai and Sir Callaghan O'Brallaghan.

The last named, the Irishman, not only gets the girl (by means of his innate gallantry) but has all the best lines.

Lover, Samuel (1797–1868), novelist and songwriter, was born in Dublin and trained as a painter, specialising in seascapes and miniatures from 1818. He began writing stories and poems for the Dublin magazines. One was the ballad 'Rory O'More', from which he devised a popular, somewhat stage-Irish novel. This he dramatised into a popular and definitely stage-Irish play. He moved to London in 1833 and became a well known figure in literary circles and a friend of Dickens, with whom he founded *Bentley's Miscellany* (1837–68). For that publication he wrote his 'tale of Irish life' *Handy Andy* (1842) and the name became a byword in Ireland for any large, awkward, amiable, clumsy youth. When his eyesight began to fail in 1844 Lover gave up miniature work and devised a one-man show of Irish entertainment which featured songs and monologues written and performed by himself, rather in the manner of Percy French* forty years later. Of his 300 songs, 'The Low-Backed Car', 'Molly Bawn', 'The Angel's Whisper' and 'Barney O'Hea' are still heard. His grandson Victor Herbert became one of the big names of the Broadway musical of the 1920s.

Lynam, William Francis (*c.* 1845–94), humorist, was born in Galway but spent most of his civilian life in Dundrum and Clontarf. He became a lieutenant-colonel in the fifth Royal Lancashire Militia and created the character Mick McQuaid whose adventures ran in the *Shamrock* from 1867 until well beyond his creator's death. The character is the archetypal philosophical, witty Irishman, whose comical adventures are laced with acute observations upon nineteenth-century Irish life; his name was adopted for a popular brand of pipe tobacco. Lynam also wrote a play, *Darby the Dodger* (1877).

Lynch, Patricia (1898–1972), writer of children's books, was born in Cork but brought up and educated in London, Scotland and Belgium. She became a journalist and feminist, covering the Easter Rising* for Sylvia Pankhurst. She married the socialist R. M. Fox in 1922 and settled in Dublin. Her children's stories, beginning with *The Turfcutter's Donkey* (1935), the first of a series, became international favourites, as did the 'Brogeen the Leprechaun' stories from 1947. She published nearly fifty books, including a slightly fictionalised autobiography, *A Storyteller's Childhood* (1947).

Lynd, Robert [Wilson] (1879–1949), essayist and critic, was born in Belfast, the son of a Presbyterian minister, and educated at Inst and QUB. On graduation he went to London and lived on occasional journalism until he joined the staff of the *Daily News* in 1908, becoming its literary editor in 1913. He stayed with the paper until his death, by which time it had long been the *News Chronicle*. For all those years he wrote an essay for its Saturday edition and as

'YY' contributed a longer piece to the weekly *Nation* and the *New Statesman*, as it afterwards became. He was also a regular contributor to *John o'London's Weekly* and served as editor during its last years. He joined the Gaelic League* at its foundation and became a friend of Roger Casement at the Cloghaneely summer school. (It was as a voluntary Irish teacher in London in 1904 that he met his wife Sylvia Dryhurst, poet and novelist, who was nine years younger. Their two daughters Sigle and Máire were brought up speaking Irish.) A dedicated Connollyite, writing an introduction to Connolly's *Labour in Irish History* (1917), he was also one of Bulmer Hobson's young men, a strong supporter of Arthur Griffith's Sinn Féin and, like his friend Tom Kettle*, greatly dismayed by the Easter Rising*. He published in all thirty books, mainly collections of his witty, companionable essays, though there were several sound, unacademic works of criticism and a brilliant evocation of *Dr Johnson and Company* (1927). A 100-cigarette-a-day man, he died of emphysema. Sean MacBride, then Minister for External Affairs, represented the Irish government at his burial in Belfast.

LYRIC THEATRE, THE (estd. 1951), founded in Belfast by Mary O'Malley in an annex of her own house and eventually sited in a custom-built theatre at Ridgeway Street. Its particular ghostly patron was Yeats*, all of whose plays have been staged there, and it continues to offer work by most significant writers, Irish and international.

Lysaght, Edward (1763–*c.* 1810), poet, was born in Brickhill, County Clare, and educated at TCD and Oxford before being called to both the Irish and English bars. He was a Volunteer and a vocal opponent of the Union, writing the squib 'A Prospect' about Ireland's coming economic depression: 'Through Capel-street soon as you'll rurally range,/You'll scarce recognise it the same street;/ Choice turnips shall grow in your Royal Exchange/ And fine cabbages down along Dame-street.' He was a member of John Philpot Curran*'s society, the Monks of the Screw*, and noted for his impersonations of other members. Known as 'Pleasant Ned', he is credited as the author of 'The Rakes of Mallow', 'Donnybrook Fair' and the exquisite 'Kitty of Coleraine', but there is no proof. His poetry was published in *Poems* (1811).

M

Mac Ádhaimh, Roibeárd (1808–95), Irish scholar, was born in Belfast to a prosperous Presbyterian family, and educated at Inst, where he came under the influence of Gaelic and classical scholar William Neilson. In 1833 he was among the founders of The Ulster Gaelic Society (*Cuideachta Gaeilge Uladh*) and later both founded and edited the *Ulster Journal of Archaeology* (1853–62). Among the scholars to whom he was patron was Aodh Mac Dómhnaill*. Their valuable work of collecting and studying Irish manuscripts was in preparation for an English-Irish dictionary which was never published.

Mac Aingil, Aodh (1571–1626), poet and religious writer in Irish, was born in Downpatrick and became tutor to the sons of Hugh O'Neill, Earl of Tyrone. He joined the Franciscan order in Salamanca in 1600 and in the order's house at Louvain wrote and published in simple and clear Irish the text *Sgáthán Shacramuinte na hAithridhe* (*Mirror of the Sacrament of Penance*) in 1618. Mac Aingil was very much a counter-Reformation philosopher of his time, as his works on Duns Scotus show. Among his best known poems is the Christmas ode, 'Dia do bheatha, a naoidhe naoimh'.

Mac Amhlaigh, Dónal (1926–89), journalist and novelist in Irish, was born in Galway. His family moved to Kilkenny and it is from that city that he emigrated, leaving a bleak and impoverished Ireland for England in 1951. He spent the rest of his life in Northampton where he worked as a navvy (labourer). *Dialann Deoraí* (literally: the diary of an exile) was published in 1960 and is the work for which he is best known. Although giving naught for the reader's comfort, it provided a welcome change from the predominantly rural style of prose writing in Irish, and became a modern classic. Mac Amhlaigh's other works include short story collections *Sweeney agus Scéalta Eile* (1970) and *Deoraithe* (1986). He contributed a column in Irish to the *Irish Times* for many years.

Mac Annaidh, Séamus (b. 1961), novelist in Irish, was born in Enniskillen, educated there at St Michael's and at NUU. He worked as a librarian and later was writer-in-residence in NUU. He has published a trilogy of novels in Irish – *Cuifeach Mo Lóndubh Buí* (1983), *Mo Dhá Mící* (1986) and *Rubble na Mickies* (1990) – which are wildly humorous and as deconstructed as any modern academic could desire. Mac Annaidh draws on his experiences as a teacher in Gaeltacht summer schools, and a relentless logic reminiscent of Flann O'Brien characterises his anti-hero Mící Mac Crosain who lives up to the literary pun on his name.

Macardle, Dorothy (1899–1958), novelist and historian, was born in Dundalk, the daughter of a well known brewing family. She was educated at Alexandra and UCD and taught at her old school until her arrest for republican activities in 1922. *The Irish Republic* (1937), her account of the years 1916–23, though written from the republican point of view (as is her booklet *Tragedies of Kerry*), is the fullest documentary account of the period. Apart from anti-Free State propaganda work, she wrote *Children of Europe* (1949), an account of the fate of refugee children after WWII. She also wrote novels and plays, one of which, *Uneasy Freehold* (1942), about a revenant, was filmed in 1944 as *The Uninvited* (its American title) with Ray Milland and Gail Russell. *Earth-Bound* (1924) is a collection of short stories written in prison; they are set in Ireland and reflect her usual themes, the fight for freedom and the supernatural.

McAughtry, Sam (b. 1923), was born in the 'Tiger Bay' area (though it was not called that in his time) of unionist Belfast and served as navigator in the RAF (1940–6). On demobilisation he became a civil servant (1947–79) and later a full-time writer and broadcaster. His sketches of working-class Belfast life are kindly and funny, though the dark aspects of his native city are not balked. This is specially true of his novel *Touch and Go* (1993), which, apart from its unlikely melodramatic conclusion, is a realistic picture of Belfast immediately postwar, when sectarian fires only smouldered and local animosities seemed trivial after the Holocaust. *McAughtry's War* (1985) and *Hillman Street High Roller* (1994) are *seanchaí*-style reminiscences, while *Down in the Free State* (1987) describes the author's wary affection for 'them wans over the Border'.

McBreen, Joan (b.1946), poet, was born in Sligo and educated at Sion Hill College in Dublin. She now lives in Tuam, County Galway. She worked for many years as a primary schoolteacher and raised a family of six children. Her first poem, prompted by the death of a child, was submitted to a local newspaper. Her poetry, which is very well regarded, deals wittily with the condition of women and the trials and rewards of intimate relationships. It is collected in *The Wind Beyond the Wall* (1990) and *A Walled Garden in Moylough* (1995). Her most recent collection is *Poems Selected and New* (1998).

McCabe, Eugene (b. 1930), playwright and novelist, was born in Glasgow and returned with his family to Ireland when he was nine. He was educated at Castleknock and UCC and in 1964 took over the running of the family farm on the Tom Tiddler's ground of the Monaghan-Fermanagh border. His play *King of the Castle* (1964), one of two hits of the 1964 Dublin Theatre Festival (the other being Brian Friel*'s *Philadelphia, Here I Come!*), is the story of a childless couple and of the husband's arranging to have his wife impregnated by another man. In 1976 he wrote *Victims*, a trilogy of contemporary plays for RTÉ about the Northern Troubles in his violent area, and developed them as prose fiction. His novel *Death and Nightingales** (1992), though set in the 1880s, is full of contemporary resonance.

McCabe, Patrick (b. 1955), novelist, was born in Clones, County Monaghan, and taught in Balbriggan and London. He won the Hennessy Award for a short story in 1979 and began writing novels, producing *Music on Clinton Street* (1986), about the breakdown of the old order of Irish life among young people, and *Carn* (1989), an anatomy of a southern border town which, having suffered a slump with the closing of the railway and been restored to temporary boom by the entrepreneurial ability of a native son, succumbs again to hopelessness as the Northern Troubles seep south. The townspeople are drawn with a raw sympathy and the IRA characters have an appropriate cold ruthlessness. *The Butcher Boy* (1992) was shortlisted for the Booker Prize and won *The Irish Times*/Aer Lingus Award. It became a play as *Frank Pig Says Hello* and was made into an outstanding film by Neil Jordan. The character of Francie Brady, the ultimate victim of rogue genes, parental neglect and small-town prejudice, survives sexual abuse and

various institutions to wreak a logical revenge on the town. *The Dead School* (1995) is also about madness and conscious mental deterioration. McCabe's humour takes some of the sting out of his black vision of Irish life. His most recent novel is *Breakfast on Pluto* (1998).

McCall P[atrick] J[oseph] (1861–1919), ballad-maker, was born in Dublin, the son of a Patrick Street grocer, and educated at the Catholic University. Later he kept a pub that was frequented by Douglas Hyde* and other members of the National Literary Society. His *Fenian Nights' Entertainment* (1897) was serialised in the *Shamrock*, the heroic tales told in racy modern language. He is remembered for his ballads of 1798, written for the centenary celebrations, notably 'Boolavogue' and 'Kelly from Killane'. His *In the Shadow of St Patrick's* (1894) is a volume of reminiscences of old Dublin.

McCann, Colum (b. 1965), fiction writer, was born in Dublin, the son of the well known journalist and writer Sean McCann (b. 1929), and educated at Rathmines College, graduating in Journalism. His stories won Hennessy Awards in 1990 and his collection *Fishing in the Sloe-Black River* (1994) won the Rooney Prize. A novel, *Songdogs* (1995), describes the quest of the son of a Mexican woman and a low-life Irish father for his missing mother. *This Side of Brightness* (1998) is a complex and ambitious novel about have-nots in New York.

MacCann, Michael Joseph (1824–83), poet, was born in Galway and taught in St Jarlath's, Tuam, before becoming a journalist and editor of the *Harp*. He died in London. His famous song 'O'Donnell Aboo' was written for *The Nation** when he was nineteen.

McCann, Sean (1905–80), playwright and politician, was born in Dublin and educated in Synge Street. He became a journalist and a Fianna Fáil politician, serving as a TD (1939–54) and as Lord Mayor of Dublin (1946–7). His comedies *Twenty Years A-Wooing* (1954), *Blood Is Thicker than Water* (1955), *Early and Often* (1956) and *Give Me a Bed of Roses* (1957), were the mainstay of the Abbey**'s exile in the Queen's Theatre after the fire of 1951. They are lower middle-class naturalistic comedies, their plots reflecting light-heartedly the mores of the 1950s.

MacCarthy, Catherine Phil (b. 1954), poet, was born in Crecora, County Limerick and educated at UCC. Her poetry collections include *This Hour of the Tide* (1994) and *The Blue Globe* (1998), her poems notable for their delicate, tactful treatment of the emotions surrounding love, death, erotic passion and children.

McCarthy, Thomas (b. 1954), poet and novelist, was born in Cappoquin, County Waterford and educated at UCC. He works as a librarian in Cork. His first collection, *The First Convention* (1978), won the Patrick Kavanagh Award. Other collections include *The Sorrow Garden* (1981), *The Non-Aligned Storyteller* (1984), and *Seven Winters in Paris* (1989) .His poetry has a quiet lyrical intensity; he deals frequently with themes of family and parenthood, but he also shows a deep interest in politics. He has also produced two novels with political themes, *Without Power* (1990) and *Asya and Christine* (1993).

McCormack, Mike (b.1965), novelist and short story writer, was born in London but grew up mainly in Louisburgh in County Mayo. He took a BA in English and Philosophy at UCG. His first collection of short stories, *Getting It in the Head* (1996), was highly praised and won the Rooney Prize for Literature. *Crowe's Requiem* (1998) is a first-person novel about a man who embarks on a quest for love that will kill him.

Mac Craith, Aindrias (1710–90), poet in Irish, was born in County Limerick and known as 'An Mangaire Súgach' [the jolly pedlar]. He was a teacher for a while but later became a wandering minstrel and one of the most regular clients of Seán Ó Tuama* (his fellow Maigue poet) in his inn at Croom. He was briefly a Protestant but was expelled from the congregation for conduct unbecoming. He was expelled from Croom for similar reasons by the local parish priest who remembered his brief apostasy. 'Slán le Croma' was written about this time and describes the loneliness of his condition in later life 'ó seoladh me chun uaignis'. Mac

Craith wrote a fine elegy on the death of his friend Seán Ó Tuama in 1775. He is buried in Kilmallock.

Mac Cruitín, Aodh Buí (?1670–1755), poet and lexicographer in Irish, was born in Corcomroe, County Clare of a family of hereditary poets, and educated by his cousin Aindrias Mac Cruitín, also a poet. A Jacobite like the other Gaelic poets of his age, he left Ireland with Patrick Sarsfield after the Treaty of Limerick (1691) and is said to have served with the famous Wild Geese battalion, Clare's Dragoons, in Flanders. On his return to Ireland he became known in Gaelic literary circles in Dublin. To refute *Hibernica Anglicana*, an anti-Irish work by Richard Cox, Chief Justice of Ireland, he wrote a history of Ireland in English, *Discourse in Vindication of the Antiquity of Ireland* (1717). Imprisoned as a result, he compiled a grammar, *Elements of the Irish Language* (1728), published by him in Louvain in 1728 after his release. There he also collaborated with Conor Begley on an *English-Irish Dictionary* (1732). On the death of his cousin Aindrias he returned to Clare to become official poet and scholar (*ollam*) to the O'Brien family, a position he held until his death.

Mac Cuarta, Séamas Dall (c. 1650–1733), poet in Irish, was born in County Louth, probably near Omeath. As his name implies, he was either blind or of defective sight. He spent his life in the region of northeast Leinster from Carlingford Lough to the Boyne.

Although trained in the bardic tradition, his nature poetry and feeling for living things makes him unusual among the more formal poets of his time. The lyrics 'Fáilte don Éan' and 'An Lon Dubh Báite', are his best known poems, the former especially much anthologised. Like his friend Carolan the harpist, who had the same disability, he depended upon patrons for survival. In the dark years of the early eighteenth century with the native Irish aristocracy in decline, he was reduced to beggary but lived to what was in his era a great age.

Mac Cumhaill, Fionn (pseudonym of Maghnas Mac Cumhaill) (1885–1965), novelist in Irish, was a native Irish speaker, born near Annagry in the Rosses of Donegal and educated at St Eunan's, Letterkenny, and for a time at UCD, which he left to travel to America. He returned to Ireland in 1913 to help run the Gaelic League* summer school at Cloghaneely in Donegal and begin writing. His best known book, *Na Rosa go Bráthach* (1939), was for many years a secondary school textbook, valued more for the quality of its Irish than as literature. Others novels were *Sé Dia an Fear is Fearr* (1928) and *Lascaire na gCiabh-Fholt Fionn* (1955). Books for children include *Maicín* (1946) and *An Dochartach* (1935). *Gura Slán le m'Óige* (1974) is a posthumously published memoir of childhood.

Macdermots of Ballycloran, The (1847), Anthony Trollope*'s first novel, set in County Leitrim and inspired by the ruin of a Big House seen by the author. In its description of the downfall of an old Catholic family it is a grim tale, far removed from the niceties of Barsetshire. Thady Macdermot tries to re-establish the family's position after its economic degeneration at the hands of his drunken father. His sister Feemie is made pregnant by her lover, Captain Myles Ussher of the constabulary, and they plan to run off together. Thady is horrified and conspires with the local chapter of the Ribbonmen to injure him but it is Thady who accidentally kills him. Feemie loses her mind and dies in childbirth, and Thady is hanged. Though there are comic scenes, they serve only to heighten the gloom and hopelessness of the main theme. The picture of pre-Famine Ireland is unusually sympathetic and authentic.

Mac Domhnaill, Aodh (1802–67), poet and philosopher in Irish, was born in Lower Drumgill, County Meath but spent much of his life in the north of Ireland. After a spell as a Protestant Bible instructor, he worked in Belfast from 1842 under the patronage of scholar Riobeárd Mac Ádhaimh, teaching Irish and transcribing manuscripts. He wrote an Irish primer and a book on natural philosophy but is now best remembered for his poem 'I mBéal Feirste Cois Cuain'. He later went to live in County Donegal and died in poverty in County Cavan.

Mac Domhnaill, Seán Clárach (1691–1754), poet in Irish, was born in Ráth Luirc (Charleville), County Cork. He trained as a teacher and was well schooled in the classics. He was the leading poet of Munster in his time and maintained the tradition of courts of poetry which met in his house at Kiltoohig, although there is evidence that he was not always on friendly terms with his confrères, who included Tadhg Gaelach Ó Suilleabháin* and Seán Ó Tuama*. Like other Irish poets of his time, he looked forward enthusiastically to a Stuart restoration, in aislings and in poems such as the powerful exhortatory 'Mo Ghille Mear'. The poem 'Taiscidh a Chlocha' [Keep fast, stones], for which he is now best known, is a powerful and bitter satire on the death of James Dawson, a hated landlord. Because of it he had to leave his home but was eventually able to return and live there in comparative peace until his death. He is buried in the ruined churchyard of Ballysallagh.

MacDonagh, Donagh (1912–68), poet and playwright, was born in Dublin, as his poem 'Dublin Made Me' proclaims, the son of Thomas MacDonagh* the poet and revolutionary, and educated at Belvedere and UCD, where he was part of a gifted and witty circle that included Flann O'Brien*, the actor Cyril Cusack and the poet Denis Devlin. After six years at the bar he became a district justice in 1941 but continued an interest in folk ballads, poetry and verse-drama as well as broadcasting. His *Happy as Larry* (1946), a ballad-opera after the manner of John Gay, uses contemporary tunes, including a splendid song from Clotho, Lachesis and Atropos, 'Three Young Ladies from

Hades' sung to the tune of 'Three Lovely Lasses'. He also wrote *God's Gentry* (1951), about travellers, and *Step-in-the-Hollow* (1957), an Irish version of Kleist's *Der Zerbrochene Krug* (1808). He was co-editor with Lennox Robinson of the important *Oxford Book of Irish Verse* (1958).

MacDonagh, Thomas (1878–1916), poet, playwright and revolutionary, father of Donagh McDonagh*, was born in Cloughjordan, County Tipperary, and educated at Rockwell. He was for some time a postulant but left in 1901 to become a teacher in Kilkenny, Fermoy and finally in Pearse*'s St Enda's. By 1911 he had graduated from UCD and was appointed lecturer in English. Disenchanted with the Gaelic League*, he joined the IRB in 1913 and was one of the signatories of the 1916 Proclamation. During the Rising he was in command of the forces in the Jacobs factory and was executed with the Pearse brothers on 3 May. His poetry, strongly influenced by his Catholicism and the Literary Revival*, was published in various volumes, notably *The Golden Joy* (1906) and *Songs of Myself* (1910) which includes the much anthologised 'John-John', an admiring address by a settled wife to a traveller husband. *Lyrical Poems* (1913) contains 'The Yellow Bittern', a sprightly version of Cathal Buí Mac Giolla Ghunna's '*An Bonnan Buí*' which gave Francis Ledwidge* the cue for his threnody for MacDonagh: 'He shall not hear the bittern's cry'. In his play *Metempsychosis* (1912) he satirised Yeats* as Lord Winton-Winton de Winton but to Yeats, after the birth of the terrible beauty, he was one who '. . . might have won fame in the end,/ So sensitive his nature seemed,/ So daring and sweet his thought.'

McFadden, Roy (b. 1921), poet, was born in Belfast and educated at QUB, qualifying as a solicitor in 1944. He has lived there all his life and his poetry reflects the troubled life of the city. His early work was published in *Lagan* and he and Barbara Edwards edited *Rann** (1948–53), a poetry quarterly. Early collections *Swords and Ploughshares* (1943) and *Flowers for a Lady* (1946) endeavour to balance the personal with the public, the poet finding it hard to countenance what passes for politics in NI. This may explain his long silence from 1947 till 1971 when at the height of the Troubles he produced *The Garryowen*, the title poem of which, ironically, is about the one thing (rugby) that unites Ireland. Other collections, including *Letters to the Hinterland* (1986) and *After Seymour's Funeral* (1990), have followed, showing a lively challenge rather than depression.

Mac Gabhann, Micí (1865–1948), autobiographer in Irish, was born in Cloghaneely, County Donegal, and hired as a *spailpín* from the age of nine. By fifteen he was a labourer in Scotland and he emigrated to America when he was twenty, working in the silver mines in Butte, Montana, and lighting out for the Yukon in the Klondyke gold rush after 1896. He returned home in 1902, a comparatively rich man. His reminiscences, recorded by the folkorist Seán Ó hEochaidh, became a book, *Rotha Mór an tSaoil* (1959), from which he emerges as a shrewd, witty, engaging man. The book was translated as *Hard Road to the Klondyke* (1962) by Val Iremonger*.

McGahern, John (b. 1934), novelist and short story writer, was born in Dublin but brought up in County Leitrim where his father was a police sergeant. This provided the material for his first novel *The Barracks* (1963). He was educated at St Patrick's College, Dublin, and UCD and taught in the city until the publication of his controversial novel *The Dark** (1965) caused him to be dismissed. Though he was refused reinstatement, the notoriety attached to the case virtually finished the system of narrow literary censorship that had bedevilled the state since 1929. After much time spent travelling and teaching abroad, he is again resident in Ireland. Other novels include *The Leavetaking* (1974), which has some elements of autobiography, and *Amongst Women** (1990), which was a critical and commercial success, being shortlisted for the Booker Prize. Like his excellent short stories, collected in 1992, his novels are remarkable for the sociological accuracy of their rendering of Irish provincial life and their grimness of outlook, occasionally mitigated by quirky humour.

McGee, Thomas D'Arcy (1825–68), journalist and poet, was born in Carlingford, County Louth, and reared in Wexford. His early manhood was spent in America where he was made editor of the *Boston Pilot* in 1844. He returned to Ireland to engage strongly in the Young Ireland movement, writing for *The Nation** and having to flee after involvement in the Smith O'Brien rising of 1848. During the next decade he lost his belief in revolutionary politics, moved to Canada in 1858 and became a prominent constitutional reformer. He was assassinated in Ottawa after vigorous denunciation of the Fenian invasion of Canada. He is remembered for such poems as 'The Celts' and 'The Man of the North Countrie'.

MacGill, Patrick (1889–1963), poet, was born in the Glen of Glenties, County Donegal, the 'Glenmornan' of his novels. He was hired out in Tyrone at twelve and went to Scotland as a 'tattie-hoker' at fourteen. He worked as a navvy on railways and building-sites, filling his sparse leisure with wide reading and writing. His early poetry, *Gleanings from a Navvy's Notebook* (1911), *Songs of a Navvy* (1911) and *Songs of the Dead End* (1912), which he hawked from door to door in Scotland, earned him the soubriquet the 'Navvy Poet'. His verse is effective and accessible, not unlike the 'sourdough' songs of R. W. Service (1874-1958), and some pieces, like 'Going Home to Glenties' have been effectively set to music. His real literary achievement is in his companion novels *Children of the Dead End** (1914) and *The Rat Pit* (1915), describing the life that he and other migrant workers experienced. These caused a sensation on publication; their strong socialist and anticlerical material had them denounced from many pulpits. The first, which autobiographically ends on a fairly optimistic note, describes the early poverty and appalling conditions under which the Donegal lad Dermod works. *The Rat Pit*, which tells the story of his sweetheart Norah, is more gloomy, describing her seduction, prostitution and death. MacGill served as a stretcher-bearer in WWI and wrote about its horrors in *The Great Push* (1916) and *The Red Horizon* (1916). *Glenmornan* (1919) is also autobiographical, describing the reaction in Ireland to the scandalous work of the writer, while *Lanty Hanlon* (1922) is a rural comedy set on the Gweebarra River. MacGill went to America where he died of multiple sclerosis in Massachusetts on the same day as Aldous Huxley, C. S. Lewis* and John F. Kennedy. The Patrick MacGill Summer School (established in 1981), dedicated to literature and politics, is held annually in Glenties.

McGinley, Patrick (b. 1945), novelist, was born in Glencolumkille, County Donegal, and educated at UCG. He taught in Ireland before becoming a publisher in England. His seven novels, including *Bogmail* (1978), *Foggage* (1984), *The Trick of the Ga Bolga* (1985) and *The Devil's Dairy* (1988), often set in Donegal, seem at first glance to be naturalistic accounts of provincial Irish life but they darken, become more extreme in violence and sexuality and often get mired in fantasy.

Mac Giolla Gunna, Cathal Buí (*c*. 1680–1755), poet in Irish, was born in County Fermanagh or County Cavan. He was, according to his own claim, destined for the priesthood but took to the more profane pleasures of drink and women. He is famous for his rakehelly life and for two excellent poems, 'Aithreachas Cathail Bhuí' ['Repentance of Cathal Buí'] written, it is said, with a burnt stick on the wall of the hut in Carrickmacross in County Monaghan where he lay dying and 'An Bonnán Buí', finely translated by Thomas MacDonagh as 'The Yellow Bittern'. 'An Bonnán Buí' describes the finding of a bittern dead by a frozen lake and points out quite a few parallels with the life of the poet. The maid servant who had been temerarious enough to give shelter to such a forbidden scoundrel claimed that his body was surrounded by a heavenly light, proof of God's forgiveness.

Mac Grianna, Seosamh (1901–90), novelist and short story writer in Irish, regarded as one of Ireland's leading writers in that language, brother of 'Máire*' (Séamus Ó Grianna, the differing surnames being caused by a family feud), was born in Rannafast in the Rosses of Donegal and educated at St Eunan's, Letterkenny, and St Columb's, Derry, qualifying as a teacher at St Patrick's College, Drumcondra, in 1921. He taught at home for some time but took the anti-Treaty side in the Civil War* and, interned by the Free State forces, found teaching jobs hard to get on his release in 1924. He worked for

An Gúm as a translator of English books, most of them pretty undistinguished, *Muintir an Oileáin*, his version of Peadar O'Donnell*'s *Islanders* (1927), being a notable exception. *An Grá agus an Ghruaim* (1929), his collection of short stories with a historical novella, showed a command of literary Irish that did not depend on local lore and idiom as did the popular work of Máire. He wrote literary criticism in *Peadar Ó Conaire agus Aistí Eile* (1936), historical biography in *Eoghan Rua Ó Néill* (1931), and a novel, *An Droma Mór*, which languished in the files of An Gúm* from 1933 till 1969, when a revival of interest in his work led to its publication and an award from the Irish-American Cultural Institute. Mac Grianna's last book, the autobiographical apologia *Mo Bhealach Féin* (1940), contains the words which marked the end of his writing life: '*Thráigh an tobar sa bhliain 1935.*' ('The well dried up in 1935') Thereafter his health gave way and he spent the next fifty years mainly in St Conall's mental hospital, Letterkenny.

McGuckian, Medbh (née McCaughan) (b. 1950), poet, was born in Belfast and educated at QUB. She graduated MA in 1974 (her thesis on Irish Gothic writers) and taught for some years before her appointment as the first woman writer-in-residence at QUB (1986-8). She has won many awards for her distinctive (and difficult) poetry which has been published in eight volumes between 1980 and 1994. Her uniting theme is the experience of being a woman and mother, but Ireland, its peace and troubles, also concern her. Among her most recent books are *Mar-coni's Cottage* (1991) (the title coming from the name of her summer house in Ballycastle, County Antrim) and *Captain Lavender* (1994). *Selected Poems 1978–1994* appeared in 1997.

McGuinness, Frank (b. 1953), playwright, was born in Buncrana, County Donegal, and educated at UCD, taking an MPhil in Medieval Studies. He was appointed to the staff of the English Department at Maynooth. Though his early plays *Factory Girls* (1983), set in a Buncrana shirt factory, and *Observe the Sons of Ulster Marching towards the Somme** (1985), a sympathetic study of soldiers of the Ulster Division in WWI, might be called conventional, later work is more experimental: *Carthaginians* (1988), taking its inspiration from the events of Bloody Sunday in Derry in 1972, *Innocence* (1986), about the troubled life of the homoerotic painter Caravaggio (1573-1610), and *Someone Who'll Watch over Me* (1992), inspired by Brian Keenan's book *An Evil Cradling* (1992) based upon his experiences as a hostage in Beirut. McGuinness has also produced versions of plays by Ibsen, Chekhov and Lorca and has written a film script for Brian Friel*'s *Dancing at Lughnasa**.

MacIntyre, Tom (b. 1931), fiction writer and playwright, was born in Cavan and educated at UCD. He taught English in Clongowes and creative writing in Ann Arbor, Michigan, and in Massachusetts. His first book *Dance the Dance* (1969), a collection of often ribald stories, was followed by *The*

Charollais (1969), a novel about a bull from the sea that stirs up an Irish community into extremes of sexuality. It is funny and nicely satirical about an Ireland on the brink of change. His drama, best interpreted by the actor Tom Hickey and directed by Patrick Mason, is very experimental, with effective use of dance and mime. The most successful was *The Great Hunger* (1983), based upon Kavanagh*'s famous poem. Others include *Dance for Your Daddy* (1987) and *Rise Up, Lovely Sweeney* (1985), the title of the latter from an Ulster ballad but the theme from *Buile Shuibhne*, the luminous twelfth-century text that has also inspired Flann O'Brien*, Seamus Heaney* and most recently Joseph O'Connor*. *Caoineadh Airt Uí Laoghaire* (1998), is a bilingual dramatic account of the background to Eibhlín Dhubh Ní Chonaill*'s famous lament for her husband. MacIntyre's poetry collections include *Blood Relations* (1972), *I Bailed Out at Ardee* (1987) and *Fleur-du-lit* (1991).

Macken, Walter (1915–67), novelist and playwright, was born in Galway, where he was educated and spent most of his life. He joined An Taidhbhearc at seventeen and learned the whole craft of theatre. After some years as an insurance salesman in London he became a member the Abbey* company and played leads on Broadway in *The King of Friday's Men** and his own *Home is the Hero* (1952). He also acted in films, notably in Behan*'s *The Quare Fellow**. His first play *Mungo's Mansions* (1946) and *Home is the Hero* tried to do for

the slums of Galway what O'Casey* had done for those of Dublin twenty-five years before, but though they are a good deal less sentimental and better made, they fall short of the older playwright's obsessive genius. Macken began to write novels which combined literary worth with popularity. *Rain on the Wind* (1950), his third book, about the life of a fisherman in the Claddagh (the medieval fishing village now part of Galway city), was so successful that he began to take less interest in the theatre. His greatest success was with his historical trilogy: *Seek the Fair Land* (1959), about Ireland in the time of Cromwell, *The Silent People* (1962), about the Great Famine, and *The Scorching Wind* (1964), about the Anglo-Irish War*. *Flight of the Doves* (1971), a children's story, was successfully filmed. He died suddenly in his home at Menlo.

MacKenna, John (b. 1952), fiction writer, was born in Castledermot, County Kildare, and educated at St Clement's College, Limerick, and UCD. He joined RTÉ as a producer (he is now a commissioning editor), making several programmes about his home place, which also bulks large in his writing. *Clare* (1994) is a brilliant, oblique account of the life of the Northamptonshire poet who ended his days in the county asylum. Four women who played parts in Clare's life – his wife, sister, mistress and patron – tell their stories, and the last word is Clare's himself in his letters. MacKenna's short story collections *The Fallen* (1992) and *A Year of Our Lives* (1995) are also impressive; the latter set of stories, set mainly on the Kildare-Carlow borders, concerns love and death, priests and rectors – and their daughters! His most recent work, *The Last Fine Summer* (1997) is a novel of remembered love.

MacKenna, Stephen (1872–1934), translator, was born in Liverpool of Irish parents and became a first-rate student of Classics, though he could not enter UCD having failed English. He became a journalist and moved to Paris where he formed a lifelong friendship with Synge*. In 1897 he fought for the Greeks against Turkey, later describing the war as 'like waiting for a train in Mullingar'. He covered the Russo-Japanese War for Pulitzer's *New York Post* and, after a quarrel with the proprietor, came to Dublin in 1907 and became a leader writer for the *Freeman's Journal*. He became one of the centres of Dublin's essentially vocal intellectual life, a member of the Gaelic League* and equally at home with the folk of the Irish Literary Revival* and the IRB. He was sent home from the GPO by Pearse because of the ill-health that plagued him for the remaining eighteen years of his life. He made his life's work the translation of the excessively difficult *Enneads* ('nines') of Plotinus (205–70), the exponent of Neo-Platonism and last of the Greek philosophers of classical antiquity. These were six volumes of nine essays, and his translation of the first volume on ethics and aesthetics appeared in 1908. He left Ireland in 1922 in disillusionment with the Civil War* and died four years after the suc-

cessful completion of his mammoth work.

Macklin, Charles (?1699–1797), actor and playwright, was born MacLaughlin in Derry or Culdaff, County Donegal, and after living with his stepfather in Islandbridge, Dublin, became a strolling player at the age of seventeen. By the age of thirty he was the only rival of the great David Garrick (1717–79) in the Theatre Royal, Drury Lane, recovering Shylock as a tragic villain and encouraging naturalism in his companies. Macklin wrote ten plays, including *The True-Born Irishman* (1762), the very popular *Love à-la-Mode** (1759) and *The Man of the World* (1781). Failing memory caused him to retire from the stage in 1789 when he was nearly ninety but he lived for eight more years.

MacLaverty, Bernard (b. 1942), novelist and short story writer, was born in Belfast and worked for ten years as a medical laboratory technician before taking a degree in QUB and moving to Scotland. His four collections of stories, *Secrets* (1977), *A Time to Dance* (1982), *The Great Profundo* (1987) and *Walking the Dog* (1994), are full of piquant characters, prostitutes, amateur musicians, bewildered adolescents and even sword-swallowers. The last-named collection has short experimental pieces interleaving more conventional stories. One story, 'My Dear Palestrina', is about a boy and his music teacher in a war-torn Ulster, also the background of his novel *Cal* (1983), which describes the relationship between a young terrorist and the widow of his victim. It was successfully filmed, as was an earlier novel, *Lamb* (1980), about a delinquent boy and a teaching brother. His most recent novel *Grace Notes** (1997), about an expatriate Ulster composer, was shortlisted for the Booker Prize.

McLaverty, Michael (1904–92), short story writer and novelist, was born in Carrickmacross, County Monaghan, in 1904 but brought up in Belfast where he taught for many years after graduating BSc from QUB in 1927 and qualifying as a teacher in 1928. He began writing short stories for such journals as the *Capuchin Annual*, and a first collection, *The White Mare*, was published by Richard Rowley*'s Mourne Press in 1943. He was already known as a novelist, having written the ever popular *Call My Brother Back** (1939), a novel of childhood and youth, partly set in Rathlin Island*, and *Lost Fields* (1941), a thematic account of the reluctant settling of country people in the city. Six novels published between 1945 and 1965 were written out of a strong Catholicism which determined the nature of the material and its treatment. To some this professional decision seemed a severe limitation for any artist since his themes were the great ones of good and evil. McLaverty's greater talent lay in his stories, which, written in a beautifully spare style, dealt with the dilemmas of unheroic people as they lived their unexceptionable lives. *Collected Stories* (1978), with an introduction by Seamus Heaney*, contains his finest work.

Mac Liammóir, Mícheál (1899–1978), actor, designer and playwright, was born Alfred Willmore in London and by 1912 was a boy actor, playing Oliver Twist. He studied art for some years and toured the continent, picking up languages with the same facility with which he later learned Irish. He came to Ireland in the 1920s, toured with his famous actor-manager brother-in-law Anew McMaster (1894–1962) and met Hilton Edwards (1903–82) who was to become his life's partner. Together they opened An Taibhdhearc* in 1928, Mac Liammóir taking the lead in his own play *Diarmuid agus Gráinne*, for which he also designed (and painted) the sets. In the same year the partners founded the Gate Theatre*, which took up residence in Parnell Square in 1930. Often on a shoestring, they provided Dublin with a theatre which was equally at home with the classical repertory and modern Irish and European plays, the strikingly handsome Mac Liammóir playing the leads. He wrote in all thirteen plays, the best known being *Where Stars Walk* (1940), based on the myth of Etain and Midir, and *Ill Met by Moonlight* (1946), about the folk tradition of the changeling. His autobiographical writings *All for Hecuba* (1946), *Put Money in Thy Purse* (1950) and *Aisteóirí faoi Dhá Sholas* (1956), translated as *Each Actor on His Ass* (1961), remain extremely entertaining and his one-man show *The Importance of Being Oscar** (1963) gave him worldwide celebrity and the partners financial security.

MacMahon, Bryan (1909–98), man of
letters, was born in Listowel, County
Kerry, and educated there and at St
Patrick's College, Drumcondra. He
became a teacher, eventually the headmaster, in Listowel, serving for forty-five
years. His charismatic life story, with his
contribution to the town in many ways
other than the pedagogical, is told with
characteristic brio in his bestselling
autobiography *The Master* (1992), the
title a universally used soubriquet that
he relished. *The Storyman*, a second
chapter describing his literary career,
was published in 1994. His writing
career began, as with so many others,
with *The Bell**, and his energetic,
eloquent short stories, first published in
book form in *The Lion Tamer* (1948),
showed him to be a writer of the quality
of O'Connor* and O'Faolain*. Other
collections were *The Red Petticoat*
(1955), *The End of the World* (1976),
The Sound of Hooves (1985) and *The
Tallystick* (1994). His novels include
Children of the Rainbow (1952) and
The Honey Spike (1967), a reworking of
his best known play, about travelling
people, for which his rare knowledge of
Shelta was a considerable advantage.
Other plays are *The Bugle in the Blood*
(1948), *The Song of the Anvil* (1967)
and a number of one-acts. MacMahon
has written books for children and
translated *Peig: The Autobiography of
Peig Sayers of the Great Blasket Island*
(1974). His 1916 pageant *Seachtar
Fear, Seacht Lá* was staged in Croke
Park as part of the fiftieth anniversary
celebration of the Easter Rising*.
MacMahon's life is an intoxicating sweep
of energetic appreciation of things Irish,
remarkable in that he was a white blackbird: a teetotal Irish writer.

MacManus, Francis (1909–65), novelist and broadcaster, was born in
Kilkenny and educated at St Patrick's
College and UCD. He taught for eighteen years before joining Radio Éireann
in 1948, eventually becoming the driving force behind the remarkable Thomas
Davis lectures. His first fiction was the
trilogy *Stand and Give Challenge* (1934),
Candle for the Proud (1936) and *Men
Withering* (1939), about the life and grim
eighteenth-century times of the Gaelic
poet Donncadh Rua Mac Conmara*. A
second trilogy, about twentieth-century
life in his native county, *This House Was
Mine* (1937), *Flow On Lovely River*
(1941) and *Watergate* (1942), shows
him to be one of the finest of Irish
realist novelists, his firmly rooted
Nationalism and Catholicism enabling
him to write with critical charity about
both those 'isms'. *The Greatest of These*
(1943) deals, with greater terseness and
austerity, with the clerical scandal in
Callan in the 1870s that also inspired
*The Big Chapel** by Thomas Kilroy*. His
finest novel (and the only one published outside Ireland) *Fire in the Dust**
(1950) describes small-town Irish
prudery in the 1940s. MacManus wrote
biographies of Boccaccio (1947) and
the fiery *peregrinus* Columban (1963),
as well as a travel book, *Seal ag Ródaíocht*
(1955).g88

MacManus, Seumas (?1870–1960),
storyteller and novelist, was born near

Mountcharles, County Donegal, and returned as a teacher to his old school. His stories and verse appeared in local papers and in Alice Milligan*'s *Shan Van Vocht*, the Belfast nationalist magazine she ran with Anna Johnston (who wrote poetry as 'Ethna Carbery*' and whom he married in 1901). He emigrated to America in 1899 (returning home each summer) where he found a ready market for his kind of Irish material. Over a long writing career he produced many popular novels such as *A Lad of the O'Friels* (1903), *Bold Blades of Donegal* (1937) and *The Little Mistress of Eskar Mór* (1960); many books of collected fairy stories and tales of local life, full of high humour and a significant measure of stage-Irishness; a number of one-act plays, including *The Townland of Tamney* (the Irish name for Mount-charles), which was presented by the Irish National Theatre Society on 4 January 1904, on the same bill as Yeats*'s *By Shadowy Waters*, in Molesworth Hall, the forerunner of the Abbey*; an epic history, *The Story of the Irish Race* (1921); and a lively auto-biography, *The Rocky Road to Dublin* (1938). His verse, and that of his wife and her partner, was published as *We Sang for Ireland: Poems of Ethna Carbery, Seumas MacManus and Alice Milligan* in 1950. He died in his nineties by falling from a nursing-home window in New York.

Mac Mathúna, Seán (b.1937), short story writer and dramatist in Irish and English, was born in Tralee, County

Kerry and educated at St Brendan's College Killarney and UCC. He has published short stories in *Combar* magazine, and a collection entitled *Ding agus Scéalta Eile* (1983). A volume of English translations of these stories was published as *The Atheist and Other Stories*, (1987). In 1992 his bilingual play *Gadaí Géar na Geamhoíche* was performed at the Peacock Theatre, Dublin.

Mac Meanmain, Seán (1886–1962), fiction writer in Irish, was born in Iniskeel near Glenties, County Donegal, and educated at Coláiste Uladh, the Gaelic League* school founded in 1906. He became a teacher at the McDevitt Institute in Glenties. He wrote many books of stories, often in the first person and based upon his own experience, in the lucid, unaffected Irish of central Donegal, including *Scéalta Goiride Geimbridh* (1915), *Fear Siubhal* (1924) and *Ó Chamhaoir go Clapsholas* (1940). His collected work was edited in three volumes in 1990, 1991 and 1992 by Séamus Ó Cnáimhsí.

MacNamara, Brinsley (pseudonym of John Weldon) (1890–1963), novelist and playwright, was born the son of a schoolmaster in Delvin, County Westmeath, a location he later made infamous in his first novel as *The Valley of the Squinting Windows** (1918). He was a member of the Abbey* company that toured America in 1911. After some freelancing there he returned home in 1913. The publication of his inflammatory first novel led to great local objections, including the boycotting of school and the public burning of his book in the town square. Three other novels continued to play a cold light on Irish life: *The Clanking of the Chains* (1919), about nationalist disillusionment, *In Clay and Bronze* (1920), a fictionalised account of his own life and artistic growth, and *The Mirror in the Dust* (1921), a tale of the blighting of young lives by the rural Ireland of the times. Of several plays written for the Abbey the finest was *Margaret Gillan* (1933), a chilling work about a jilted woman's revenge, but two comedies, *The Glorious Uncertainty* (1923) and *Look at the Heffernans!* (1926), were so popular with amateurs that they provided the author with a regular addition to his income. He became registrar of the National Gallery in 1924 in succession to James Stephens* and in 1929 produced what is regarded as his finest novel, *The Various Lives of Marcus Igoe*, which returns to the 'Garradrimna' of his first novel but is deliberately anti-realistic. *Some Curious People* (1945), a collection of idiosyncratic stories, and *Michael Caravan* (1946), a novel, represent his most significant later work.

MacNamara, Gerald (pseudonym of Harry Morrow) (1866–1938), playwright, was born in Belfast of a family of painters and decorators, one of whom, George (1870–1955), became art editor of *Punch*. He was one of the young men who founded the Ulster Literary Theatre* and wrote its most famous comic squib, *Thompson in Tír na nÓg* (1912), about the confusions that arise when an Orangeman from Scarva (scene of a yearly sham rerun of the Battle of the Boyne) is transported to the Land of Youth and tries to explain his politics to Cuchulain and Finn. An earlier, unfortunately unpublished piece, *The Mist That Does Be on the Bog* (1909), effectively satirised Synge*, and its title passed into currency as a label for that kind of language. Though Morrow, who was one of the company's finest actors, wrote six other plays, none is in print. His satires were the more effective because of his knowledge of the Irish history and culture that he guyed.

McNamee, Eoin (b. 1961), novelist and poet, was born in Kilkeel, County Down and educated at QUB where he graduated in Law. A novella, *The Last of Deeds*, was published in 1989. *Resurrection Man* (1994) deals with the murders of the sectarian 'Shankill' butchers in Belfast, holding the mirror up to evil in unflinching but controlled prose. His début collection of poetry is *The Language of Birds* (1995).

MacNeice, Louis (1907–63), poet and playwright, was born in Belfast 'between the mountains and the gantries' and educated at Marlborough and Merton College, Oxford. He graduated with a double first in Classics and Philosophy and his poetry is irradiated with classical attitudes. (His version of Aeschylus's *Agamemnon* (1936) is a classic in its own right.) He taught Classics at Birmingham (1929-36) and Greek at Bedford College in London (1936-40) but, after the break-up of his marriage, joined Laurence Gilliam's Features Department in the BBC in 1941, staying more than twenty years and contributing to its reputation for excellence. He wrote a number of memorable radio plays, notably *Out of the Picture* (1937) and *The Dark Tower* (1946). *One for the Grave*, his modern Everyman, was part of the 1966 Dublin Theatre Festival. He was primarily a poet, and a prolific one, equally at home in love lyrics and prophecy. His *Autumn Journal* (1939), a long poem recording London life after the Munich crisis, combines art with readability, and even the less successful *Autumn Sequel* (1946), three times as long, is still marvellously readable. Ireland, which both amused and exasperated him, recurs as a theme for verse, sometimes savagely chided, as in 'Neutrality', but always fascinating him and claiming his love and allegiance: 'The woven figure cannot undo its thread.' He never lost a salutary fear of 'darkest Ulster' but, by appointing the liberal Sam Hanna Bell* as Features Producer for BBC NI in 1946, hoped to thaw intransigent attitudes. He died after contracting a viral infection while looking for a special sound effect deep in a coal mine.

MacNeill, Janet (b. 1907), novelist, was born in Dublin, the daughter of a Presbyterian minister, and educated in Birkenhead and St Andrews. She came to live in Ulster to tend her failing father and worked for some time with the *Belfast Telegraph*. She married in 1933 but did not begin writing until 1951 when she entered a BBC play competition and came second with *Gospel Truth*, based upon her own life. This was followed by other successful radio work and a number of books for children, many featuring a hero called Specs McCann. One radio play, *A Child in the House*, was so popular that she was persuaded to render it as fiction. She wrote in all ten novels, mostly dealing with middle age and the reluctance of her literate but unexpressive characters to admit their emotional sterility. They happen to be middle-class Belfast Protestants and her work charts a kind of economic decay and waning influence. In *A Child in the House* (1955) a visit by the wife's niece might possibly have irrigated the marriage of Henry and Maud but the chance is lost. Her best known work *The Maiden Dinosaur* (1964) is a study of a middle-aged spinster schoolteacher who has taken refuge in a kind of frigid, rarely expressed lesbianism. She has many married friends of her own age and in time finds a settled low content. *The Small Widow* (1967) describes the discovery by a widow that her husband had had a long-time affair with his unstable cousin. On her suicide the widow realises that she played an important part in her husband's life after all. MacNeill's novels, if short on drama, are beautifully written, subtle, adult works about real life.

Mac Piarais, Pádraig, *see* Pearse, Patrick*

Mac Síomóin, Tomás (b. 1938), poet in Irish and translator, was born in Dublin and educated at UCD and Cornell.

His published collections include *Damhna agus Dánta Eile* (1974) and *Scian* (1989). He became editor of *Combar** in 1988.

Madden, Deirdre (b. 1960), novelist, though born in Belfast, was brought up in Toomebridge on the northern shore of Lough Neagh and educated in St Mary's, Magherafelt, TCD and the University of East Anglia. Her first work was published in David Marcus's *Irish Press* 'New Irish Writing' page. She has published five novels: *Hidden Symptoms* (1988), about the shocking effect of the bursting out of the sectarian evil, the symptoms of which were hidden in the euphoric 1960s, as a girl comes to terms with the murder of her twin brother by Protestants; *The Birds of the Innocent Wood* (1988), the story of a mother and her two daughters; *Remembering Light and Stone* (1992), which focuses on the experiences of a young Irishwoman in a small Italian town; *Nothing Is Black* (1994) about three women in crisis coming to terms with their lives; and her latest novel *One by One in the Dark* (1996), which won the Listowel Writers' Week Award and in which Madden returns to the theme of troubled Ulster, treating of the mistaken killing of the father of a family by Loyalist paramilitaries. Her work, especially when dealing with the female psyche, shows great depth and passion.

Maginn, William (1793–1842), man of letters and child prodigy, was born in Cork and educated at TCD, having entered it at the age of twelve. He was back teaching in his father's school at sixteen and ran it when his father died in 1813. In 1821 he left Cork for London and began contributing to the '*Noctes Ambrosianae*' series in *Blackwood's*. He founded *Fraser's Magazine* in 1830 and his coterie, which included Francis Sylvester Mahony*, became known as the Fraserites. He was for a time the typical drunken hack, with deadlines only just met but with a wide circle of friends. He was deeply affected by the accidental death of his partner Letitia Landon (1802–38) who as L. E. L. had supported herself from an early age by writing. He was noted even in those days for his wit and the clever humour of his verses, and his friend Thackeray* immortalised him in *Pendennis* (1850) as Captain Shandon, a subtle tribute to his birthplace.

Mahon, Bríd (b. 1922), novelist, children's writer, journalist and folklorist, was born in Dublin and early established herself as a working journalist, beginning her radio career while still a schoolgirl. She wrote hundreds of scripts for Radio Éireann and the BBC, and was Irish theatre critic for the British *Sunday Express* and women's editor for the *Sunday Press* (1970-80). She was for many years a member of the Irish Folklore Commission* under Seamus Ó Duillearga (Delargy), and when its activities were transferred to UCD at Belfield she became a senior research lecturer in the Department of Irish Folklore. Her career in folklore is described in a fascinating memoir, *While Green Grass Grows* (1998), while an earlier book on traditional Irish food, *Land of Milk and Honey* (1991), blasted forever the myth of 'praties and tay'. *A Time to Love* (1992) is a picaresque novel based on the life of David Garrick's partner, the Dublin-born Peg Woffington, while *Dervorgilla* (1994) does the same for the wayward wife of Ua Ruairc of Breifne. Her best known children's books are *Loo the Leprechaun and Báinín the White Cat* (1943) and *The Search for the Tinker Chief* (1968).

Mahon, Derek (b. 1941), poet, was born in Belfast and educated at Inst and TCD, where he studied Classics. He worked as a teacher and journalist, and was writer-in-residence at Coleraine (1978–9) and TCD (1988) and now divides his time between Dublin and New York. He has published many collections of poetry, among them *The Hunt By Night* (1982) and *Antarctica* (1985). A *Selected Poems* was published in 1990, *The Hudson Letter* in 1996 and *The Yellow Book*, a meditation on decadence in literature and culture, in 1997. He has also published a selection of journalistic writings, *Journalism: Selected Prose*, (1996). Because of the coincidence of place and date of birth, Mahon's name was conveniently linked with his near coevals Heaney* and Longley*, but he is more instinctively representative of Protestant middle-class Ulster even than Longley and more consciously apocalyptic in his work. *Night Crossing* (1968) portrays a kind of spiritual exile, cut off not only from home but also from history. The mocking, ambivalent lines from his poem 'Rage for Order' (which gave Frank Ormsby* the title for his anthology of the Ulster Troubles): 'Somewhere beyond the scorched gable and the burnt-out buses/ there is a poet indulging/ his wretched rage for order/ or not as the case may be   .   .   .' will do as an interim testament. John Banville* has described his poem 'A Disused Shed in County Wexford' as 'the most beautiful single poem produced by an Irishman since the death of Yeats*'. *High Time*, Mahon's version of Molière's *L'École des Maris* (1661), had its première in a Field Day* production in 1994.

Mahony, Francis Sylvester (aka 'Father Prout') (1804–66), humorist and journalist, was born in Cork, son of the owner of the well known woollen mills of Blarney, the village near Cork famous for its groves and stone of eloquence. It was Mahony who added the extra verse to Milliken*'s squib, which contains the lines that helped confirm the stone's reputation: There is a stone there,/ That whoever kisses,/ Oh! he never misses/ To grow eloquent. Mahony was educated at Jesuit seminaries in Paris and Rome and was a teacher at Clongowes (with Canon Sheehan* among his pupils) when he was asked to resign from the order as unsuitable – one story concerns a drunken spree with pupils at Celbridge – but was ordained in Lucca as a secular priest in 1832. He served heroically as a curate during a cholera outbreak in Cork but left for London after a row with his bishop in 1834. Witty, clever and gifted in Classics and modern languages, he was an obvious contributor to his friend Maginn*'s *Fraser's Magazine*. His writings (including the squib 'The Bells of Shandon') were published by Hugh Fraser, the magazine's publisher, as *The Reliques of Father Prout* in 1837. (Father Prout was the name of an actual parish priest of Watergrasshill who died in 1830.) He became Rome correspondent of the *Daily News*, the paper founded by Dickens, in 1846 and finally settled in Paris where he died. He is buried in the vault of Shandon church.

Máire (pseudonym of Séamus Ó Grianna) (1889–1969), novelist and short story writer in Irish, was born in Rannafast in the Rosses of Donegal, to a family renowned for its *seanchas*. His brother Seosamh Mac Grianna* was also a writer, and another brother Seán Bán and sister Máire Bhán were noted *seanchaithe*. Like his brothers, he took the Republican side in the Civil War* and was interned until 1924. In 1932 he joined the Customs and Excise service in Dublin. He was a contributing editor to both De Bhaldraithe*'s and Ó Dónaill*'s dictionaries. He wrote many novels and short stories about his native place, using his mother's name and with her often as narrator, which were treasured for their idioms and their picture of Donegal life at the turn of the century, but he set his face against the *nua-litríocht*, refusing to allow his best known novel *Caisleáin Óir* (1924) to be standardised. Other works were *Mo Dhá Róisín* (1921) and a collection of short stories, *Cioth is Dealán* (1927). His work, and that of others like him,

was paid the ultimate accolade of parody by Myles na Gopaleen* in *An Béal Bocht* (1941).

Mangan, James Clarence (a name adopted from *Richard III* as poetical) (1803–49), poet, was born in Dublin, the son of a small grocer who went bankrupt. He was educated by a Father Graham who taught him something of the modern European languages at which he afterwards became proficient but he had to begin miserable work as a copy clerk at fifteen and continue in this drudgery until he was thirty. Then he was able to eke out a living by his writing and occasional work in the library of TCD. Of generally poor health, and later addicted to opium and alcohol, his happiest times were those spent working with Petrie*, O'Curry* and O'Donovan in the Ordnance Survey offices (1833-39). Under such pseudonyms as 'Clarence' and 'The Man in the Cloak' he wrote much prose and poetry for periodicals like the *Dublin University Magazine*, his most popular poems being versions of prose translations from Irish made by the Ordnance Survey scholars. He also published translations from German. He was a great admirer of John Mitchel and contributed to the first number of *The Nation*. With such poems as 'Dark Rosaleen', 'O'Hussey's Ode to the Maguire', 'The Time of the Barmecides', 'The Nameless One', 'Gone in the Wind', 'Twenty Golden Years Ago', 'And Then No More' and 'The Women of Three Cows', which show great imagination and technical proficiency, he is now regarded as the significant Irish poet of the mid-nineteenth century. His work (and life) shows a remarkable affinity with that of the American Edgar Allan Poe (1809–49). Worn out by malnutrition, he finally died during the cholera epidemic of 1849.

Marcus, David (b. 1924), editor and novelist, was born in Cork and educated by the Presentation Brothers and at UCC and King's Inns, Dublin. Though qualified in Law, he rarely practised, preferring to write and edit *Irish Writing* (1946–54) with Terence Smith, and *Poetry Ireland* (1948–54). He worked in London for thirteen years, returning to Ireland in 1967. For twenty years (1968–88) he ran a 'New Irish Writing' page in the Saturday edition of the *Irish Press*, discovering and publishing many talented young Irish writers who had no other outlet and reminding readers of the excellence of the continuing work of established authors. He also ran a fresh and exciting book page. In 1954 he published a semi-autobiographical novel, *To Next Year in Jerusalem*, but did not return to serious writing for more than thirty years, when he wrote two historical novels, *A Land Not Theirs* (1986), a story of the Jewish community in Cork during the War of Independence, which in O'Faolain's phrase 'gave Cork city its epic', and *A Land in Flames* (1987), set somewhat earlier in the same period in Kerry and ending with the burning of a Big House and the coming of the Black and Tans. A book of excellent short stories, *Who Ever Heard of an Irish Jew?*, was published in 1988. He has also produced a marvellously witty version of *The Midnight Court* written in modern colloquial English. Famous for his advocacy of the Irish short story as a superb literary form, he has continued to edit many anthologies which resoundingly prove his case. He is married to the writer Ita Daly*.

Marshall, W[illiam] F[rederick] (1885–1959), poet and novelist, was born in Dereband, County Tyrone, and brought up in Sixmilecross where his father was a schoolmaster. He was educated at the Royal School, Dungannon, UCG and Assembly's College, Belfast, where he was ordained a Presbyterian minister, spending the main years of his ministry in Castlerock, County Derry. He was an authority on the Ulster dialect, and one of the drama highlights of the prewar BBC NI was his production of *A Midsummer Night's Dream* in Tyrone accents. His best known dialect poem 'Me an' Me Da' was included in *Ballads and Verses from Tyrone* (1929), and his novel *Planted by a River* (1948), set in the reign of Queen Anne, considers the Ulster Plantation from the point of view of the austere, industrious settlers. *Ulster Speaks* (1936) is a collection of essays on dialect and *Ulster Sails West* (1950) describes the eighteenth-century Protestant emigration to the New World.

Mathews, Aidan [Carl] (b. 1956), poet, playwright, novelist and short story writer, was born in Dublin and educated at TCD and Stanford University,

California. He has published two collections of poetry, *Windfalls* and *Minding Ruth*, and written several plays, including *The Diamond Body*, *The Antigone* and *Exit/ Entrance* (1990). His first short story collection, *Adventures in a Bathyscope*, which uses diverse settings and moves from a style of dark tragedy to metaphysical comedy, was published in 1988 to critical acclaim. The equally brilliant collection, *Lipstick on the Host* (1992), is remarkable for its humanity and great complexity of characterisation. A novel, *Muesli at Midnight*, was published in 1990. Aidan Matthews works as a radio producer with RTÉ.

Maturin, Charles Robert (1782–1824), novelist and playwright, born in Dublin of Huguenot stock, was educated at TCD before serving as an Anglican curate in Loughrea, County Galway, and Dublin. He wrote many forgotten tragedies and six novels, including *The Wild Irish Boy* (1808) and *The Milesian Chief* (1812), but his lasting contribution was *Melmoth the Wanderer* (1820), a classic of Gothic literature, in which a man who has sold his soul to the devil in exchange for knowledge, power and prolonged life helps a number of people in terrible situations, hoping that they will take on his wanderer's curse, but in the end he is claimed by Satan.

Maude, Caitlín (1941–82), poet and playwright in Irish, was born in Connemara and educated at UCG. She worked as a teacher and actor and was famous for her *sean-nós* (unaccompanied singing in the traditional style) renditions, especially of love songs of the people. Her work was collected and published posthumously, *Caitlín Maude, Dánta* in (1984) and *Drámaíocht agus Prós Caitlín Maude* (1988).

Maxwell, W[illiam] H[amilton] (1792–1850), fiction writer, was born in Newry and educated at TCD. It is unlikely that he served, as he claimed, as Captain Hamilton Maxwell in the Peninsular War and at Waterloo, though his rollicking novels with dashing Irish officers are full of impressive lore. His family insisted on the other resort of younger sons and he was ordained an Anglican minister, being given the sinecure of Balla, County Mayo, in 1820. This left him free to hunt over Lord Mayo's estates and produce the book for which he is still known, *Wild Sports of the West* (1832), a collection of sketches and ripe gossip about hard-riding country gentlemen which provided Charles Lever* with the material for his more successful novels, Maxwell's *Hector O'Sullivan and His Man Mark Antony O'Toole* (1842) and *Luck is Everything, or The Adventures of Brian O'Linn* (1856) being weak and stiff by comparison. He wrote a life of Wellington (1839) and history of the '98 rebellion. He died in poor circumstances in Musselborough near Edinburgh.

Mayne, Rutherford (pseudonym of Samuel Waddell) (1878–1967), actor and playwright, was born, like his sister Helen Waddell*, in Tokyo, the son of a

Presbyterian missionary. He was educated at Inst and QUB before qualifying as an engineer from the Royal University and joining the Irish Land Commission where he rose to be Chief Inspector and stayed until retirement in 1950. He joined the Ulster Literary Theatre* in 1904 and soon became their most significant writer. *The Drone* (1908), a comedy of rural Ulster, established a genre which attracted such playwrights as Lynn Doyle* and George Shiels*. An earlier play, *The Turn of the Road* (1906), was a light treatment of the serious theme of the artistic versus the pragmatic. Robbie John Granahan, a violinist of talent, has to choose between music and farming. Both plays were done so often that even as late as the 1950s an actor in a revival of *The Drone*, unsure of his lines, was reassured by the producer: 'Don't worry; if you need a prompt the audience will prompt you' and a radio programme about the ULT written by David Kennedy and produced by Sam Hanna Bell* was called *Enter Robbie John* (1954). *The Troth* (1909) is an allegory of Ulster life in which a Catholic and a Protestant unite to murder an oppressive landlord, while *Peter* (1930) has the slightly daring theme of a young engineering student turning gigolo. Mayne was married to Josephine Campbell, sister of Joseph Campbell* the poet.

Meehan, Paula (b. 1955), poet, was born in Dublin and educated at TCD, where she was greatly influenced by Brendan Kennelly*. She has been Writer Fellow of the English Department at TCD. She has published five collections of poetry, *Return and No Blame* (1984), *Reading the Sky* 1986), *The Man Who was Marked by Winter* (1991), *Pillow Talk* (1994) and *Mysteries of the Home* (1996). Childhood and the problematic question of Irish womanhood are recurring themes in her poetry; her mother appears frequently as a source of inspiration.

Merriman, Brian (?1745–1805), poet in Irish, was born near Ennistimon in County Clare, the son of a stonemason, or perhaps the illegitimate son of a gentleman. He taught school in Feakle, County Clare and after 1790, married and with two daughters, continued his profession in one of Limerick's schools. He died suddenly in 1805, his death notice referring to him as a teacher of mathematics. Such a calling does not necessarily preclude literary talent and certainly *Cúirt an Mheán-Oíche**, written about 1780, is an original and exuberant work. Very few of his other poems are known. For several decades now there have been Merriman Summer and Winter Schools (the former in the poet's own county), which provide a forum for academic and cultural lectures and discussions.

Mhac an tSaoi, Máire (b. 1922), poet in Irish, critic and translator, was born in Dublin but immersed from childhood in the Irish of Dunquin, in the west Kerry gaeltacht. The daughter of politician and minister Seán McEntee and niece of Monsignor Pádraig de Brún*, she was educated at UCD and the Sorbonne and worked with Tomás de Bhaldraithe* on his *English-Irish Dictionary* (1959) and abroad with Ireland's Department of External Affairs. Her work unites the best of the traditional and the modern and she is capable of great lyric intensity. Her collections include *Margadh na Saoire* (1956), *An Galar Dubhach* (1980) and *An Cion go dtí Seo* (1987). She is married to politician and man of letters Conor Cruise O'Brien.

Midnight Court, The, see *Cúirt an Mheán Oíche**.

Milligan, Alice (1866–1953), poet and editor, was born in Omagh and educated at Methodist College, Belfast, and London University. On her return to Belfast she was an active worker for the Gaelic League* (and its laureate). She and Ethna Carbery* edited the *Shan Van Vocht* (1896–9) and she composed the first dramatic scena in modern Irish for Letterkenny Feis in 1898. *The Last Feast of the Fianna*, produced at the Gaiety by the Irish Literary Theatre on 19 February 1900, was the fourth play of the Literary Revival to be staged. Her patriotic poems were published in *We Sang for Ireland* (1950). She grew silent after Partition and wrote little, dying in the Omagh house where she was born.

Milliken, Richard (1767–1815), journalist and satirist, was born in Castlemartyr, County Cork, and qualified as an attorney but practised little, preferring to edit a magazine, *The Casket* (1797–8). It ceased publication because of the 1798 rising and Milliken joined the notorious Cork Yeomanry which, with that of Donegal, put down the Wexford rebellion with great savagery. He is famous for his extempore burlesque on the anonymous poem 'Castle Hyde', a bathetic hedge-schoolmaster's attempt to write a Gaelic poem in English. 'Groves of Blarney' met the fate of many squibs: it was taken seriously, as was 'The Bells of Shandon' by Mahony*, who had added to Milliken's poem the verses about the famous Blarney Stone.

Molloy, M[ichael] J[oseph] (1917–94), playwright, was born at Milltown, County Galway, and educated at St Jarlath's, Tuam. Studies for the priesthood were terminated because of illness and he became a farmer, retaining a love of drama and fine language that had begun with a childhood visit to the Abbey*. His best known works are *The King of Friday's Men** (1948), an evocation of late-eighteenth-century Irish peasant life, and *The Wood of the Whispering* (1953), which mixes the realism of Connacht depopulation with fantasy.

MONKS OF THE SCREW, THE (1780–95), a literary and social club which met in John Philpot Curran*'s house, the Priory in Rathfarnham. The members included Grattan, Henry Flood, Ned Lysaght* and others, and were on the whole opponents of the Act of Union.

Montague, John (b. 1929), poet, was born in Brooklyn, NY, but brought up in Garvaghey, County Tyrone ('From the Rough Field I went to school/In the Glen of the Hazels'). He was educated at UCD and Yale and taught at Berkeley and UCC, retiring in 1988. He has published more than a dozen collections of poetry, notably *Poisoned Lands* (1961), *The Rough Field* (1972), A *Slow Dance* (1975), *The Great Cloak* (1978) and *The Dead Kingdom* (1988). His work reflects his Northern Nationalism, his pleasure in and regret for the Gaelic past, and the intensity of personal relationships. *Death of a Chieftain* (1964) and *A Love Present* (1997) are collections of short stories, while the novella *The Lost Notebook* (1987) recalls a love affair in and with Italy. Montague edited *The Faber Book of Irish Verse* (1974) and his excellent criticism is available in *The Figure in the Cave* (1990). In 1998 he was appointed to the Chair of Irish Poetry, to be held for a year each in QUB, UCD and TCD.

Moore, Brian (b. 1921), novelist, was born in Belfast the son of a nationalist surgeon and educated in St Malachy's College. After WWII he worked in Europe and North Africa for the British Ministry of Transport and for a UN relief agency in Warsaw, then emigrated to Canada in 1948. In Montréal, he became a successful journalist and writer of several bestselling and lucrative pulp crime novels but, ever a serious reader of Joyce and of contemporary fiction, adhered to his ambition to write literary novels. His breakthrough came with *Judith Hearne* (1955), (later published as *The Lonely Passion of Judith Hearne**),

which received critical acclaim on both sides of the Atlantic. (It and its successor *The Feast of Lupercal* were banned in Ireland, one supposes on account of the – for the time – explicit sex scenes.) A *bildungsroman*, *The Emperor of Ice-Cream*, followed before Moore moved to New York in 1959, thence several years later to California, settling in Malibu with his second wife Jean. He has been regarded as a Canadian as well as an Irish novelist and won high literary honours in the country of which he has for many years been a citizen. Moore's output has been prolific – twenty novels in little more than forty years – and consistent, his work always treated with critical respect. His themes have included the displacement and loneliness of the expatriate, the role of memory and identity for an individual in crisis and the search for meaning in a world where God has ceased to matter. He has also been praised for his depiction of the interior world of women in novels such as *I Am Mary Dunne* and *The Doctors's Wife* (1976). Among the more successful of his other works are *An Answer from Limbo* and *Black Robe*. Moore is an experimenter with different forms and a superb stylist; his is the art that conceals art. He has himself expressed the view that fiction has to compete successfully with electronic entertainment in our age, and the wish that a novel of his might be read in one sitting. His most recent novels, including *Lies of Silence* (1990) and *The Magician's Wife* (1997), bear some of the hallmarks of the thriller genre in which he first wrote fiction.

Moore, George (1852–1933), novelist, was born the son of a Catholic landlord and Nationalist MP in the family home, Moore Hall, Ballyglass, County Mayo, and educated at Oscott College near Birmingham. He trained as a painter in Paris but, admitting his lack of talent, turned to literature. His poetry was as unsuccessful as his art but his first novel *A Modern Lover* (1883), strongly influenced by Zola, was both good and shocking, and a career was found. Other novels included *A Mummer's Wife* (1885), *A Drama in Muslin* (1887), about Irish society, and *Esther Waters* (1894), an early feminist book describing the travails of an independently-minded woman who survives unmarried pregnancy and lives to see her son safely to adulthood. This last made his name as a writer and, though he wrote other books, including *The Brook Kerith* (1916) and *Héloïse and Abelard* (1921), none was as popular. He was to prove the *enfant terrible* of the Irish Literary Revival*, soberly writing *The Untilled Field* (1903), a collection of short stories – models for young Irish writers– and the plays *The Strike at Arlingford* (1893) and *The Bending of the Bough* (1900), but cherishing anecdotes that would cause his account of his Irish times in the three-volume *Hail and Farewell* (1911–14) – even franker and much funnier than his earlier *Confessions of a Young Man* (1888) – to be the most entertaining document of the Revival.

Moore, Thomas (1779–1852), poet, was born in Aungier Street, Dublin, the son of a grocer, and educated at TCD, one of the first Catholics to be so. His friendship with Robert Emmet caused him to consider joining the United Irishmen but he was no revolutionary. He was in the Middle Temple when Emmet led his abortive rising and he wrote several of his early *Irish Melodies* (1808) 'O, Breathe Not His Name' and 'She Is Far from the Land' in sentimental regard for the old friendship. He became a close friend of Lord Byron, characteristically after a farcical failed duel, and, adopted by the Whigs and gifted with a fine tenor voice which made him the best renderer of his own melodies, seemed to lose any real Nationalism. William Hazlitt (1778-1830) accused him of turning 'the wild harp of Erin into a musical snuff-box'. In fact he did not compromise his Irishness and as an unofficial ambassador did much to prick the English conscience about 'Erin with the tear and the smile in her eye'. He was a brilliant song-lyricist, an effective satirist and much more than a minstrel boy.

Morgan, Lady (née Sydney Owenson) (?1776–1859), novelist, was born at sea and educated at the Huguenot School, Clontarf. Her father Robert Owenson was an unsuccessful actor-manager who had been born MacOwen and a Catholic. Sydney became a governess and anticipated Tom Moore*'s *Irish Melodies* (1808) with *Hibernian Melodies* (1801). She drew upon her Irish-speaking relatives from Mayo to write her best-seller *The Wild Irish Girl* (1806) which, though a romance with the author as heroine, is sound on such things as women's freedom and Catholic Emancipation. She was taken up by the Marchioness of Abercorn, whose surgeon Charles Morgan was urged to marry the celebrity and was given a knighthood as a wedding present. Lady Morgan's salon in her house in Kildare Street became one of the highlights of Dublin society and her books, whether fiction or accounts of her frequent travels, made her a rich woman. Her will included a benevolent fund for actors and governesses.

Morrison, Danny (b. 1953), novelist, was born in West Belfast and became a republican activist with the outbreak of the Northern Troubles in the late 1960s. He was later Publicity Director of Sinn Féin and imprisoned for republican activities from 1990–5, after his release devoting himself full-time to writing. He has published three well regarded novels: *West Belfast, On the Back of the Swallow,* which is set in prison but which deals with personal suffering rather than political matters, and *The Wrong Man,* which confronts in graphic style the pivotal issue of informers in the republican movement.

Morrissy, Mary (b. 1957), novelist, short story writer and journalist, was born in Dublin. Her published works are a novel, *Mother of Pearl* (1993), and a short story collection, *A Lazy Eye* (1996), for which she has won several awards. Her prose is lyrical although her themes are often dark.

Morrow, John (b. 1930), novelist and short story writer, was born in Belfast and apprenticed to the linen trade. He worked in the shipyard and sold insurance before joining the Arts Council of NI, eventually becoming Director of Combined Arts. He has published two novels, *The Confessions of Prionsias O'Toole* (1977), a wacky look at that humourless topic the Northern Troubles, and *The Essex Factor* (1982). *Northern Myths* (1979) and *Sects and Other Stories* (1987) contains his short pieces, which vary from sketches and squibs to serious stories.

Muldoon, Paul (b. 1955), poet, was born near Moy in County Armagh and educated at QUB. He worked as a producer in Radio Ulster before moving to America in the late 1980s. He is Director of the Creative Writing Programme at Princeton. His published work includes *New Weather* (1973), *Mules* (1977), *Quoof* (1983), *Meeting the British* (1987), and *Madoc: A Mystery* (1990), his latest volume being *New and Selected Poems* (1996). His poetry is obstinately personal and wittily allusive, though as a child of the Northern Troubles he cannot altogether avoid political considerations. He is editor of *The Faber Book of Contemporary Irish Poetry* (1986). He is regarded as one of the finest of the younger Irish poets and his work has been honoured with many awards.

Mulholland, Rosa (Lady Gilbert) (1841–1921), novelist, was born in Belfast and gave up artistic ambition to become a writer on the urging of Charles Dickens who printed her early stories in *Household Words*. She married John (later Sir John) Gilbert (1829–89), the antiquarian and historian of Dublin, in 1891. She wrote many novels about Irish Catholic life, determined, like Anna Hall*, to persuade the Victorian British of the true gentility of the Irish, but, as with so many others, she ultimately despaired of getting her message across. Her most popular novels were *The Wild Birds of Killeevy* (1883) and *A Fair Emigrant* (1888).

Mulkerns, Val[entine] (b. 1925), novelist and short story writer, was born in Dublin and educated at the Dominican College, Eccles Street. She became a drama critic and associate editor of *The Bell** under Peadar O'Donnell*. Two lyrical novels, *A Time Outworn* (1951) and *A Peacock Cry* (1954), partly based upon her own life, showed her as a writer of controlled passion and the possessor of a lucid, witty style. Though she continued to write for Dublin papers, she published nothing until 1978 when *Antiquities*, a series of linked stories, showed a new maturity. Later collections, *An Idle Woman* (1990) and *A Friend of Don Juan* (1988), are witty, sympathetic and slightly mournful about the deteriorating quality of life in her native city, one of the themes of her novel *Very Like a Whale* (1986). *The Summerhouse* (1984), a faultless study of south-coast life, won the Allied Irish Bank Prize for Literature.

Murphy, Dervla (b. 1931), travel writer, was born in Lismore, County Waterford, and educated at the Ursuline Convent in Waterford and at TCD. Her first book *Full Tilt* (1965), best described by its subtitle: 'Ireland to India on a Bicycle', was a bestseller because of the skill, humour, curiosity and intrepidity of the author, and her many other books have the same virtues. A worldwide traveller, she turned her rover's eye on NI in *A Place Apart* (1978), like *First Tilt* a prizewinner, with interesting results. Her autobiography is aptly called *Wheels within Wheels* (1979) and recent work includes *Transylvania and Beyond* (1992), *The Ukimwi Road* (1993), which follows the AIDS trail in Central and South Africa, and *South from Limpopo: Travels through South Africa* (1997).

Murphy, Michael J[oseph] (1913–96), folklorist, was born in Liverpool of south Armagh parents and educated in Dromintee near his magic mountain Slieve Gullion. He left school at fourteen to work for local farmers and made himself such an expert on folkways and local lore that he was a natural to be appointed to the Irish Folklore Commission* in 1942. He had already begun broadcasting for BBC NI and Radio Éireann, collaborating most effectively with Sam Hanna Bell* in such series as *Fairy Faith*. He wrote many stories and had plays in the Abbey* and the Belfast Group Theatre. His best known books are *At Slieve Gullion's Foot* (1940), *Mountain Year* (1964) and *Tyrone Folk Quest* (1973), the latter describing the years spent in the locked Sperrin valley of Glenhull, because 'the folklore collector knows he has to spend months, even years, with one mind'.

Murphy, Richard (b. 1927), poet, was born in Milford House, his family home in County Galway. His father was in the British colonial service and his boyhood was spent in Ceylon and the Bahamas. He was educated at Wellington, Magdalen College, Oxford, and the Sorbonne. He ran a school in Crete before coming to live on Inishbofin off the Connemara coast which is the inspiration for much of his poetry. *Sailing to an Island* (1963) contains many of the poems for which he is famous, notably the title poem, 'The Last Galway Hooker' and 'The Cleggan Disaster'. *The Battle of Aughrim* (1968) contains a commentary on the aftermath of the Williamite wars. Other work includes *High Island* (1974) and *The Price of Stone* (1985).

Murphy, Tom (b. 1935), playwright and novelist, was born in Tuam, County Galway, and educated by the Christian Brothers before becoming a metalwork teacher. *On the Outside* (1959), his first play, written with Noel O'Donoghue, is set outside a dancehall and deals with the violent frustration of young men too poor to enjoy the pleasures within, a neat symbol for the Ireland of the time. Violence and inarticulacy (in an Irish family in England) are also the themes of *A Whistle in the Dark* (1961) which, like *A Crucial Week in the Life of a Grocer's Assistant* (finally produced in 1969), was rejected by the con-

servative Abbey* management of the time. Later work, distinguished by great power and some experimentation, includes *The Morning after Optimism* (1971), *The White House* (1972), *The Sanctuary Lamp* (1975), *The Gigli Concert** (1983), *Bailegangaire* (1985) and *Too Late for Logic* (1989), all of which deal in some way with Irish people and their troubled engagement with their distressful country. *The Seduction of Morality* (1994), Murphy's first novel, is about the effect of the return of a prostitute who inherits a family business. It formed the basis of *The Wake*, which was produced in the Abbey in 1998.

Murray, T[homas] C[ornelius] (1873–1959), playwright, was born in Macroom, County Cork, and trained as a teacher at St Patrick's College, Drumcondra, graduating in 1893. From 1909 he contributed many plays to the Abbey*, the best and most successful being *Autumn Fire** (1924) which has a *Phaedra*-theme. The realism of his dialogue and the daring choice of subject caused him some clerical criticism and he was happy to accept the post of headmaster of Inchicore Model Schools (1915–32). He was called 'the doyen of the Munster realists', with such grim dramas as *Maurice Harte* (1912), about a clerical student without a vocation, and *Michaelmas Eve* (1932), in which a young man, on the advice of his mother, jilts the girl he loves to marry a woman with land.

My New Curate (1900), Canon Sheehan*'s best known novel, about

'Daddy' Dan the parish priest and his new curate Father Letheby and how they learn from each other. The young man is full of ideas about improving the lot of his parishioners but his schemes tend to go awry: a shirt factory fails and an uninsured fishing-boat is lost. He is saved from bankruptcy by the people and leaves the parish to become the bishop's chaplain. The novel gives a useful picture of post-Land War, pre-revolutionary Ireland.

N

NATION, THE (1842–8; 1849–96), a weekly newspaper founded by Thomas Davis*, Charles Gavan Duffy (1816–1903) and John Blake Dillon (1814–66) to promote the ideas of Young Ireland. It was the journal of a highly successful initiative in adult education, reaching an audience of 250,000 each week and succeeding in restoring in the sorely deprived Irish a sense of national and cultural identity and an awareness of the culture of other nations. Its ballads and songs, contributed by, among others, Davis, Duffy, John Keegan Casey*, 'Speranza' (Lady Wilde*), John Kells Ingram* and Richard D'Alton Williams*, which were mocked and praised with equal force, renewed an old interest in poetry, and the essays on history and economics prepared a depressed nation for eventual independence. The journal was suppressed in 1848 after the Smith O'Brien rising and, though the second series, which ran for nearly fifty years more, had less impact, it continued as an important organ of Irish nationhood.

Ní Chonaill, Eibhlín Dubh (?1743–?80), poet in Irish, was born in Derrynane, County Kerry, one of the twenty-two children of Dónall Mór Ó Conaill, the grandfather of the Liberator, Daniel O'Connell. In 1767, against the wishes of her people, she married Colonel Art Ó Laoghaire of the Hungarian army who had returned from the continental wars. They settled in Macroom and there he fell foul of Abraham Morris, the High Sheriff. It is said that Morris had demanded Ó Laoghaire's charger at a price of £5, as he was entitled to do under the largely inactive but still binding Penal Laws. Ó Laoghaire set out to kill Morris on 4 May 1773 but was himself killed by the sheriff's military bodyguard in Carriginima, County Cork. 'Caoineadh Airt Uí Laoghaire,' written in elegant but simple language as a traditional 'keening' or lament – and written down from the oral tradition many years after its composition – is one of the most beautiful love poems in modern Irish and has been much translated. Eibhlín contrived to have the members of the picket who shot her husband transported and Morris himself was later killed by Ó Laoghaire's brother.

Ní Chuilleanáin, Eiléan (b. 1942), poet, was born in Cork, the daughter of Eilís Dillon*, and educated at UCC and Oxford before becoming a lecturer in Medieval and Renaissance Literature at TCD in 1966. She has published seven collections of verse, notably *Acts and Monuments* (1972), *Site of Ambush*

(1975), a good description of her poetry, *Cork* (1977), about the dire effects of urban renewal, and *The Magdalene Sermon* (1989), which, as the title suggests, has woman in all her aspects as theme. *Brazen Serpent* was published in 1994.

Ní Dhomhnaill, Nuala (b. 1952), poet in Irish, was born in Lancashire but spent most of her childhood in the Kerry gaeltacht area near Ventry. She was educated at UCC, at the time of the remarkable flowering of Irish language poetry which involved Michael Davitt*, Liam Ó Muirthile* and *Innti* magazine. Her first collection, *An Dealg Droighin* (1991), features the Munster fertility goddess Mór and Ó Domhnaill's themes have always included femaleness, sexuality and fertility; her style is uncluttered and direct but also at times very lyrical. As well as being highly gifted, she is one of the most popular and accessible of the younger poets in Irish, being a formidable performer of her own work with the capacity to reach even those who do not understand the language in which she writes. Other collections include *Féar Suaithinseach* (1984) and *Feis* (1991). She has attracted translators of the highest rank, including Michael Hartnett*, Seamus Heaney*, Michael Longley* and Paul Muldoon* and in collaboration with translators has published bilingual collections, such as *Pharaoh's Daughter* (1990) and *The Astrakhan Cloak* (1992). Her most recent collection is *Spíonáin is Róiseanna*. (1993).

Ní Dhuibhne, Eilís (b. 1954), novelist, short story writer and dramatist, was born in Dublin, educated at UCD, and works in the National Museum in Dublin as an ethnographer. A highly talented and versatile writer, her vision is original, often quirky, surreal or disturbing, casting a caustic eye on the emotional and social life of women. Her first short story collection, *Blood and Water (1988),* was followed by a futuristic novel, *The Bray House* (1990), and a second collection, *Eating Women Is Not Recommended* (1991). She has also published several well regarded books for children, among them the historical novels *The Hiring Fair* and *Blaeberry Sunday* and has had published and had performed a play in Irish, *Milseog an tSamhraidh* (*Summer Pudding*) (1997). *The Inland Ice and Other Stories* was published in 1997.

Ní Ghlinn, Áine (b. 1955), poet and journalist, was born in County Tipperary and works in Irish-language radio. She has published three collections of poetry, *An Chéim Bhriste* (1984), *Gáirdín Pharthais* (1988) and *Deora Nár Caoineadh/Unshed Tears* (1996).

Ní Ghráda, Mairéad (1899–1971), playwright in Irish, was born in County Clare and educated at UCD. She took part in the War of Independence as a member of Cumann na mBan and was secretary to Ernest Blythe* at the time of the first Dáil. She worked as an announcer with RTÉ from 1927–35. She wrote many books in Irish, including textbooks, a novel and a collection of short stories. But it is for her plays, many of which were performed in amateur drama festivals, that she is best known. They include *An Uacht* (1935), *Súgán Sneachta* (1962) and *Stailc Ocrais* (1966). *An Triail* was staged successfully at the Dublin Theatre Festival in 1964 and also broadcast as a television play.

'Night before Larry Was Stretched, The' (18th century), a famous Dublin low-life ballad, cherished for its authentic urban slang and thieves' cant, which describes a visit to the condemned cell by friends of the soon-to-be-deceased. It is attributed to Robert Burrows (1756–1841), Dean of Cork, one of the Monks of the Screw*, though he always denied it.

Ní Laoire, Máire Bhuí (?1770–?1849), poet in Irish, was born near Inchigeelagh in west Cork and lived after her marriage in the district of Ballingeary near Céim an Fhia, the place she has made famous. Her poetic output comprised aisling*s, ballads and laments about the distressful state of the Ireland of her time which were handed down orally in her locality. Her most famous work, 'Cath Chéim an Fhia' is a vigorous, rousing and partisan account of a battle between local Whiteboys and a battalion of yeomanry in 1822.

Noonan, Gilman (b. 1937), short story writer, was born in Kanturk, County Cork, and educated at UCC before moving to Hamburg to work as a journalist. He has published two collections: *A Sexual Relationship* (1976) and *Friends and Occasional Lovers* (1982), the themes of which are neatly hinted by the titles. Some of his work stands comparison with that of McGahern* or Trevor*.

North (1975), Seamus Heaney*'s fourth poetry collection in which he addresses both obliquely and directly the political realities of his own province. The book is divided into two parts and carries also two separate introductory poems in celebration of peaceful rural rituals. 'Funeral Rites' takes up the theme of healing ritual, evoking the ancient burial-place of Newgrange: 'Now as news comes in/of each neighbourly murder/we pine for ceremony,/customary rhythms:/. The collection is rich and allusive, making reference to the long buried in 'The Bog Queen' and 'The Grauballe Man' and to the Vikings. 'Whatever You say, Say Nothing' and 'The Minstry of Fear' contrast a militarised Northern Ireland with the gentler former days of 'A Constable Calls', while in the final poem the poet, in ironic commentary on his own situation, describes himself as a wood-kerne, camouflaged, 'escaped from the massacre'.

Northern Iron, The (1907), an unusually serious novel by the humorous George A. Birmingham* set in County Antrim just before the rebellion of 1798. The hero is Neal Ward, the son of Micah Ward, a radical clergyman who has found biblical justification for rebellion.

Neal is in love with Una, the daughter of Lord Dunseveric, who protects them from the violence of the yeomanry. Micah, having served a prison sentence for sedition, elects not to go to the freedom of the United States but to stay on with the revolutionary Antrim weaver Jemmy Hope (editor of the *Northern Star*, the United Irishmen's paper) 'since there is no other land but this lost land for me and him'.

Northern Star (1984), play by Stewart Parker* about Henry Joy McCracken as he awaits execution after the failure of his 1798 insurgency in Antrim. The main events of his life are dramatised in a pastiche of the styles of such Irish playwrights as Farquhar*, Boucicault*, Wilde*, Shaw*, Synge*, O'Casey*, Behan* and Beckett*. The play ends, oddly, on a note of hope (Jemmy Hope was editor of the *Northern Star*, the United Irishmen's paper), unlike *Pentecost* (1987), which was set during the UWC strike of 1974.

Norton, [Hon. Mrs] Caroline (1808–77), poet and novelist, was famous for her beauty, her unhappy marriage, her independence and her successful agitation for women's rights. Granddaughter of Richard Brinsley Sheridan* and sister of Lady Dufferin*, she was unlucky in her husband William Norton, a brutish, lecherous villain straight from Victorian fiction, whom she supported and who when they separated prevented her, though the innocent party, from seeing her children for six years. Her pamphlets eventually changed the law about custody and the rights of married women. She supported herself by her pen, writing lengthy novels which rehearse the unhappiness of her own marriage and isolation, though *A Voice from the Factories* (1836) and *Child of the Islands* (1845) deal with the exploitation of children. She is remembered today for such parlour poetry as 'The Arab's Farewell to His Steed', 'Not Lost but Gone Before' and 'Bingen on the Rhine'.

O

O'Brien, Conor Cruise (b. 1917), politician and man of letters, was born in Dublin and educated at Sandford Park and TCD. He joined the Department of External Affairs in 1944 and was part of the United Nations team in the Congo in 1960, an experience recounted in *To Katanga and Back* (1962). Later work included a university vice-chancellorship, a chair of humanities, politics (TD from 1969 and Minister of Post and Telegraphs 1973–7) and editing the London *Observer*. He is much exercised by the intersection of violence and politics and shows a consequent distaste for the IRA that amounts to an obsession and an attitude to Unionism that seems to mix fear with appeasement. As 'Donat O'Donnell' he published *Maria Cross* (1952), a critical view of modern Catholic writers, including Sean O'Faolain*. Other work includes collections of essays and reviews, such as *The Shaping of Modern Ireland* (1960), *States of Ireland* (1972) and *Ancestral Voices* (1994), about literature and politics. His most recent major work *The Great Melody* (1992) is a biography and anthology of the writings of Edmund Burke*. He is married to the poet Máire Mhac an tSaoi*.

O'Brien, Dillon (1817–82), novelist, was born in Turnabeg, County Roscommon, and went to America as a teacher at the Indian mission at La Pointe, Minnesota. He later settled in St Paul and began to write literally Irish-American novels since they are set in both countries. His best known novel *The Dalys of Dalystown* (1866) has the recurrent nineteenth-century theme that the solution to Ireland's problems lies in the re-establishment of a Catholic aristocracy, kind hearts being less than green coronets. *Dead Broke* (1882), set mainly in America, deals with the clash between old Catholic values and American life.

O'Brien, Edna (b. 1930), novelist and short story writer, was born in Tuamgraney, County Clare, and educated at Loughrea, County Galway, and in Dublin where she qualified as a pharmacist. She followed this profession for some time before marrying Ernest Gébler (b. 1915) in 1951; they were divorced in 1967. Her (automatically) banned novels about Kate and Baba, the 'country girls' – *The Country Girls** (1960), *The Lonely Girl* (1962) and *Girls in Their Married Bliss* (1963) – were extremely successful, as much for their black humour and deceptively untutored style as for their rejection of puritan Ireland. Subsequent novels, including *August Is a Wicked Month* (1964) *A Pagan Place* (1971), *The High Road* (1988), *Time and Tide* (1992), *Johnny, I Hardly Knew You* (1994), and *House of Splendid Isolation* (1995), usually have as protagonist a sensual woman who suffers for love. The last-named is unusual in that it deals with the occupation of a house by the IRA. Her short story collections include *The Love Object* (1968), *A Scandalous Woman* (1974), *Returning* (1982) and *Lantern Slides* (1988). Her play *The Gathering*, about the apparently put-upon mother of a family, was staged in the Abbey* in 1974. Her most recent novel is *Down by the River* (1996).

O'Brien, Fitz-James (1828–62), fantasy writer, was born in County Cork and reared in County Limerick. His first poem, about the horrors of the Famine, was published in *The Nation** when he was seventeen, and by the age of twenty-one he had squandered a large patrimony and emigrated to America where he supported himself with such strange tales as 'The Diamond Lens', about a man who falls in love with a creature seen in his microscope, and 'What Was It?', about an invisible man. He enlisted in the Union army in 1861, was promoted to captain and died of wounds a year later.

O'Brien, Flann (most common of the many aliases of Brian O'Nolan) (1911–66), novelist and columnist, was born in Strabane, County Tyrone, the son of a customs officer who moved eventually to Dublin in 1923. Irish was the language of the home and English was learned from books. O'Brien began writing as an undergraduate at UCD, finding an outlet as 'Brother Barnabas' for his polyglottal, paronomastic humour in *Comhthrom Féinne* (Fair Play) edited by Niall Sheridan. He joined the civil service in 1935 and published his first uncategorisable novel-complex *At Swim-Two-Birds** in 1939. The war prevented the acceptance of *The Third Policeman* (1940) but by then he had begun in *The Irish Times* the column 'Cruiskeen Lawn' (Full Jug) which he signed as Myles na Gopaleen, from a character in Boucicault*'s *The Colleen Bawn**, the name he also used for the Gaelic squib *An Béal Bocht* (1941). The column was originally written in Irish but gradually English took over. The tri-weekly (health and hangover permitting) ration of jokes, puns and increasingly savage satire continued for more than twenty-five years and made him the best known journalist in Ireland. By comparison the postwar novels *The Hard Life* (1961) and *The Dalkey Archive* (1964) were less inventive and at times distinctly sour. A series of television playlets with Jimmy O'Dea and David Kelly called *O'Dea's Your Man* (1963–4) introduced O'Brien to a wider audience. *The Third Policeman* was published in 1967, a year after his death from cancer.

O'Brien, Kate (1897–1974), novelist and playwright, was born in Limerick to wealthy parents and educated at Laurel Hill Convent and by scholarship at UCD, the family business having failed with the death of the father. She worked as a journalist in London and in Spain as a governess, married and quickly divorced, and when her play *A Distinguished Villa* (1926) was a success in London she became a full-time writer. Her first novel *Without My Cloak* (1931) describes the rise to economic success of a family like her own and paints an alternative picture of nineteenth-century Catholic Ireland. *The Ante-Room* (1934) develops the story of some minor characters from her first book. The protagonists in her remaining seven (implicitly feminist) novels are women, the Irish ones facing the clash of passion and morality (or rather what they have been trained to accept as morality). Her books were given the accolade of banning by the mean-minded, unctuous members of the Censorship Board, because, as with most writers of the time, she wrote novels not tracts, but she responded with scorn: *Pray for the Wanderer* (1938) was a riposte to the banning of *Mary Lavelle* (1936) and *The Last of Summer* (1943) was written when *The Land of Spices** (1941), a magnificent novel about women in the religious life, was banned because of a single sentence. *That Lady* (1946) describes the clash between Philip II of Spain and a free-souled aristocrat, Aña de Mendoza, with whom he was in love. Her final novels *The Flower of May* (1953) and *As Music and Splendour* (1958) were followed by highly personal travel books: *Farewell Spain* (1937), about the country from which she was banned for eleven years because of her portrayal of Philip II in *That Lady*, and *My Ireland* (1962). *Presentation Parlour* (1963) is a book of reminiscences about the convent where two of her aunts were nuns. The work of Kate O'Brien was reprinted and rediscovered by a new generation of readers and academic critics during the 1980s and 1990s.

O'Brien, Kate Cruise (1948–98), short story writer and novelist, was born in Dublin, the daughter of Conor Cruise O'Brien*, and educated at TCD. Her first book *A Gift Horse* (1978) was a collection of short stories, most of which first appeared in David Marcus*'s 'New Irish Writing' page in the *Irish Press*, 'Henry Died' winning the Hennessy Award. *The Homesick Garden* (1991) described adolescence in a self-consciously eccentric household. For several years she was literary editor at Poolbeg Press in Dublin.

O'Brien, William (1852–1928), novelist and political journalist, was born in Mallow, County Cork, and educated at Queen's College, Cork. He became Parnell's deputy and, because of the militancy of his writings in *United Ireland*, the organ of the Land League, suffered the first of nine spells of imprisonment. He was an MP (1883–1918) and the chief hope of reconciliation between Parnell and his adversaries. He was aware of the need for reconciliation between unionist and nationalist and took no part in politics after the establishment of the Irish Free State. His best known book is *When We Were*

Boys (1890), a long account (it was written in prison 'which left a lot of weary time on my hands') of life in Cork during the Fenian campaign and the struggle between nationalist and Ultramontane clerics. *A Queen of Men* (1898) is based on the career of the 'most famous, feminine sea-captain' Grainne Ní Mhaille (*c.* 1530–1600). O'Brien died suddenly in England and is buried in Mallow.

Ó Bruadair, Dáibhí (c. 1625–98), poet in Irish, was born in East Cork. He was of comfortable means and had a good education in English, Latin, Irish and history. He was also trained in bardic poetry and genealogy. From about 1660 he lived in Limerick and his poetic output was prodigious. As the century progressed the destruction of the Gaelic world he represented became more certain. Indeed his consciousness of the cataclysm makes his poetry a valuable historical source for the period in poems like 'Caithréim Phádraig Sáirséal', which celebrates Sarsfield's famous if minor victory over the Williamites, and 'An Longbhriseadh' which laments his country's plight after the Treaty of Limerick and the flight of the Wild Geese. His patrons, the Fitzgeralds, left with the other Wild Geese, and Ó Bruadair was reduced for a time to working as a farm labourer. His distaste for the louts who replaced the old aristocracy is clearly seen in the poem 'Mairg Nach Fuil 'na Dhubhthuata' ['A pity not to be an utter boor']. He died in January 1689, sustained at the end by some of the older Irish families who still had property.

Observe the Sons of Ulster Marching towards the Somme (1985), Frank McGuinness*'s play about the relationships between members of a patrol of the Ulster Division in WWI as they prepare for the 1916 battle in which eventually a million men were killed. The events are recalled by a survivor, Kenneth Pyper, whose lover was one of the fatalities. The refusal of the soldiers to relinquish old shibboleths is starkly symbolised by their wearing of Orange sashes over their uniform as they march out to death.

Ó Cadhain, Máirtín (1906–70), novelist and short story writer in Irish, was born in the Connemara gaeltacht area of Cois Fharraige and educated at St Patrick's College in Dublin, qualifying as a primary schoolteacher in 1926. Over the following ten years as a teacher in County Galway he began to write fiction. A fervent Irish-language activist and campaigner for the development of the gaeltacht, he was often embroiled in controversy. He became a member of the army council of the IRA and was interned in the Curragh during the 'Emergency' of WWII for his republican activities. It is likely that his later fiction was influenced by his period of internment and the opportunity for wide reading it gave him. The theme and atmosphere of his finest and best known work, *Cré na Cille**(1948), are very far from a traditional view of Gaelic Ireland, and the short story collections *An tSraith ar Lár* (1967) and *An tSraith Dhá Thógáil* (1970) are modernist works in which the protagonists are at sea in a hostile world. Ó Cadhain found it difficult to get congenial employment after his internment during WWII but he was appointed lecturer in Irish in TCD in 1956 and Professor of Irish in that university the year before his death.

O'Casey, Sean (1880–1964), playwright, was born in Dublin of working-class Protestant parents, one of a large family made even poorer by the premature death of the father. He left school at fourteen, a persistent eye-complaint having made his attendance sporadic. The colourful account of his childhood in a series of garrulously impressionistic *Autobiographies* (1939 to 1954) is morally if not factually accurate, the author's general verbal exuberance, also shown in his plays, being the mark of the relentless and uncontrolled autodidact. He learned his dramaturgy, like Shaw*, by attendance at the generally sentimental and melodramatic fare of the Queen's Theatre, for which he had free passes, but his own work did for the slum-dwellers of Dublin what Synge* did for the peasants of Connacht and Wicklow, earning the same gratitude. His Dublin trilogy, *The Shadow of a Gunman* (1923), *Juno and the Paycock** (1924) and *The Plough and the Stars** (1926), staged at the Abbey*, was brilliantly shocking, the underclass being invested with an eloquence and gritty humour that distracted the critical ear from the sentimentality and the predictable plots. They proved too much for the self-conscious patriotism of the new state, especially in the treatment of the already mythologised Easter Rising* in the last-named play. It was greeted with riots, shouts of 'There are no prostitutes in Ireland!' and a happily magisterial, 'You have disgraced yourselves again!' from Yeats*. O'Casey's next play, *The Silver Tassie* (1928), about football and the horrors of WWI, had elements of rather undigested expressionism and was rejected by the Abbey*, and the author shortly afterwards went into permanent exile in Devon. Later plays *The Star Turns Red* (1940), *Red Roses for Me* (1942), *Purple Dust* (1945) and *Oak Leaves and Lavender* (1947) combine socialist propaganda, anticlericalism and sentimentality, while retaining interesting characters and at times a farcical humour. A later trio, *Cock-a-Doodle Dandy* (1949), *The Bishop's Bonfire* (1955) and *The Drums of Father Ned* (1959) (which was due to be part of the Theatre Festival but was withdrawn by the author because of perceived interference by Archbishop McQuaid), are experimental and their occasional production is more a mark of respect than of worth. His greater plays are his earlier ones and once out of Ireland he lost the richest source of his inspiration.

Ó Catháin, Liam (1896–1969), novelist in Irish, was born in Emly, County Tipperary and worked in England and locally as a schoolteacher. He wrote a trilogy based on the life of local poet Liam Dall Ó hIfearnáin*: *Ceart na Sua* (1964), *Ceart na Bua* (1968) and *Ceart na hUaighe* (1986), another novel, *Eibhlín a' Ghleanna* (1954), and a play, *UNO i bPollachliste* (1962).

Ó Ceallaigh, Seán ('Sceilg') (1872–1957), journalist and politician, was born in Valentia Island in County Kerry. Coming from a gaeltacht area though relatively unproficient as a child, he was encouraged to write in Irish by Torna* and in time became president of the Gaelic League (1919–23) and Ceann Comhairle of the Dáil (1925–30). Involvement in politics from 1919 on meant he wrote little in the latter part of his life but until that date he was responsible for many, generally educational works in Irish, including books of stories, biographies of such figures as St Laurence O'Toole (1905) and Brian Boru (1906), and (in English) *Gill's Irish Reciter* (1907).

Ó Céileachair, Donncha (1918–1960), writer and lexicographer in Irish, was born in Coolea, County Cork, the son of Dónal Bán, who dictated the well-known Irish autobiography *Scéal mo Bheatha* (1940). He was a teacher for a number of years before working with Tomás de Bhaldraithe on the *English-Irish Dictionary* (1959). He wrote (with Prionsias Ó Conluain) a life of the great Kerry lexicographer Pádraig Ó Duinnín* (1958) and a biography of St Ignatius Loyola (1962). *Bullaí Mhártain* (1955), a fine collection of modern short stories, was written in collaboration with his sister Síle.

Ó Ciobháin, Pádraig (b. 1951), poet, novelist and short story writer in Irish, was born in An Ghráig, Ballyferriter, in the Kerry gaeltacht and educated at St Brendan's College Killarney and UCC.

He is a teacher in Cork City. His published work includes *Le Gealaigh* (1991), An *Grá Faoi Cheilt* (1992), *An Gealas i Lár na Léithe* (1992), *Desiderus a Dó* (1995), and *Ar Gach Maoilinn Tá Síocháin* (1998)

Ó Coileáin, Seán (?1754–?1816), poet in Irish, was born near Clonakilty, County Cork of people who had enough wealth to have the boy sent to Spain to study for the priesthood. He gave up his clerical studies and returned to Ireland to set up a hedge school at Myross, near Union Hall. He was known as the 'silver tongue of Munster' and is most famous now for 'An Buachaill Bán' the last of the Jacobite *aislingí* and for the romantic 'Machtnamh an Duine Dhoilíosaigh' [Musings of the Melancholy Man] (1813), set in the atmospheric ruins of Timoleague Abbey. Some scholars believe it may be a translation of a friend's English poem and there is a strong tradition that was written as a Gaelic response to Gray's *Elegy* (1751). Ó Coileáin was prone to melancholy anyway, a not unexpected condition for a poet of the period, especially one who sensed that he was the last of his kind.

Ó Coistealba, Seán (b. 1930), poet and dramatist in Irish, was born in Indreabhán in the Connemara gaeltacht in County Galway. He has written many poems, collected in *Buille faoi Thuairim Gabha* (1987), and a number of very popular plays in which he appeared, including *An Tinceara Buí* (1962), *Ortha na Seirce* (1968) and *Pionta Amháin Uisce*. Recent work has included *An Crústóir* (1985) and *An Mhéar Fhada* (1992).

Ó Conaire, Pádraic Óg (1893–1971), novelist and short story writer in Irish, was born in Ros Muc in the Connemara gaeltacht, County Galway, and educated locally and on scholarship at Patrick Pearse*'s Scoil Éanna in Dublin. He was a *múinteoir teastail* for the Gaelic League, a government translator (1931–58) and Irish-language newsreader for RTÉ. His fiction, which portrays the life of the western people with whom he grew up, won many Oireachtas* prizes.

Ó Conaire, Sean-Phádraic (1882–1928), novelist and short story writer in Irish, was born in Galway but reared in Ros Muc and educated in Rockwell and Blackrock College. He went to work as a civil servant at the Ministry of Education in London and there became a teacher for the Gaelic League and involved socially with the Irish expatriate community, including at the time Michael Collins and P. S. O'Hegarty*. He was also made welcome in cultured English homes and was a good friend of Robert Lynd*. His best writing was done in London; he spent the last decade of his life back in Ireland, much of it homeless and in poverty. The short story collections *Nóra Mharcuis Bhig agus Sgéalta Eile* (1909) and *An Chéad Chloch* (1914) and his novel *Deoraíocht* are considerable achievements, owing more to the influence of the Russian writers Dostoievesky and to modernist trends than to any vision of rural Gaelic Utopia. His best stories were collected

as *Scothscéalta* and translated by Eoghan Ó Tuairisc* and others as *The Finest Stories of Pádraic Ó Conaire* (1982).

Ó Conghaile, Mícheál (b. 1962), poet, short story writer and publisher in Irish, was born in Inis Treabhair in County Galway and educated at UCG. He established a vibrant Irish-language publishing house, Cló Iar-Chonnachta, in 1985. His published works include two collections of short stories, a collection of poetry, *Combrá Cailí* (1987), and non-fiction. His most recent short story collection, *An Fear a Phléasc* (1987), was widely praised as innovative and surreal. In 1997 he won first prize in the Hennessy Literary Awards for New Irish Writing and was named Young Writer of the Year.

O'Connor, Clairr (b. 1951), novelist, poet and playwright, was born in Limerick and educated at UCC and Maynooth. She has taught in Ireland and England and published a book of verse, *When You Need Them* (1989). Her two novels, *Belonging* (1991) and *Love in Another Room* (1995), are complicated, readable stories in which many characters, primarily women, engage with love, work and families.

O'Connor, Frank (name adopted by Michael O'Donovan) (1903–66), short story writer and translator, was born and reared in poverty in Cork and educated locally but was given early adult education by Daniel Corkery* who taught him (and his older colleague Sean O'Faolain*) Irish and national culture.

O'Connor was his mother's maiden name and it was in tribute to their close relationship (the father being in the British army) that he made it his for all practical purposes. Like O'Faolain, he took the Republican side in the Civil War* and, like Peadar O'Donnell*, was interned in 1923. His paramilitary experiences provided the material for his first book of stories *Guests of the Nation* (1931), the title story of which is one of his best, and a strongly slanted biography of Michael Collins, *The Big Fellow* (1937). After release he joined the library service and soon made his name as a literary gadfly (encouraged by the Censorship Board whose implacable and effective enemy he became) and probably the best short story writer Ireland has produced, the only near rival being William Trevor*. The stories were published in such collections as *Bones of Contention* (1936), *Crab Apple Jelly* (1944), *The Common Chord* (1947), *Traveller's Samples* (1951) and *The Stories of Frank O'Connor* (1953). Later collections appeared simply as *Collection Two* (1964) and *Collection Three* (1969). The label 'anticlerical', applied with equal inaccuracy to O'Faolain* because of his straight talking in *The Bell*, was attached to him because of his tricky stories of Father Ring, the foxy curate of his Everytown 'Asragh', but in fact few people have ever written with such accuracy and sympathy about priests as O'Connor did, as an anthology edited by his widow Harri et Sheehy and called *The Collar* (1993) makes clear. He contributed many stories and essays to the early numbers of *The Bell* but by the end of the 1940s had had enough of tight little Ireland and began a successful career as a maverick, heretical academic in America. His lectures resulted in a study of the novel, *The Mirror in the Roadway* (1956), that tended towards the wayward – his own novels *The Saint and Mary Kate* (1932) and *Dutch Interior* (1940) were not particularly good – a more successful account of the short story, *The Lonely Voice* (1962), and *A Backward Look* (1967), a survey of the literature of Ireland from the beginning of its civilisation. His versions of early Gaelic poetry in the *A Golden Treasury of Irish Poetry 600–1200* (1959), done with David Greene (1915– 81), and of Middle and Modern Irish verse, including the banned *Cúirt an Mheán-Oiche*, in *Kings, Lords and Commons* (1959) did much to stimulate interest in an unrecognised treasure. O'Connor, for all of his quirks and crotchets, remains a major figure in twentieth-century Irish literature.

O'Connor, Joseph (b. 1963), novelist and short story writer, was born in Glenageary, County Dublin, and educated at UCD, graduating MA in 1986 with a thesis on the poet Charles Donnelly (1914–37). He has travelled widely and written much, often comic, journalism, becoming the voice of the young, mobile, frontier-lepping Irish. One effective non-fiction book, *Sweet Liberty* (1996), uproariously describes his visits to all nine towns in the United States called Dublin. O'Connor has written three novels: *Cowboys and Indians*

(1991), *Desperadoes* (1994), about young, confused and irreverent Irish people, and *The Salesman* (1997), a reworking of *Buile Suibhne* in a one-man crusade for justice. *True Believers* (1991), which contains 'The Last of the Mohicans', an earlier adventure of Eddie Virago the anti-hero of *Cowboys and Indians*, is a collection of short stories.

O'Connor, Joseph K. (1878–1961), sketch writer, was born in Ashford, County Limerick, and educated at Clongowes and King's Inns, becoming a barrister and eventually a judge. As 'Heblon' he contributed many sketches of Dublin life to the *Evening Mail*, mainly police court stories, which were published as *Studies in Blue* (1903). He also had a hand in a slum play of Gogarty* called *Blight* (1917) which was written as by Alpha and Omega.

O'Connor, T[homas] P[ower] (1848–1929), journalist and politician, known universally as 'Tay Pay', was born in Athlone and educated at Queen's College, Galway. He was a Nationalist MP for Galway (1880–5) and for the Scotland division of Liverpool (1885-1929). He broke fresh ground in journalism with the *Star* (1887) and followed it with the more literary *T. P.'s Weekly* (1902), both leading the field in the golden age of literate popular journalism. He was the first British film censor (1917–29), a Privy Councillor (1924–9) and father of the House of Commons for many years. His most important books are *The Parnell Movement* (1886) and *Memories of an*

Old Parliamentarian (1929).

O'Connor, Ulick (b. 1929), biographer, was born in Dublin and educated at UCD, Loyola College, New Orleans, and King's Inns, being called to the Irish bar in 1951. An accomplished sportsman and journalist, he has written biographies of Oliver St John Gogarty (1964) and Brendan Behan (1970), the latter controversially revealing the subject's bisexuality. *A Terrible Beauty Is Born* (1975) and *The Celtic Dawn* (1984) are popular accounts of the Troubles and the Irish Literary Revival*.

Ó Criomhthain, Tomás (1856–1937), autobiographer in Irish, was born on the Great Blasket* Island off the west coast of Kerry. A fisherman and small farmer, he and his wife reared ten children and he was the first islander to be able to read and write in Irish. He was encouraged to write by Irish and foreign visitors to the island, who came in search of one of the few unsullied remnants of Gaelic culture, most notably by Irish scholar Brian Ó Ceallaigh from Killarney and Englishman Robin Flower. Ó Ceallaigh assembled Ó Criomhthain's day-by-day accounts of life on the island and had them edited by Pádraig Ó Siochfhradha ('An Seabhac') as *Allagar na hInise* (1928) (translated by Tim Enright as *Island Cross-Talk* in 1986). The greatest of all Blasket books, *An tOileánach**, appeared in 1929.

O'Curry, Eugene (1796–1862), Gaelic scholar, was born in Carrigholt, County Clare into a family which, though lacking in formal education, was steeped in

Gaelic tradition. He spent his youth working at a variety of occupations in Clare and in Limerick City and moved to Dublin in about 1834. There he began to work for the Ordnance Survey under George Petrie*, who spearheaded a Topographical section from 1830–41. Petrie had assembled a number of Irish scholars, including O'Curry's brother-in-law, John O'Donovan and Samuel Ferguson*, to do field-work and research on manuscripts and O'Curry also came in contact with other scholars based in TCD and the RIA who were deeply interested in the manuscript sources for Gaelic culture. He studied and catalogued Irish manuscripts at various stages in the RIA and the British Museum and edited the legal text, *The Book of Achill*, held at TCD. Thereafter he became an expert on Gaelic law and customs, basing his research on manuscript sources. He and John O'Donovan worked together on an edition of *Senchas Mór*, another legal text. In 1854, O'Curry was made Professor of Irish History and Archaeology at the Catholic University (now UCD). His most sgnificant contribution to Gaelic scholarship were the volumes based on series of lectures he delivered there and published as *Lectures on the Manuscript Materials of Ancient Irish History* (1861) and *On the Manners and Customs of the Ancient Irish* (1873), in which he reconstructed Gaelic life and customs from the evidence of the manuscripts. He edited versions of stories from the heroic cycle, such as *The Sick Bed of Cuchulainn* and *The Only Jealousy of Emer* and translated from the Irish love poems such as '*An Cuimhin Leat an Oíche Íd?'/'Do You Remember that Night?*' With George Petrie, he collected traditional music and songs in the Aran Islands, which Petrie published in *The Ancient Music of Ireland* (1855). The influence of his pioneering work on manuscript sources is incalculable; he and scholars like him paved the way for the Gaelic League and language revival and recreated the concept of an ancient and sophisticated Gaelic society.

Ó Direáin, Máirtín (1910–1988), poet in Irish, was born in Inis Mór in the Aran Islands*. As a young man he went to work in the post office in Galway, later moving to the civil service in Dublin where he spent the remainder of his working life until retirement in 1975. One of the finest and most assured of the modern Irish poetic voices, Ó Díreáin was recognised as a major poet by Seán Ó Tuama* in his *Nuabhéarsaíocht* (1950), a year after the publication of Ó Direáin's *Rogha Dánta* (1949). Ó Direáin's verse is beautifully lyrical and rhythmic; in many of his poems he uses a language that denotes the natural features of his native Aran Islands both to celebrate their unchanging beauty – in lyrics such as 'An tEarrach Thiar' and 'An Nollaig Thiar' – and to point up the contrast with the bleakness of contemporary urban life. Later collections included *Ó Morna agus Dánta Eile* (1957) and *Ceacht an Éin* (1980). A *Tacair Dánta/ Selected Poems* was published in 1984.

Ó Doibhlin, Breandán (b. 1931), novelist, critic and scholar in Irish and translator, was born in County Tyrone and educated at St Columb's College, Derry, Maynooth and Rome. He was appointed Professor of French and Modern Languages in Maynooth in 1958. He was influential in the development of a critical idiom for the study of modern Irish literature, many of whose practitioners he promoted while editor of *Irisleabhar Mhá Nuad*. His own novels include *Néal Maidine agus Tine Oíche* (1960) and *An Branar Gan Cur*1979), which describes the disaffection of a Catholic in Northern Ireland. *Smaointe Phascal* (1994) and *Fabhalscéalta La Fontaine* (1997) are recent published works.

Ó Doirnín, Peadar (?1704–69), poet in Irish, seems to have been born near Dundalk, County Louth, and to have been a schoolmaster. There is considerable confusion about his life, as Seán de Rís, the editor of his surviving poems, makes clear in *Peadar Ó Doirnín, a Bheatha agus a Shaothar* (1969). He may have been destined for the priesthood but is thought to have become tutor to the family of one Arthur Brownlow, a Protestant from Lurgan, who had then in his possession the *Book of Armagh*. Ó Doirnín may have taught Brownlow Irish. They parted after some years because of inevitable disagreements about politics and Ó Doirnín married Rose Toner and settled near Forkhill, County Louth, where he became a teacher. He wrote satirical verse and came in for constant persecution by a local government agent known as Johnston of the Fews. Among his best known works are 'Úr-Chnoc Chéin Mhic Cáinte' and 'Mná na hÉireann', love poems with a strong element of fantasy and exaggeration. Ó Doirnín died in his classroom on 3 April 1768 and is buried at Urney churchyard near Dundalk. Seosamh Mac Grianna's story 'Codladh an Mháistir' is based on the circumstances of Ó Doirnín's death.

Ó Dónaill, Niall (1908–94), scholar and lexicographer in Irish, was born in County Donegal, a native Irish speaker, and educated at St Eunan's Letterkenny and UCD. He worked as a translator for An Gúm* and wrote many books and articles on biographical subjects, on Donegal and on the Irish language. His greatest contribution to that language was his decades of work as the editor of the classic *Foclóir Gaeilge-Béarla* (1977), which has never been superseded.

Ó Donnchadha, Tadhg (aka 'Torna') (1874–1949), poet, editor and scholar in Irish, was born in Carrignavar near Cork City and educated at the North Monastery in Cork and St Patrick's College in Dublin. While a teacher in Dublin he joined the Gaelic League and became acquainted with the figures of the Literary Revival*, translating into Irish some of the work of Yeats* and George Moore* and also publishing a collection of his own poetry, *Leoithne Andeas* (1905). He was Professor of Irish at UCC from 1916–44. He produced editions of several great Gaelic poets, among them Aogán Ó

Rathaile* (with Pádraig Ó Duinnín*) and Pádraigín Haicéad*.

Ó Donnchadha, Séafraidh (an Ghleanna) (?1620–?80), poet in Irish, was born in Killaha Castle near Killarney, County Kerry, the seat of the O'Donoghue clan of which he became chief on the death of his father in 1643. Although he took part in the 1641 Rebellion he retained his patrimony and made Killaha castle a haven both for fugitives from the fighting and for men of letters and poets. He himself composed poetry mainly in the formal *dán díreach* syllabic style, although he is known to have written more personal lyrics. His poetry was edited by fellow Kerryman Pádraid Ó Duinnín* and published in 1902. He is one of the four 'Kerry poets' apostrophied 'Aogán, Séafraidh, Piaras, Eoghan' by Ó Duinnín on a memorial in Killarney.

O'Donnell, Mary (b. 1954), short story writer, poet and novelist, was born in Monaghan and educated at Maynooth. She has published three collections of strongly emotional, sensual verse, *Reading the Sunflowers in September* (1990), *Spiderwoman's Third Avenue Rhapsody* (1993) and *Unlegendary Heroes* (1998). She has also published a book of powerful short stories, *Strong Pagans* (1991), which deals with the old themes of love, motherhood and passion, and two novels *The Light Makers* (1992), in which a childless woman is married to a unfaithful architect, and *Virgin and The Boy* (1996).

O'Donnell, Peadar (1893–1986), writer and socialist, was born at Meenmore near Dungloe, County Donegal, and educated at St Patrick's College, Dublin. He became a teacher and union organiser, using his personal knowledge of the appalling conditions of migrant workers in Scotland. He took the Republican side in the Civil War*, recording his experiences in *The Gates Flew Open* (1932), and edited the IRA paper *An Phoblacht* (1926–34). His agitation against the Land Annuities helped bring down the Cosgrave government and he was a local recruiter for the International Brigade during the Spanish Civil War. In 1940 he persuaded Sean O'Faolain* to edit *The Bell** and took over as editor (1946–54) when O'Faolain retired. Of O'Donnell's novels, three – *The Storm* (1925), *Islanders* (1928) and *Proud Island* (1975) – are set in the islands of the Rosses of Donegal, which he knew from boyhood and where he taught. *The High Windows* (1953), set in the heart of the Donegal Mountains, which he remembered from a time spent 'on the run' when he was nursing a wound, is about a woman who has left her bright island home for life in the dark interior glens. *The Knife* (1930) and *On the Edge of the Stream* (1934) are about small-town Irish life, the former dealing with the lot of Protestant farmers caught on the Free State side of the border. *Ardrigoole* (1929) is based on a true incident in which a mother and child died of starvation in a pro-Treaty area while her Republican husband was imprisoned. For most of the ninety-three years of his life O'Donnell was a fighter for social justice, his writings in fiction implicitly furthering his undoctrinaire socialism.

O'Donoghue, D[avid] J[ames] (1866–1917), literary historian, was born in London of Cork parents and, apart from primary schooling, was self-educated, using the Reading Room in the British Museum to excellent effect. In 1886 when he was thirty he came to live in Ireland to work in his brother's bookshop, becoming librarian of the new UCD in 1909. His work *Poets of Ireland* (1892–3), a biographical dictionary, is in its enlarged form (1912) still one of the standard works of Irish bibliography. He compiled an anthology of *Humour in Ireland* (1894), happily ignoring charges of 'stage-Irishness', wrote a life of Carleton* (1896) and edited the works of Mangan* (1897).

O'Donovan, Gerald [Jeremiah] (1871–1942), novelist, was born in County Down, the son of a Cork pier-builder, and was educated at Maynooth, being ordained for the diocese of Clonfert in 1895. He was a white blackbird among the clergy of the time: liberal, aesthetically inclined, a strong supporter of the Gaelic League* and the Irish Renaissance, making the cathedral of Loughrea (of which he was administrator) a centre for culture as well as liturgy. He was the inspiration for George Moore*'s aesthetic priest in the story 'Fugitives' and for his Father Gogarty in *The Lake* (1905). Though the diocesan clergy's choice, he was passed over for bishop by the Vatican because of his 'modernistic' views, and relations between him and Dr O'Dea, the new bishop, deteriorated rapidly. O'Donovan resigned in 1904 and eventually went to London where, after some hack work, he married Beryl Verschoyle, the daughter of an Irish colonel, who supported him until he joined the Italian desk of the War Office in 1914, becoming its head in 1918. It was here that he met the novelist Rose Macaulay (1881–1958), with whom he had a relationship until his death of cancer and whose literary mentor he became. His first and best novel *Father Ralph** (1913) is largely autobiographical, and four others, *Waiting* (1914), *Conquest* (1920), *Vocations* (1921) and *The Holy Tree* (1922), deal with Irish themes, religious and political.

O'Driscoll, Dennis (b. 1954), poet and critic, was born in Thurles, County Tipperary and educated at UCD, where he studied Law. He works as a civil servant in Dublin. His poetry, published in three collections, *Kist* (1982), *Hidden Extras* (1987) and *Long Short Story* (1993), is precise and powerful, treating frankly of the human condition. His latest collection is *Quality Time* (1996).

O'Duffy, Eimar (1893–1935), novelist, was born in Dublin, the son of a society dentist, and educated at Stonyhurst and UCD, graduating BDS, but he did not practise. Though a member of the IRB, he was strongly opposed to the Easter Rising*, becoming MacNeill's informant of Pearse*'s intentions, and was dispatched to Belfast to call off the mobilisation there. This unfashionable attitude is reflected in his novel *The Wasted Island* (1919, revised 1929) and his future in the new bourgeois state looked bleak, though he managed to keep a job with the Department of External Affairs, supplementing his salary with the income from such novels as *The Lion and the Fox* (1922), about Hugh O'Neill in Munster at the time of Kinsale, and two lighter books, *Printer's Errors* (1922) and *Miss Rudd and Some Lovers* (1923), set in the Ireland of the time, until 1925. He then left for England with his wife Kathleen Cruise O'Brien and two children. He supported himself by writing detective stories and began the trilogy of satirical fantasies about the unregretted Ireland he had left and upon which his literary reputation rests. *King Goshawk and the Birds* (1926), *The Spacious Adventures of the Man in the Street* (1928) and *Asses in Clover* (1933) use Celtic mythology and Swiftian savagery to pillory all aspects of the Free State, including its economics and acquiescence in clerical domination.

Ó Dúill, Gréagóir (b.1946), poet in Irish, was born in Dublin. His family moved to Belfast and he was educated at St Malachy's College and QUB, later studying also at UCD and Maynooth, where he was awarded a PhD for his research on Samuel Ferguson. He has published many collections of poetry, including *Innilt Bhóthair* (1981), *Blaoscoileán* (1988) and *Saothrú an Ghoirt* (1994).

Ó Duinnín, an tAthair Pádraig (Fr Patrick Dineen) (1860–1934), scholar, editor and lexicographer in Irish, was born in Rathmore, County Kerry. In 1880 he joined the Jesuit Order, studying at Milltown Park in Dublin and at UCD. He was ordained in 1984 and subsequently taught at the Jesuit schools, Mungret in Limerick and Clongowes Wood in County Kildare. Like many of his contemporaries he joined the Gaelic League* and was exposed to the influence of language revivalists such as Patrick Pearse*. Although he wrote drama and fiction it is as an editor of Irish poetry and a lexicographer that he made a lasting contribution to Gaelic scholarship. He left the Jesuit order (although remaining a priest to the end of his rather eccentric life) and in the first decades of the century completed the herculean labour of editing for publication the work of the four great Kerry Poets (Piaras Feiritéar* (1903), Séafraidh Ó Donnchadha* (1902), Aogán Ó Rathaile* (1900) and Eoghan Rua Ó Súilleabháin* (1901) as well as those of Seán Clárach Mac Dómhnaill* (1902) and Tadhg Gaelach Ó Súilleabháin* (1903). Later he edited Seathrún Céitinn's *Foras Feasa ar Éirinn* (1908–14). The first edition of his *Foclóir Gaedhilge agus Béarla* (*Irish-English Dictionary*) was published in 1904, calling itself 'a thesaurus of the words, phrases and idioms of the modern Irish language'. It is a Johnsonian achievement in its idiosyncracy and breadth of learning, uniting scholarship with a genial understanding of and respect for local lore and history and a most entertaining read, particularly strong on the spoken Irish (and Hiberno-English) of Kerry.

O'Faolain, Eileen (née Gould) (1900–88), writer of folktales and children's books, was born in Cork, like her husband Sean O'Faolain* whom she met at Ballingeary Irish College and whom she married in Boston in 1927. She wrote lively fairy stories for children, including *The Little Black Hen* (1940), *The King of the Cats* (1941) and *Miss Pennyfeather and the Pooka* (1949). Her classic *Irish Sagas and Folktales* (1954) and *Children of the Salmon* (1965) tell the old stories in a mode as acceptable to adults as to children.

O'Faolain, Julia (b. 1932), novelist and short story writer, was born in Twickenham, where her father Sean O'Faolain* was a lecturer, and was educated at UCD, Rome and the Sorbonne. Her first book *We Might See Sights* (1968) had seven Irish and six Italian stories, the home-grown ones showing the revolution in the attitudes of Irish women, the others the unchanged *machismo* of Italian men, but all marvellously readable and wonderfully expressed. The same themes are covered with greater seriousness and sharper satire in other collections, *Man in the Cellar* (1974) and *Daughters of Passion* (1982). *Godded and Codded* (1970), O'Faolain's first novel, withdrawn because of fears of a libel suit, describes a 'liberated' young woman's life in Paris, the males still dreaded by 'Mummy' as 'a dangerous hybrid – part jelly, part tyrant, part snake-in-the-grass'. *Women in the Wall* (1975), a spare and beautiful account of the remarkably autonomous life of nuns in Merovingian Gaul, has as much to say about modern feminism as her account of women in history, *Not in God's Image* (1973), co-authored with her academic husband Lauro Martines. Later work darkened as 'daddy's girl' reacted to the Troubles in *No Country for Young Men* (1980) and in some of the stories in *Daughters of Passion. The Obedient Wife* (1982), *The Irish Signorina* (1984) and *The Judas Cloth* (1992), the latter a novel set in the reign of the reactionary Pio Nono, all rehearse, sharply and sometimes cruelly, her themes of women, the Church and life in academic America and a still medieval Europe.

O'Faolain, Sean (1900–91), man of letters, was born John Whelan in Cork, the son of an RIC constable and a theatrical landlady. Educated by the Presentation Brothers, like Lennox Robinson* he was nudged towards Nationalism by Abbey* plays, though Daniel Corkery* helped with his lessons in Irish and Irishness. He graduated from UCC in 1921, using the Irish form of his name, having been a student by day and a revolutionary at night. He took the Republican side in the Civil War* but gradually turned against violence and extremism. After some years teaching in Ennis, now with an MA, he spent three years in Harvard and a further four lecturing at St Mary's Education College at Strawberry Hill, Twickenham, from which he was eased when his first book of short stories, *Midsummer Night*

Madness (1932), was given the honour of being banned in Ireland. He went to live in Wicklow, supporting himself there by his pen for the rest of his long life. He wrote many short stories, some of the finest for *The Bell** (as had his friend and fellow-citizen Frank O'Connor*) which he edited from 1940 to 1946 with genial kindness to its often unprofessional contributors and for which, with righteous wrath, he wrote editorials excoriating 'our bourgeoisie, Little Islanders, chauvinists, puritans, stuffed-shirts, pietists, Tartuffes, Anglophobes, Celtophiles, *et alii hujus generis*'. He wrote luminous biographies of such people as de Valera (1933), Constance Markievicz (1934), Daniel O'Connell (1938), Hugh O'Neill (1942) and John Henry Newman (1952), travel books about Italy, his second favourite country, works of criticism – *The Short Story* (1947) and *The Vanishing Hero* (1956), a study of the modern novel – and one stage comedy, *She Had to Do Something* (1938). His novels *Bird Alone* (1936), about lifelong self-punishment for an act of passion, and *Come Back to Erin* (1940), about distance lending green enchantment to the exile's view of 'oul' Ireland', a book all but disowned by its author, are not as successful as his stories. His first novel *A Nest of Simple Folk* (1934), written in deliberate imitation of Turgenev, is still a brilliant evocation of the recovery of Irish nationhood as exemplified in the career of Leo Foxe-Donnell, product of a mixed marriage, who becomes a Fenian and lives to be aware of the Easter Rising*. Set in the lush rural isolation of County Limerick, the home of O'Faolain's forebears, it is, in a sense, a prologue to his patriotic autobiography *Vive Moi!* (1964), in the updated (1993) version of which, at his daughter Julia*'s behest, he recounted his affairs with Elizabeth Bowen* and Honor Tracy*. A late novel *And Again* (1979) is interesting mainly for its reversal of time in the story of a man's life. O'Faolain is arguably the premier Irish man of letters of the century, since no one else had his cultural breadth, his moral courage or his sense of nationhood. Others were undoubtedly of greater literary and artistic ability but his was the greater service.

Ó Faracháin, Roibeárd (aka Robert Farren) (1909–84), poet, was born in Dublin and educated at St Patrick's College, Drumcondra and UCD. He taught for ten years before joining Radio Éireann in 1939, becoming Controller of Programmes (1953–74) and a director of the Abbey Theatre*. With Austin Clarke* in 1940 he founded the Dublin Verse-Speaking Society which grew into the Lyric Theatre Company in 1944, presenting verse-dramas biannually in the Abbey. His own work for the company included *Convention at Druim Ceat* (1943), about the assembly near Limavady, County Derry, attended by Colum Cille* to settle, among other matters, the succession of the kingdom of Dál Riata and the position of poets in Ireland, and *Lost Light* (1943). His best known books of verse are *Rime, Gentlemen, Please* (1945) and an epic version of the career of Colum Cille,

The First Exile (1944). His mildly chauvinistic but entertaining *The Course of Irish Verse* was published in 1948.

Ó Fiaich, Tómas (1923–90), scholar in Irish and ecclesiastic, was born in County Armagh and educated at St Patrick's College Armagh and Maynooth. He was ordained to the priesthood in 1948 and studied in UCD and in Belgium. A distinguished academic, he taught history at Maynooth before becoming President of the university in 1974. He was elevated to the primatial see of Armagh in 1977 and made a cardinal two years later. He was an authority on the missionaries of early Christian Ireland who rekindled the faith in a pagan Europe, as his two most significant publications, *Gaelscrínte i gCéin* (1960) and *Irish Cultural Influences in Europe* (1966) attest.

Ó Fiannachta, Pádraig (b. 1927), poet, scholar and translator, was born near Dingle in County Kerry. He was educated at St Brendan's College, Killarney, UCC and Maynooth. He was ordained a priest in 1953. An authority on Welsh as well as early and modern Irish, he was Professor of Modern Irish at Maynooth from 1981–92. He is a biographer (*de Valera*, with Thomas P. O'Neill, 1968 and 1970), poet, among his collections being *Ponc* (1970), *Donn Bó* (1976), *Rúin* (1971) and *Deora Dé* (1988), novelist, literary historian and travel writer. Editor and main translator of the new Irish Bible, *An Bíobla Naofa* (1981), he was also editorial director of

An Sagart, Maynooth's Irish-language imprint and editor of the periodical *Irishleabhar Mhá Nuad*.

Ó Flatharta, Antaine (b. 1953), playwright and scriptwriter in Irish, was born in Lettermullen in County Galway and educated in Carraroe. He has written many plays and television scripts, in Irish and in English, and five of his plays have been published: *Gaeilgeoirí* (1986), *Imeachtaí na Saoirse* (1986), *Grásta i Meiriceá* (1990), *Ag Ealaín in Éirinn* (1994) and *An Fear Bréige* (1996).

O'Flaherty, Liam (1896–1984), novelist, was born on Inis Mór the largest of the Aran Islands*, and educated there and at Rockwell, County Tipperary, where he was a postulant of the Holy Ghost Fathers. He had been enrolled by them in UCD when he decided he had no vocation and joined the Irish Guards in 1915 as Bill Ganly (his mother's maiden name). He was wounded and badly shellshocked in 1917 and took several years to recover, years which included his seizure of the Rotunda to set up a socialist state and fighting on the Republican side in the Civil War*. He left Ireland in 1922 and became a full-time writer, producing over the next thirty years many remarkable novels and short stories in English, including *Thy Neighbour's Wife* (1923) and *The Black Soul* (1924), which give a memorable picture of Aran life and the author's vision of himself as the 'black soul'. A long novella, *The Return of the Beast* (1929), describes how the humanity of ordinary men is eroded under 'no-man's-land' bombardment, much as Gypo Nolan – in *The Informer* (1929), O'Flaherty's best known novel, which became a powerful film in the hands of John Ford – changes from a slow-witted, decent man to a shambling animal in whom a dawning conscience comes too late. *Spring Sowing* (1924), O'Flaherty's first collection of stories, deals as much with animals and even inanimate nature (as in 'The Wave') as with humans. A historical trilogy, *Famine* (1937), *Land* (1946) and *Insurrection* (1950), shows the best and the worst of the author. Æ* once summed up O'Flaherty's work as follows: 'When O'Flaherty thinks, he is a goose; when he feels, he is a genius.' His sympathetic delineation of the mute and inarticulate is his greatest strength; his artistic 'agony', though sincere, rings false. His women, apart from mothers, are unconvincing, and his admiration for cold-blooded fanatics such as Gallagher, the IRA commander in *The Informer*, Tyson in *The Martyr* (1933) and Dwyer in *Land* may be a recognition of his own mercurial temperament. His short stories are better than his novels, and in the language of *Dúil (Desire)* (1953) – a significant title – a collection of stories in Irish, some of them versions of earlier English ones, there is a marvellously appropriate terseness. *Shame the Devil* (1934) was a striking autobiography and, considering the length and drama of O'Flaherty's life, one wishes that he had written about the next fifty years with the same frankness and elegance.

Ó Floinn, Críostóir (b. 1927), man of letters, was born in Limerick, which he enthusiastically celebrates in his memoir *There is an Isle* (1998), educated there and at St Patrick's College Drumcondra. He has worked as teacher, broadcaster and lecturer and written plays, poetry and short stories in Irish and English, mostly polemical and critical of the changing Ireland. His best known work *Cóta Bán Chríost* (1966), about the effects on a priest's vocation of a visit by a pregnant young woman on Christmas Eve claiming to be a virgin still, won the Oireachtas Prize and, in its English version, *The Order of Melchizedek*, was the sensation of the Dublin Theatre Festival of 1967. *Sanctuary Island* (1971) is a collection of largely satirical short stories. Other plays include *Is É A Dúirt Polonius* (1973), a modern morality, and *Mise Raifteirí an File* (1974). *Aisling Dhá Abhainn* (1977) is a collection of verse.

Ó Gadhra, Nollaig (b. 1943), biographer, historian and journalist in Irish and English, was born in Feenagh, County Limerick and educated at De La Salle College in Waterford. He is a graduate of UCC and also studied at Harvard and Salzburg. A bilingual journalist, he worked for various newspapers as well as for RTÉ News and Current Affairs. He is a lecturer in Communications and European Studies at the Galway-Mayo Institute of Technology and was a member of Comhairle Teilifís na Gaeilge which supervised the launch of Ireland's first national Irish television channel (T na G) in 1996. He has published biographies of Gandhi (1969), John Boyle O'Reilly (1976), Edward Ignatius Rice (1977) and Richard J. Daley (1979). His political trilogy, *Guth an Phobail* (1984), *Ríocht Roinnte* (1985) and *Éire agus Polaitíocht na hEorpa* (1986) won several awards. His other books include *Margáil na Saoirse* (1988), which deals with the Feakle peace talks of the 1970s, *An Chéad Dáil Éireann 1919 – 21* (1989) and *An Ghaeltacht (Oifigiúil) agus 1992?* (1990).

Ó Gramhna, An tAthair Eoghan (Fr Eugene O'Growney) (1863–99), Irish enthusiast, scholar and grammarian, was born in Ballyfallon, County Meath, and educated at St Finian's College, Navan, and Maynooth, where he was ordained a priest in 1889. His enthusiasm for Irish dated from his youth and as a student he spent summers in gaeltacht areas. He was appointed curate in a parish in County Westmeath and wrote articles for *Irisleabhar na Gaedhilge*, the periodical of the Gaelic Union (the precursor of the Gaelic League*). In 1891, he became its editor, and Professor of Celtic Literature and Language at Maynooth. When the Gaelic League* was founded in 1893, with his friend Douglas Hyde* as its President, he became Vice-President. His book *Simple Lessons in Irish* (1894), based on a series of lessons he wrote for *Irisleabhar na Gaedhilge* and *The Weekly Freeman* was a great popular success. Chronic ill-health caused him to leave Ireland for America and led to his premature death in Los Angeles. He was reinterred in Maynooth in 1901.

O'Grady, Standish James (1846–1928), novelist, a man often confused with his cousin Standish Hayes O'Grady (1832–1915), the Gaelic scholar, was born in Castletown Berehaven, County Cork, the son of an Anglican rector who was also a viscount. He was educated at TCD and called to the bar in 1872. His interest in Irish myth led to the extensive research that produced *History of Ireland* (1878–80) and a corrective volume in 1881, and made him one of the enablers of the Irish Literary Revival*, having a profound effect on Yeats*. This was particularly true of his re-writing of the saga tales as adventure novels, with a trilogy about Cuchulain – *The Coming of Cuculain* (1894), *In the Gates of the North* (1901) and *The Triumph and Passing of Cuculain* (1924) – and a similar treatment of Fionn and the Fianna in *Finn and His Companions* (1892). Other novels, written mainly with children in mind, include *The Bog of Stars* (1893), *Lost on Du-Corrig* (1894), *Ulrick the Ready* (1896), *In the Wake of King James* (1896) and *The Flight of the Eagle* (1897), about Red Hugh O'Donnell. O'Grady was a Liberal Unionist who correctly anticipated the coming resort to arms and left Ireland in 1918, spending the rest of his life in the Isle of Wight.

O'Grady, Timothy (b. 1951), novelist, was born in Chicago and worked as a fiction editor for literary magazines in the USA, Ireland and Britain. He is the author of the novels *Motherland* (1988) and *I Could Read the Sky* (1997) (with photographer Steve Pike). He also collaborated with Kenneth Griffith on *Curious Journey: an Oral History of Ireland's Unfinished Revolution* (1982).

O'Hegarty, P[atrick] S[arsfield], (1879–1955), historian and biographer, was born in Carrignavar, County Cork. He worked in the post office in England until in 1918 he returned to Dublin to run the Irish Bookshop in Dawson Street. He was Secretary of the Department of Posts and Telegraphs from 1922–45. He wrote biographies of Irish patriots John Mitchel (1917) and Terence MacSwiney (1922), books on politics such as *The Victory of Sinn Féin* (1924) and *A History of Ireland Under the Union 1801–1922* (1952) from a strongly nationalistic viewpoint.

Ó hEigeartaigh, Pádraig (1871–1936), was born in Iveragh, County Kerry. He was taken to America when he was twelve and went to work in a cotton mill. He became interested in Irish when he bought an Irish book, *Filidheacht Chúige Mumhan*, in a second-hand bookshop. He taught himself the language and helped to found the Springfield Irish Society, in which he became a teacher of Irish. The poem 'Ochón, A Donncha', for which he is best known, was written on the death of his small son in a boating accident. It was published by Pádraig Pearse in *An Claideamh Soluis*.

Ó hEithir, Breandán, (1930–90), novelist and journalist in Irish and English, was born on Inis Mór in the Aran Islands*, where his parents were schoolteachers. He was the nephew of Liam O'Flaherty*. He was educated locally and at Coláiste Éanna in Galway, the school being evacuated during WWII. (This and other diverting episodes of his first twenty or so years are drolly recounted in the sporting memoir, *Over the Bar*, which ostensibly deals with his life-long obsession with Galway hurling.) He spent a brief ill-starred period on scholarship to UCG (which provided him with material for the partly autobiographical *Lig Sinn i gCathú* (1976; translated by the author as *Lead Us Into Temptation* in 1978) and after some years working at a variety of occupations, including that of travelling salesman, turned to writing. He was a gifted political journalist in Irish and in English and in the three decades' span of his varied career was at different times Irish editor of the *Irish Press* (1957–63), editor of *Comhar**, presenter of RTÉ's Irish current-affairs programme, *Féach*, a long-standing columnist with the *Irish Times* and a scriptwriter for film and TV. The cynical and amusing *The Begrudger's Guide to Irish Politics* (1986) was another product of his immersion in Irish politics. His second novel, *Sionnach ar Mo Dhuán* (1988), was both controversial and successful. He settled in Paris with his German-born wife in the period before his death, maintaining his professional, personal and sporting links with Ireland and his reputation as a brilliant talker and shrewd observer. *An Nollaig Thiar* (1989), an outstanding autobiographical book for children, was the last he published before his death.

Ó hIfearnáin, Liam Dall (?1720–1803), poet in Irish, was born at Shronell near Tipperary town and spent his whole life in the same area. As the name by which he was known suggests, he was blind or very weak-sighted from birth. He wrote personal poetry, laments and patriotic verse, Jacobite in sympathy like that of his contemporaries, and is credited with having invented the name 'Caitlín Ní Uallacháin' for Ireland. The aisling* 'Pé in Éirinn í' is probably the poem by which he is best remembered and 'Ar Bhruach na Coille Móire,' as well as being beautiful and lyrical, is an energetic political composition in which the poet claims that if he heard that the English were defeated, he would rise from the grave itself. He was a regular participant at the court of poetry which was held at the home of Seán Clárach Mac Domhnaill* at Kiltoohig. He died as he had lived in poverty in County Tipperary.

Ó hOdhráin, Micheál (b. 1932), novelist, short story writer, and playwright in Irish, was born in County Mayo and educated at St. Jarlath's College, Tuam and UCG. He worked as a teacher, university lecturer and civil servant. He has published two collections of short stories, Slán leis an gComhluadar (1961) and Sléibhte Mbaigh Eo (1964), novels for children including Ar Son na Treibhe (1964) and An Tine Bheo (1966), and many radio plays for RTÉ.

tOileánach, An (1929), autobiography of Tomás Ó Criomhthain which gives an account of all aspects of the harsh but culturally rich life on the Great Blasket*. The book, regarded as a classic, is dignified and elegiac in tone, its author conscious of preserving a record of a culture that is coming to an end, as its most famous line, 'Ní bheidh ár leithéidí arís ann' ('We are the last of our kind') testifies. A translation by Robin Flower was published as The Islandman in 1934.

tOIREACHTAS, An, the annual festival of Gaelic culture initiated by the Gaelic League in 1897 on the models of the Scottish Mod and the Welsh Eisteddfod. Its literary competitions played a significant part in the establishment of a modern Gaelic literature.

O'Keeffe, John (1747–1833), playwright, was born in Dublin and studied painting before becoming an actor and author for Smock Alley*. He went to London, where he had already spent two years, in 1784. Though his weak eyesight finally turned in 1790 to total blindness which spelled the end of his acting career, he wrote in all sixty-eight pieces for the theatre, mostly comedies. His first effort was Tony Lumpkin in Town (1778), a sequel to Goldsmith*'s She Stoops to Conquer*. As with Macklin*, his plays are full of sympathetic Irish characters and he retained his Catholicism and mild Nationalism until his death. His play Wild Oats (1791) was revived in 1976 by the RSC and ran for two years in

London; there was an Abbey* production in 1977 and it had another successful season at the RNT in 1996. 'I Am a Friar of Orders Grey' is one of the songs of his comic opera *Merry Sherwood* (1798) and 'Amo, Amas, I Love a Lass' of *The Agreeable Surprise* (1781); the phrase 'fair and fat and forty' is in *The Irish Mimic* (1795) and 'You should always except the present company' in *The London Hermit* (1793).

O'Kelly, Seumas (?1875–1918), playwright and fiction writer, was born near Loughrea, County Galway, and, though of minimal education, rose to become editor of various papers, including the *Leinster Leader*, which he took over when his brother was arrested in 1916, and *Nationality*, replacing Arthur Griffith when he was deported in 1918. It was on the premises of *Nationality* that he died after the invasion of the office by soldiers and their wives, celebrating the Armistice by attacking Sinn Féin. O'Kelly wrote two novels, *The Lady of Deerpark* (1917) and *Wet Clay* (1922), which are very much melodramas of their time, a children's book, *The Leprechaun of Kilmeen* (1920), several Abbey* plays, including *The Shuiler's Child* (1909), and many short stories. His masterpiece, which, adapted as a play for radio by Mícheál Ó hAodha, won the Prix Italia in 1961 and was later filmed for television, was the novella *The Weaver's Grave* (1919), a version of Petronius's *Widow of Ephesus*.

Ó Laoghaire, An tAthair Peadar (1839–1920), novelist in Irish and translator, was born in Clondrohid in County Cork and educated at Maynooth, where he was ordained in 1867. He served as a priest in the diocese of Cloyne for the rest of his life. He began writing in Irish in the 1890s, after the foundation of the Gaelic League* and his insistence on using '*caint na ndaoine*', the living language still spoken in gaeltacht areas, rather than any more literary form of Irish as the basis of his works had a strong influence on the Gaelic revival and on future developments in literature and education. He produced a large body of work, original novels such as *Séadna** and *Niamh*, translations into Irish of devotional and religious works, and versions in modern Irish of older texts. His autobiography, *Mo Sgéal Féin*(1915), was a classic for decades. His detractors criticise him for narrow-mindedness, which took the form of bowdlerising texts, and for glorifying Irish peasant culture at the expense of everything else.

Old Lady Says 'No!', The (1928–9), satirical play by Denis Johnston* which uses many of the lines of Hiberno-English drama and verse that formed the oral treasury of the literate Irish of the time to underline the unheroic nature of the Free State. It begins with a performance of a melodrama about Robert Emmet (1778–1803) in which the actor playing the hero is concussed and wanders out into the Dublin of the 1920s. Its original title, *Shadowdance*, was changed when the script was returned from the

Abbey* with pencilled words suggesting that Lady Gregory* had rejected it, or so the story goes. It provided Mac Liammóir* with one of his recurring starring roles.

O'Loughlin, Michael (b. 1958), poet, short story writer, novelist and critic, was born in Dublin. He lived in Barcelona and Amsterdam before returning to live in Dublin. He has published three collections of poetry, *Stalingrad: the Street Dictionary*, *Atlantic Blues* (1982) and *Diary of a Silence* (1985), a volume of translations from the Dutch and a study of Patrick Kavanagh: *After Kavanagh: Patrick Kavanagh and the Discourse of Contemporary Irish Poetry* (1985). His latest collection is *Another Nation: New and Selected Poems* (1995). He has also published a collection of short stories, *The Inside Story* (1989), which has been translated into Dutch.

O'Malley, Mary, poet and broadcaster, was born in County Galway and educated at UCG. She has lectured in Europe (she spent a long period in Lisbon) and the USA and written for radio and television. She has published three collections of poetry, *A Consideration of Silk* (1990), *Where the Rocks Float* (1993) and *The Knife in the Wave* (1997). She now lives with her family in the Moycullen gaeltacht in County Galway.

Ó Maoileoin, Pádraig (b. 1913), novelist and editor in Irish, was born in Dunquin in the Kerry gaeltacht, the grandson of Tomás Ó Criomhthain*. He

wrote many of his earlier works while employed as a garda, but left the force to work on Niall Ó Dónaill*'s *Irish–English Dictionary* (1977). His best known work is the autobiographical *Na bÁird Ó Thuaidh* (1960) but he wrote a number of novels, among them *Bríde Bhán* (1967) and *Ó Thuaidh* (1983). He edited several Blasket works: Ó Criomhthain*'s *An tOileánach* (1973) and *Allagar na hInise* (1977) and Peig Sayers*'s *Machtnamh Sean-Mhná* (1980).

Ó Muimhneacháin, Aindrias (b. 1905), was born in County Cork and trained as a teacher. He was a member of the Gaelic League* executive, An Coiste Gnó, for many years, and a historian of the League. His works include *An Claidheamh Solais – Tríocha Bliain de Chonradh na Gaeilge* (1955) and *Na Múinteoirí Taistil* (1962). *Seanchas an Táilliúra* (1978) records in Irish the humour and chat of Tim Buckley, the tailor of *The Tailor and Ansty**.

Ó Muircheartaigh, Aogán (b. 1948), poet in Irish, was born in Port Laoise of Kerry parents, his father a native speaker, and educated at Coláiste Mhuire, UCD, and Maynooth. He worked as a teacher before becoming a producer with Radio na Gaeltachta in Baile na nGall, County Kerry. He has published two collections of poetry, *Oíche Gréine* (1987) and *Drúcht ar Chneas* (1992) and versions of *An Táin* (1992) and *Cath Fionn Trá* (1994).

Ó Muirithe, Diarmuid, playwright, lexicographer and journalist, was born in New Ross, County Wexford. He became a lecturer in Irish Language and Literature in UCD and is the author of ten books, including works on Anglo-Irish lexicography, and twelve broadcast radio plays. He contributes a popular long-running column to *The Irish Times* called 'The Words We Use', which has twice been published in book form.

Ó Muirthile, Liam (b. 1950), poet, journalist, novelist and playwright in Irish, was born in Cork City, the eldest of a large and talented family with roots in west Cork. He was educated at Coláiste Críost Rí and UCC, where he was taught by Seán Ó Tuama* and Seán Ó Ríordáin*, who had by then been appointed to a part-time lecturership. He was involved with Michael Davitt* and Nuala Ní Dhomhnaill* on the magazine *Innti*, which was the outward show of a significant resurgence in Irish-language poetry at the time. After graduation, he worked with Gael Linn and as a broadcaster and producer with RTÉ. He has published several volumes of poetry, including *Tine Chnámh* (1978) and *Dialann Bóthair* (1992). A play, *Fear an Tae*, was staged in 1995. His work is sensitive and humanistic, combining a deep appreciation of pagan and Gaelic Ireland with a similar appreciation of other cultures. He has been a regular columnist with the *Irish Times* since 1989; his column, 'An Peann Coitianta', was collected in a volume under that title in 1991. He has also produced a novel, *Ar Bhruach na Laoi* (1995).

Ó Neachtain, Seán (?1650–1729), poet and scholar in Irish, was born in County Roscommon to a prosperous family. He left his home county as a young man and thereafter lived in County Meath and Dublin where he worked at various jobs, including that of schoolmaster. He wrote in a wide variety of forms: lyric poetry, elegies, verse-plays and comical poems lampooning his friends, society and satirising himself. *Stair Éamuinn Uí Chléire* is a substantial work of comic prose, an allegorical *bildungsroman*. Ó Neachtain and his son Tadhg* are also of particular interest for providing glimpses of a Irish-speaking (and bilingual) community in early eighteenth-century Dublin.

Ó Neachtain, Tadhg (1670–1749), poet and lexicographer in Irish, was born in Dublin, the son of Seán Ó Neachtain*. He was a leading light in Irish-speaking society in Dublin, entertained all the Irish scholars (of whom there appears to have been a substantial number) in his house and was also a teacher of Irish. In the 1730s he compiled an *Irish–English Dictionary*, which was never published but the manuscript of which survives in TCD.

O'Neill, Joseph (1886–1953), novelist, was born in Tuam and educated at UCG and Maynooth, which he left after a crisis of faith. He gave up studies in Old Irish to become a civil servant in 1908 and was Permanent Secretary for Education (1923–44). He is remembered for a number of strange novels, some of which combine fantasy with history: *Wind from the North* (1934) is set in Viking Dublin at the time of

Clontarf (1014) but the protagonist is a Dublin clerk who was injured in a tram-car accident; *Land under England* (1935) is an account of a subterranean life terrorised by automata descended from the Roman legionaries; *Philip* (1940) is set in the Jerusalem of the Crucifixion; and *Chosen by the Queen* (1947) is about the Earl of Essex (1566–1601). He was the husband of Mary Devenport O'Neill*.

O'Neill, Mary Devenport (1879–1967), poet, wife of Joseph O'Neill*, was born in Loughrea, County Galway, and educated at the Metropolitan School of Art. Her verse was published in *Prometheus* (1929), and individual poems and her verse-plays *Bluebeard* (1933) and *Cain* (1945) were printed in the *Dublin Magazine*. She was famous as a literary hostess in the 1920s and 1930s. 'Thursdays' in her house in Kenilworth Square, Rathgar, being part of Dublin's informal intellectual life.

O'Neill, Moira (pseudonym of Nesta Skrine, née Higginson) (1865–1955), poet, was born in Cushendun at the foot of one of the nine Glens of Antrim, which were the inspiration for her popular two-volume *Songs of the Glens of Antrim* (1901, 1921). She was the mother of Molly Keane*.

Ó Néill, Séamus (1910–81), poet, novelist, short story writer and playwright in Irish, was born in County Down. He was educated at QUB, UCD and Innsbrick and became a lecturer at Carysfort College in Dublin. A versatile writer in many genres, he tackled contentious modern themes such as marital breakdown in *Tonn Tuile* (1947) and sectarianism in Ulster in *Máire Nic Artáin* (1959). His short story collections include *Ag Baint Fraochán* (1955), his plays *Faill ar an bhFeart* (1967) and he published two collections of poetry, *Dánta* (1944) and *Dánta do Pháistí* (1949).

Ó Raifteirí, Antoine (?1784–?1835), poet in Irish, was born near Kiltimagh in County Mayo. He was blinded by smallpox at the age of nine and became a travelling fiddler who entertained households and crowds at fairs with his own rather homespun poetry. His patch was the area including Gort, Athenry and Loughrea as well as Mayo, and he responded in verse to local and national events. He was in a sense the last Gaelic poet to write unselfconsciously in his own language. 'Cill Aodáin,' a hymn to spring, is one of the best known and most often quoted poems in modern Irish and 'Eanach Dhúin,' the lament for the drowned in the Corrib tragedy in 1822 shows his vigour and fluency. 'Máire Ní Eidhin', his Beatrice, died shortly after the writing of the poem in her praise, creating for the poet a reputation for bringing ill-luck. His poetry recaptures a lost age, not entirely mournful, and full of a rough vigour that was lost with the Famine years and never totally recovered. His Irish is accessible and it is no surprise that he was one of the poets who was taken as a patron saint of both the Gaelic revival and the Literary Renaissance, cultivated by both Lady Gregory and Douglas Hyde. His most famous poem, 'Mise Raifteirí', is probably not entirely his own work.

Ó Rathaile, Aogán (1675–1729), one of the four great Kerry poets and regarded by many as the greatest of all Gaelic poets, was born at *Screathan a' Mhíl* in the Sliabh Luachra district east of Killarney. He belonged to a family of small landowners that owed fealty to the native chieftains, the MacCarthys. These were supplanted by the Jacobite Brownes. Much of Ó Rathaile's poetry is the mournful cry of the client who fell with the fall of his master. Frank O'Connor*, who translated some of Ó Rathaile's finest work, described him as 'one of the great snobs of literature', and 'Vailintín Brún', written in satirical disparagement of his would-be patron, who failed to restore him to his lands when he himself was reinstated, shows considerable disdain from a beggar. Ó Rathaile was not a nationalist or patriot in the modern sense but longed for the restoration of the Stuart dynasty which would in turn restore a natural and more rightful aristocracy, both Gaelic and old English. 'Gile na Gile' is one of the finest of *aisling** poems. In it Ireland, more beautiful than any woman, is apostrophied and consoled with the hope of a Stuart success. 'Mac an Cheannaí', also much anthologised, is another superb *aisling*. Ó Rathaile combined the highest skills of bardic poetry and the conventions of *aisling* and satire with immense rhythmic power and intensity of personal and political feeling. The sense of degradation and the hardship he suffered are the more poignant because he was conscious of his superior education, obtained at what was the period's equivalent of a university at Killarney. He died in poverty in Corca Dhuibhne in 1729 and is buried with his true patrons the MacCarthys at Muckross Abbey.

O'Reilly, John Boyle (1844–90), poet, was born in Dowth Castle, the son of a schoolmaster, and worked as a printer and journalist in Drogheda before joining the British army in 1863. He was arrested as a Fenian mole and, after much harsh treatment, transported to Australia. He escaped to America and became editor of the *Boston Pilot*, which became a kind of transatlantic *Nation**. He wrote *Moondyne* (1879), a novel about his convict life in Australia, and many patriotic ballads and sentimental love lyrics. One of his poems was quoted by President Kennedy in his address to the Dáil during his Irish visit of 1963. He died of an overdose of chloral taken to cure a cold.

Ó Ríordáin, Seán (1917–77), poet in Irish, was born in Ballyvourney, at that time a gaeltacht area, but moved with his family to Iniscarra, nearer to Cork City, when he was a teenager. He was educated at North Monastery CBS and worked in an administrative capacity for Cork Corporation from 1937. He suffered from ill-health, including the TB which he contracted while still a young man, and retired early from his position in 1965. His first collection, *Eireaball*

Spideoige (1952), broke new ground in Irish poetry with its tone of isolated personal enquiry (often angst), its obsessive search for an authentic language and its broad philosophical speculations married to a deep attachment to the integrity of the Gaelic tradition. Further collections which enhanced Ó Ríordáin's reputation as both a poet and a highly original thinker were *Brosna* (1964), *Línte Liombó* (1976) and *Tar Éis Mo Bháis* (1978), published posthumously. A collected poems, *Scáthán Véarsaí*, was published in 1980. Ó Ríordáin was a major poet; his integrity evidenced by everything he wrote. Seán Ó Tuama*, Professor of Irish at UCC, became a friend and supporter and Ó Ríordáin was appointed to a part-time lectureship in Irish in UCC in 1969, greatly influencing a new generation of poets, among them Michael Davitt*, Nuala Ní Dhomhnaill*, Liam Ó Muirthile* and Gabriel Rosenstock*. He was also a long-standing columnist for the *Irish Times*.

Ormsby, Frank (b. 1947), poet and anthologist, was born in County Fermanagh and studied English at QUB, where he took an MA. He now teaches English at Inst and edits *The Honest Ulsterman*. His collections of poetry include *A Northern Spring* (1993), *A Star of Candles* (1993) and *The Ghost Train* (1995).

Ó Séaghdha, Pádraig (1855–1928), short story writer, novelist and playwright in Irish, was born near Kenmare, County Kerry. His home language was Irish but the educational system of the time meant that he was divorced from his Irish heritage until he reclaimed it for himself as an adult. He entered the British Customs Service as a bright young man and began to write in English under the name 'John Desmond' while stationed in Cardiff. He joined the Gaelic League* when he was posted to Belfast and wrote a column in Irish for *An Claidheamh Soluis* * for several years. Thereafter he wrote in Irish under the pseudonym 'Conán Maol' (one of Fionn Mac Cumhaill's close associates). His published work includes a collection of stories, *Buaiceas* (1903), and novels *Eoghan Paor* (1903) and *Stiana* (1930). His interest in Irish history was reflected in his book on Shane O'Neill, *Seághan an Díomais* (1901), and his play about Hugh O'Neill, *Aodh Ó Néill* (1902).

Ó Sandair, Cathal (b. 1922), children's author in Irish, was born in England of an English father and an Irish mother, and educated in Dublin after the family moved to Ireland. He worked as a civil servant and wrote a great number of formulaic schoolboy's adventures in Irish, featuring Reics Carlo and Réamonn Óg, Captaen Toirneach and Captaen Speirling. They were remarkable for being mass market books and for their – by Irish language standards – vast sales. The first, *Na Mairbh a dh'Fhill*, was published in 1942; *Réics Carlo ar Oileán Mhanann* in 1984. Ó Sandair also published a collection of short stories, *Mo Chara, Mo Namhaid* (1967).

Ó Searcaigh, Cathal (b. 1956), poet in Irish, was born in Gortahork in the County Donegal gaeltacht and educated at NIHE, Limerick and Maynooth University. In his collections, which include *Miontragéide Cathrach* (1975), *Súile Shuibhne* (1983) and An *Bealach 'na Bhaile* (1991), he unites the traditions of the great Irish poets with modern cultural influences and a kind of personal celtic spirituality. Some of his work bears comparison with the best work of the great Irish poets. His work has been translated into English by Seamus Deane*, Gabriel Fitzmaurice* and others. His latest, highly regarded collection, *Na Buachaillí Bána* (1996), treats of sexual themes frankly and in a way that is highly original for the Irish language. *Out in the Open*, an English-language version with translations by Frankie Sewell, was published in 1997.

O'Siadhail, Micheal (b. 1947), poet in Irish and English and scholar, was born in Dublin and educated at TCD and in Oslo. He was lecturer in Irish in TCD and later worked as a researcher and Associate Professor in DIAS until in 1987 he became a full-time writer. He has published several collections of precise, powerful and lucid poems in Irish, including *An Bhliain Bhisigh* (1978), *Runga* (1980) and *Cumann* (1982). His English-language collections include *Springnight* (1983) and *The Chosen Garden* (1990). His most recent collection is *Our Double Time* (1998).

Ó Siochfhradha, Pádraig (An Seabhac) (1883–1964), novelist in Irish, was born in Dingle, County Kerry. He became a teacher and later editor for the Gaelic League*, and was interned during the War of Independence as a Volunteer. After the establishment of the Free State he became a civil servant, then editor for the Educational Company of Ireland, where he produced many textbooks, plays and versions of Irish stories. He is best known for *Jimín* (1921), the hilarious first-person narrative of the mischievous Jimín Mháire Thaidhg, which was enjoyed more than many other Irish texts by generations of schoolgoers until the radical changes in the educational curriculum of the late 1960s and early 1970s. *An Baile Seo' Gainne* (1913), which was also very popular, is a series of gentle, humorous sketches, a sort of *Lake Woebegone* of gaeltacht life.

Ó Snodaigh, Pádraig (b. 1935), poet, critic and publisher in Irish, was born in Carlow and educated locally and at UCD. He was Assistant Keeper of the National Museum from 1963–88. He was President of the Gaelic League* from 1974–79 and chairman of Clódhanna Teo, a Gaelic League* imprint. He is the owner and publisher of Coiscéim, which has been a major force in Irish-language publishing since the 1980s. Among his own writings, *Hidden Ulster* (1973) is a treatment of Northern Ireland involvement in Irish culture and Ó *Pharnell go Queenie* (1991) a novel. His poetry collections include *Cumha agus Cumann* (1985) and *Cúl le Cúl* (1988).

Ó Súilleabháin, Amhlaoibh (1780–1837), diarist, was born in Killarney, County Kerry, but his father, a hedge-schoolmaster, moved the family to Kilkenny. Amhlaoibh became a teacher and also ran a shop in Callan after his marriage. His *Cín Lae* is the first known autobiographical writing in Irish, a lively mixture of reflection, observation and social commentary by a man who had read widely in English and Irish. A selection from this very lengthy work was edited by Tomás de Bhaldraithe* as *Cín Lae Amhlaoibh* (1970) and translated by the same author as *The Diary of Humphrey O'Sullivan* (1979).

Ó Súilleabháin, Eoghan Rua (1748–84), poet in Irish, was born at Meentogues, eight miles east of Killarney* in County Kerry. He was the archetypal roistering poet, amorous, hard-drinking, generous-hearted and so talented that he was known for years after his death as 'Eoghan an Bhéil Bhinn' [Eoghan of the sweet mouth]. His name was, until the advent of television and other mass media, frequently on the lips of the people of Sliabh Luachra, usually in connection with apocryphal stories in which he got the better of landords, priests, schoolmasters and other people of pretension. He is a kind of Irish Burns except that life for a Gaelic poet in Ireland was much grimmer than for the society pet of Edinburgh, however much Burns may have sold himself as a simple plowman. Ó Súilleabháin studied at a bardic school at Faha, west of Killarney, where poetry, music and the classics were taught, and when he was eighteen set up his own school at Gneeveguilla.This respectability did not last and he took to the roads as a *spailpín*. He spent the next decade labouring, writing poetry, school-mastering and acting as tutor to a Fermoy family called Nagle, a post which ended when he was discovered in dalliance with Mrs Nagle. He joined the British navy and served with Rodney in the West Indies, in celebration of which he wrote a piece of doggerel in English called 'Rodney's Glory.' When he left the navy he became a soldier. It was during this period of military service that he wrote his most famous aisling*, 'Ceo Draíochta', and it is for aislingí such as this and 'Ag Taisteal na Blárnan' that he is most celebrated. He was discharged from the army on medical grounds (self-inflicted sores) and returned home to his beloved Sliabh Luachra in 1784. He opened a school at Knocknagree, offering a wide range of subjects from the Classics to Mathematics – all to be taught by himself – but died soon afterwards of fever caused by injuries inflicted in Killarney by the servants of a landowner whom he had satirised. He was one of the greatest poets of the Jacobite eighteenth century and is one of the four great Kerry poets commemorated in Killarney.

Ó Súilleabháin, Muiris (1904–50), autobiographer in Irish, was born on the Great Blasket, one of the Blasket Islands* but reared until the age of seven in an orphanage in Dingle after the death of his mother. His father brought him back to the island and he lived there until he joined the Garda Síochána (police force) and moved to Dublin. He was stationed in Indreabhán in the Connemara gaeltacht and there wrote his classic autobiography, *Fiche Blian ag Fás**(1933), which was translated into English by his mentor, the scholar George Thomson, and Moya Llewelyn Davies and published in the same year under the title *Twenty Years A-Growing*. Ó Súilleabháin wrote a second volume of memoirs, *Fiche Blian Faoi Bhláth*, which was never published. He died, tragically young, while bathing in Galway.

Ó Súilleabháin, Seán (1903–96), folklorist and writer, was born in Tuosist in County Kerry and worked as a primary schoolteacher before joining the Irish Folklore Commission* in 1935. He was one of the most celebrated of Irish folklorists for many decades. His published work includes *A Handbook of Irish Folklore* (1942) and *Caitheamh Aimsire at Thórraimh* (1964), published in English as *Irish Wake Amusements* (1967)

Ó Súilleabháin, Tadgh Gaelach (1715–1915), poet in Irish, was born near Drumcollogher in County Limerick. He was a light-hearted wanderer about south Munster, writing occasional political verse of a pro-Jacobite nature that earned him a spell in Cork gaol. In middle age he settled in Dungarvan, County Waterford and as a result of a sudden religious conversation wrote mainly confessional poetry. His 'dánta diaga' (religious poems) were published in 1802 as *Timothy*

O'Sullivan's Irish Pious Miscellany with the support of Dr Coyle, the Bishop of Raphoe. The book was reprinted forty times and the poems set to folk-tunes, were sung as hymns in church throughout the nineteenth century. 'Duan Chroí Íosa' is his best known religious poem.

O'Sullivan, Seumas (pseudonym of James Starkey) (1879–1958), poet and editor, was born in Dublin and educated mainly at home, becoming apprenticed to his pharmacist father. He was a minor figure of the Irish Literary Revival*, producing several books of verse. *The Earth-Lover* (1909) contains unforgettable pictures of the city, including the famous 'A Piper'. He founded the *Dublin Magazine** (1923–58) which complemented the *Irish Statesman* and *The Bell** in forming the main cultural outlet for the new state. His collections of essays include *Essays and Recollections* (1944) and *The Rose and the Bottle* (1946).

Ó Tuairisc, Eoghan (aka Eugene Watters) (1919–82), poet and novelist, was born in Ballinasloe, County Galway, educated at Garbally and served as an officer in the army (1939–45). He trained as a teacher at St Patrick's College, Drumcondra, after the Emergency, and taught in Dublin until 1961 when he became a full-time writer, travelling the country in a horse-drawn caravan with his wife, the artist Una McDonnell. *L'Attaque** (1962), his first significant work, a novel written in Irish and set in County Mayo during the 1798 Rising, was followed by *The Weekend of*

Dermot and Grace (1964), a long poem based on the epic *Tóraigheacht Dhiarmada agus Ghráinne* and dealing with modern pursuers of lovers. Ó Tuairisc's wife died suddenly in 1965 while he was working on *Dé Luain* (1966), a novel about Easter Week, and for a number of years afterwards he was unable to work, living in isolation in rural Leinster. In 1972 he married Rita Kelly and together they produced a sizeable body of work, including a joint poetry collection, *Dialann sa Díseart* (1981), a play about Pearse*, *Fornocht do Chonac* (1981), and *The Road to Bright City* (1981), brilliant translations of early short stories by Mairtín Ó Cadhain.

Ó Tuama, Seán (?1707–75), poet in Irish, known as Seán 'an Ghrinn' [of the fun], was born near Kilmallock County Limerick in 1707. He was briefly a schoolteacher and then kept an inn at Mungret Gate in Croom at which all poets were said to have been served without charge. Seán Clárach Mac Domhnaill, Aindrias Mac Craith and he comprised the school known as *Filí na Máighe* [poets of the Maigue valley]. It was he who gathered the southern poets together on the death of their leader Seán Clárach in 1754 to see how both poetry and the Irish language should be preserved. An ardent Jacobite like other Gaelic poets of his time, Ó Tuama is now best known for 'A Chuisle na hÉigse', which ardently anticipates the return of the Stuarts and the support they will receive from all the Gaelic poets. Ó Tuama's concerns and hospitality cost him his livelihood and he experienced periods of financial hardship.

He died in Mungret, County Limerick and was buried in Croom.

Ó Tuama, Seán (b. 1926), poet in Irish, playwright and critic, was born in Cork and educated at UCC, where he was taught by Daniel Corkery*. He became Professor of Modern Irish at UCC and an influential teacher and apologist for the Irish language. His anthology *Nuabhéarsaíocht* (1950) recognised the quality of rising Irish poets such as Seán Ó Riordáin*, Máirtín Ó Díreáin* and Máire Mhac an tSaoi*. In 1960 he published a major scholarly work, *An Grá in Amhráin na nDaoine*, in which he studied the traditional love poetry of the ordinary people as both a French and an Irish phenomenon. He subsequently produced *An Grá i bhFilíocht na nUaisle* (1988) and *Cúirt, Tuath agus Bruachbhaile* (1991). A collection of essays in English were published as *Repossessions: Selected Essays on the Irish Literary Heritage* (1995). He has also published several volumes of poetry, including *An Bás i dTír na nÓg* (1988) and plays such as *Gunna Cam agus Slabhra Óir* (1969). He collaborated with Thomas Kinsella* on *An Duanaire 1600–1900: Poems of the Dispossessed* (1981). *Death in the Land of Youth*, a *Selected Poems* with versions in English by the poet and by Peter Denman, was published in 1997.

Ó hUid, Tarlach (1917–90), novelist, poet and journalist in Irish, was born in London. Although his background was unionist he learned Irish and was interned in Northern Ireland during WWII as a member of the IRA. He later became disenchanted with violent Republicanism. *Ar Thóir Mo Shealbha* (1960) and *Faoi Ghlas* (1985) are autobiographical works and he also published several novels, including the historical *An Bealach chun a' Bhearnais* (1949) and *An Dá Thrá* (1952), as well as novels for teenagers and short stories. *Rachtanna* (1975) is a collection of poems. He worked as an Irish-language journalist and became editor of *Inniu*, the Irish-language weekly, in 1979.

Ó hUiginn, Tadhg Dall (1550–91) poet in Irish, was born in County Sligo, a member of the famous Ó hUiginn family of bards or hereditary poets, whose traditional patrons were the Ó Conchobhair family of Sligo. Tadhg Dall, blind as his name suggests, had several patron families among the Gaelic aristocracy of the region, including the Burkes, the O'Rourkes and the O'Haras. His poetry is mostly of the conventional bardic type, written in praise of his patrons and urging them on to heroic feats of arms against one another or against the English, but very fine of its kind, lucid and sophisticated. Tadhg Dall settled in some style with his family near his home place of Leyney in County Sligo. There, it is said, members of the O'Hara family killed him, his wife and child in revenge for his having satirised them in a poem: 'six men of the O'Haras', he alleged, had come and eaten all the food and drink in the house.

P

Park, David (b. 1954), fiction writer, was born and educated in Belfast and now teaches in County Down, the background of his novel *The Rye Man* (1994), about a man returning to his old primary school as principal and his involvement with a retarded pupil. *The Healing* (1992) is an unusually sensitive novel about people caught up in the Ulster violence, while *Oranges from Spain* (1990) is a collection of variegated stories with the same horrific background. His most recent work is *Stone Kingdoms* (1996).

Parker, Stewart (1941–88), playwright, was born in Belfast and educated at QUB where he was a member of Philip Hobsbaum's poetry discussion group. He taught for some years before becoming a professional playwright. His work, though often very funny and punctuated by popular song – sometimes misheard, as in *I'm a Dreamer, Montreal* (1979) – is fundamentally serious about the need for the positive living of life. *Spokesong* (1974), about love, bicycles and the Northern Troubles, the hit of the 1975 Dublin Theatre Festival, was followed by *Catchpenny Twist* (1977), about two Belfast teachers who try to bridge the sectarian divide by writing political ballads for both sides and meet an appropriate fate. *Northern Star** (1985), a pastiche tour de force about the United Irishman Henry Joy Mc Cracken, was succeeded by the much grimmer *Pentecost* (1987), which was written for Field Day* and set in Belfast during the 1974 UWC strike. Parker wrote much for television, including *The Kamikaze Ground Staff Reunion Dinner* (1980). His premature death from cancer led to the establishment of the Stewart Parker Trust and Award to encourage young Irish playwrights.

Patrick, St (d. ?493), missionary and patron of Ireland, was born probably on the Severn shore of Roman Britain, the son of a deacon. Tradition has it that his six-year period as a slave in Ireland convinced him of a religious vocation and that, having been trained for the priesthood by St Germanus of Auxerre (*c.* 378–*c.* 448), he asked to be sent back to the Celtic island as a Christian missionary. He was instrumental in setting up ecclesiastical structures that survived, with effective acculturation of druidical practices. Patrick's extant work consists of *Epistola ad Milites Coritici*, an admonition against the soldiers of the British prince Coroticus who had attacked some of Patrick's followers, and *Confessio*, his account of his own life and failings.

Patterson, Glenn (b. 1961), novelist, was born in Belfast and educated at QUB. *Burning Your Own* (1988) describes the cataclysmic events of August 1969 as seen from the perspective of an eleven-year-old Protestant misfit. *Fat Lad* (1992) is a Protestant acronym of the six counties – Nationalists would never accept the 'L' of Londonerry – and the book is steeped in the Northern Troubles, in spite of which the author has returned to Ireland to be writer-in-residence at various campuses. His most recent novel is *Black Night at Big Thunder Mountain* (1995).

Paulin, Tom (b. 1949), poet, playwright and critic, born in Leeds but brought up in Belfast, was educated at Hull and Lincoln College, Oxford. He is a director of Field Day*, for which he wrote *Riot Act* (1985), a version of Sophocles's *Antigone* (441BC) and a pamphlet 'A New Look at the Language Question' (1983). He has also written *Seize the Fire* (1990), a version of Aeschylus's *Prometheus Bound* (456BC). His poetry, which includes *A State of Justice* (1977), *Liberty Tree* (1983), *Fivemiletown* (1987) and *Walking a Line* (1994), has won several awards. His criticism has been collected in *Ireland and the English Crisis* (1984). His most recent work is *Day-Star of Liberty: William Hazlitt's Radical Style* (1998).

Pearse, Patrick H[enry] (1879–1916), poet and revolutionary, was born in Dublin and educated at Westland Row CBS, the Royal University and the King's Inns. He joined the Gaelic League* in 1896 and became the editor of *An Claideamh Soluis** (1903-9) before resigning to work full-time in Scoil Éanna, the bilingual school based upon his own educational theories, that he had founded the previous year. He was one of the founders of the Irish Volunteers in 1913 and a member of the IRB, and became President of the Provisional Government and leader of the Easter Rising*. He was executed by firing-squad in Kilmainham on 3 May 1916. Political and educational writings occupied him most, but he found time to write stories, poems and plays in English and Irish. Of his English poems, 'The Mother', 'I Am Ireland', 'Renunciation', 'The Fool' and 'The Wayfarer' (written on the day before his death) are the best known. His play *The Singer* (1915) is about his self-fulfilling prophecy of the blood sacrifice which obsessed him. *Iosagán agus Sgéalta Eile* (1907) and *An Mháthair agus Sgéalta Eile* (1916) are collections of stories, while *Suantraidhe agus Goltraidhe* (1914) contains his poems in Irish, some of which are versions of his English poems.

Petrie, George (1790–1866) archaeologist and scholar, was born in Dublin and educated at the RDS Art School. His conversion to a passionate interest in Irish antiquities dated from his travels as a illustrator of guide books, when he became acquainted with some of the great archaeological treasures of the country. In 1833, the year of publication of his *Essays on the Round Towers of Ireland*, he was employed by the Ordnance Topographical Survey, along with John O'Donovan and Eugene O'Curry*. When funding for this work ceased in 1841 he continued to strive for the preservation of relics of ancient life, writing of Irish antiquities in *The Dublin Penny Journal* and later in *The Irish Penny Journal*. To him must be given credit for the preservation of manuscripts like *The Annals of the Four Masters** and such treasures as The Cross of Cong in museums and public institutions in Ireland.

Philibín, An (pseudonym of John Hackett Pollock) (1887–1964), novelist, was born in Dublin and qualified as a pathologist at the Royal University, where his reports were models of elegance. He was briefly a Benedictine postulant at Buckfast Abbey in Devon but returned to the Richmond Hospital. He wrote nineteen novels using his pseudonym (meaning 'The Plover') including *The Valley of the Wild Swans* (1932), about middle-class Dublin in 1916, and *The Last Nightingale* (1951), about John Dowland (1563-1626) the lutenist and madrigal composer. *The Moth and the Star* (1937) tells the story of Sarah Curran's sister Amelia.

PIKE THEATRE, THE, founded in Dublin by Alan Simpson (b. 1921) and Carolyn Swift in 1953. Though not comparable in size to the Abbey* or the Gate*, it was to have a major influence on Irish theatre. Behan*'s *The Quare Fellow** was premièred there in 1954, and the following year, simultaneously with the Arts Theatre in London, the Pike presented the English language première

of Beckett*'s *Waiting for Godot**.

Playboy of the Western World, The (1907), Synge*'s best known play, about the effect on a County Mayo village of a blustering, eloquent Munster stranger who has killed his bullying father. His 'gallous deed' is treated as heroism and he becomes a 'playboy', fêted by men and women alike. His betrothal to Pegeen Mike, the desirable daughter of the local merchant, whom he has wooed with high talk and physical feats, is interrupted when his father, with heavily bandaged head, appears to seek his son. The people turn on him but he rejects the offer of escape by the Widow Quin, who understands his true nature, and he leaves to travel the roads with a tamed father. The plays ends with Pegeen's lament, 'I've lost the only Playboy of the Western World.' The romantic language (partly inspired by Hyde*'s translation of *The Love Songs of Connacht* in 1893) and the suggestion of amorality and unruliness among decent Irish peasantry caused its first performances at the Abbey* to be picketed by Nationalists and members of the Gaelic League*.

Plough and the Stars, The (1926), Sean O'Casey*'s anti-heroic play about slum life in Dublin around the time of the Easter Rising* of 1916. The play's realistic account of the reaction of the urban majority to the events, including looting and jeering at the Volunteer prisoners, and the character of Rosie Redmond, a prostitute, caused a famous

Abbey* riot. Jack Clitheroe, a Volunteer, and his new wife Nora share a tenement with a rich collection of characters, including the Covey, a slogan-repeating socialist, Bessie Burgess, a Protestant whose son is fighting in France, Fluther Good, Mrs Gogan and her consumptive daughter Mollser. Jack is strongly influenced by a speech given by the 'Man' (heard off-stage) calling for blood sacrifice, and is killed during the fighting, trying to drag the demented and miscarried Nora away from the window. As usual with O'Casey, the leads are unconvincing, the love-talk of Clitheroe contrived, and the song derived from the Edwardian ballad 'When You and I Were Young' excruciating. The play's richness lies in the tenement characters, their exuberant speech and curious optimism.

Plunkett, Sir Horace (1845–1932), social reformer, was born in Gloucester, son of Lord Dunsany, and educated at Eton and University College, Oxford. Having spent time ranching in Wyoming to improve his health, he returned to Ireland in 1888. Dismayed by the poor state of agriculture, in 1894 he set up the Irish Agricultural Organisation Society (IAOS) which helped to change the attitudes of the new Irish farmers. He appointed Æ* as organiser and editor of the society's journal, the *Irish Homestead*. His book *Ireland in the New Century* (1904) was critical of certain aspects of the Catholic Church's influence in Ireland. He was a Unionist MP for Dublin and appointed a senator of the Free State, but after the burning of his house by Repub-licans in 1923 he left Ireland for good. He died in Weymouth in Dorset.

Plunkett, James (b. 1920), fiction writer, was born J. P. Kelly in Sandymount, Dublin, and educated in Synge Street and at the College of Music. After a clerkship in the Gas Company he became a trade unionist, working for Jim Larkin, whose career he dramatised in *The Risen People* (1958). He was one of the writers who received encouragement from Sean O'Faolain*, contributing the script of *Homecoming*, a radio play (June 1954), and thirteen stories to *The Bell**, the edition of October 1954 containing a novella and four stories. These were later published as *The Trusting and the Maimed* (1955). Plunkett was one of a group of Irish writers who visited Russia in 1955 (described in his 1990 novel *The Circus Animals*) and a number of Catholic activists called for his resignation from the Workers' Union of Ireland. Though the Union stood firm, he resigned and joined Radio Éireann, later becoming one of the first producers for the new television network. Plunkett is best known for his Dublin trilogy: *Strumpet City* (1969) – the title borrowed from Denis Johnston*'s play *The Old Lady Says 'No!'** – *Farewell Companions* (1977) and *The Circus Animals*. These novels give an account of the changing fortunes of the city, from the drama days of the 1912 Lockout to the mean-minded 1950s. He has also written *The Gems She Wore* (1972), a fascinating literary travel book, and a collection of essays, *The Boy on the Back Wall* (1987). His *Collected Short Stories* was published in 1977.

Plunkett, Joseph Mary (1887–1916), poet and revolutionary, was born in Dublin and educated at Belvedere, Stonyhurst and UCD. Of poor health, he spent much time abroad, living in Mediterranean countries including Algeria. He returned to Ireland in 1911 and helped Thomas MacDonagh* edit the *Irish Review* and Edward Martyn run the Irish Literary Theatre*. Having joined the Irish Volunteers and the IRB, he was sent with Roger Casement to Germany in 1915 seeking arms for the planned rising. He was a signatory of the Proclamation of the Irish Republic and was executed on 4 May 1916 in Kilmainham, having married Grace Gifford on the eve of his execution. His poetry is in two volumes: *The Circle and the Sword* (1911), showing Arabic influences, and the posthumous *Poems* (1916). He is best known for the much-anthologised pieces 'I See His Blood upon the Rose' and 'My Lady Has the Grace of Death'.

Portora Royal school, Enniskillen, founded by James I in 1608 and having among its pupils Samuel Beckett*, Henry Francis Lyte (1793–1847), author of 'Abide with Me', and Oscar Wilde*.

Portrait of the Artist as a Young Man, A (1916), James Joyce*'s fictionalised spiritual autobiography, describing his childhood, schooldays, consideration of a vocation to the priesthood, discovery of sex with prostitutes, Thomistic disputations with staff and fellow undergraduates at the Royal University, rejection of family and Ireland ('the old sow that eats her farrow'), personal aesthetic to be attained by 'silence, exile and cunning', and assorted 'epiphanies' including the girl on Sandymount Strand: '– Heavenly God! cried Stephen's soul, in an outburst of profane joy.' The total seriousness of the book suggests that the reader may supply his own ironies.

Power, M[aurice] S. (b. 1935), novelist, was born in Dublin and educated in Ireland and France. He was a television producer in America before settling in England. He has written at least thirteen novels, all dealing with mental aberration in some form, usually psychosis. The best known form a trilogy about the Northern Troubles and the machinations of the IRA and the British army, which was called in the television version *Children of the North* (1985), a theme recapitulated in *Come the Executioner* (1991). *The Crucifixion of Septimus Roache* (1989), about the torture of a turbulent priest in Haiti, is strangely lighter than *Bridie and the Silver Lady* (1988), which is about murder, incest and psychiatry in an Irish village. *Skating round the Poppy* (1992) describes the career of a serial killer who was abused as a child, while *Dealing with Kranze* (1996) describes a cat-and-mouse game between Walwyn, a convicted crook, his evil genius Zanker (an anagram of the Kranze of the title) and an Inspector Birt. As with *Septimus Roache*, its preoccupations are less stygian than Power's usual work.

Power, Richard (1928–70), novelist, was born in Dublin and joined the civil service in 1945. He took leave to live in

Aran and improve his Irish, a period which produced *Úll i mBarr an Ghéagáin* (1959) – translated by the author's brother as *Apple on the Treetop* (1980) – a book of autobiography, and *The Land of Youth* (1966), a turn-of-the-century novel set in the islands. *The Hungry Grass* (1969) is a warts-and-all portrait of an Irish priest.

Power, Tyrone (1797–1841), actor and playwright, was born near Kilmacthomas in County Waterford, the son of a strolling player. He had service in both the army and navy before becoming an actor in 1815. His true métier was discovered when he was called upon to play a comic Irish role in 1826 and he soon became *the* stage-Irishman in the many parts available, from Teague in Farquhar*'s *The Twin-Rivals* (1707) to Sir Lucius O'Trigger in Sheridan*'s *The Rivals* (1774). He became very rich in other men's work and turned to authorship himself, producing such comedies as *St Patrick's Eve* (1832), *Paddy Cary, the Boy of Clogheen* (1833) and *O'Flannigan and the Fairies* (1836), in which he took the lead. He was a regular visitor to Dublin, appearing to great acclaim at the Theatre Royal, and was lost returning from his third visit to America when the SS *President* sank. He was the great-grandfather of the film actor Tyrone Power (1913-58).

Praeger, Robert Lloyd (1865–1953), naturalist, was born in Holywood, County Down, the son of a Dutch linen merchant. He was educated at Inst and QUB, and worked as a civil engineer before joining the staff of the National Library in 1893, becoming Chief Librarian in 1920 but retiring on full pension in 1924, making Belfast again his base. He published many works on Irish flora, fauna and landscape. His book *The Way That I Went* (1947) is an Irish travel journal of great interest. He was made first President of the National Trust in 1948.

Prút, Liam (b. 1940), poet, critic and prose writer in Irish, was born in Ballinderry, County Tipperary. He trained as a primary teacher and also worked in the translation service of Dáil Éireann (Irish parliament). He has published six collections of poetry, *Fíon as Seithí Óir* (1972), *Asail* (1982), *An Dá Scór* (1984), *An Giotár Meisce* (1988), *Loch Deirg-Dheirc* (1994) and *Plumaí* (1997). He has also published novels, including *Geineasas* (1991) and *An Leanbh sa Lamborghini* (1996), a collection of short stories, *Sean-Dair agus Scéalta Eile* (1985), and a critical study of Máirtín Ó Direáin* (1982).

Purcell, Deirdre (b. 1945) was born in Dublin and educated there and in Mayo. She became a member of the Abbey Theatre* company and in 1968 she went to Loyola University, Chicago, as actress in residence. She began writing for the *Irish Press* in 1983, then spent seven years with the *Sunday Tribune*, with which she won the two most prestigious awards in Irish journalism, the Benson and Hedges Award and the Cross Award. She is the very successful author of a number of well-constructed and accomplished novels, including *A Place of Stones* (1991), *That Childhood Country* (1992), *Sky* (1995) and *Like, Love, Hate, Adore* (1997).

Pygmalion (1914), Shaw*'s best known play because of the success of the musical *My Fair Lady* (1954) derived from it by Lerner and Loewe. It is a modern version of the story of the Cypriot king who fell in love with a statue he had created and to which Aphrodite gave life as Galataea. Henry Higgins, a phoneticist, wins a bet that it is only speech that prevents a personable woman of any class from being taken for a duchess. (The idea probably came from the effect of Shaw's own elegant Dublin accent.) The imposture succeeds but at great cost to Eliza Doolittle, the Cockney flower-girl who is declassed. The other great character, apart from the bustlingly offensive Higgins, is Eliza's father Alfred Doolittle who as 'one of the undeserving poor' is punished by becoming a millionaire. The sentimental contra-Shavian ending of the musical play is its only weakness.

Q

Quare Fellow, The (1954), Brendan Behan's genuinely humorous play about prison life and the convicts' reactions to the execution of a prisoner, 'Silver-top', who has killed his wife. Warder Regan is compassionate and abolitionist but the prisoners, especially the recidivists, are sanguinely ribald about this and all other aspects of prison life. It was first performed in Dublin's Pike Theatre*.

Querist, The (1735–7, 1750), a series of 900 questions posed, at first anonymously, by Bishop Berkeley* of Cloyne, mainly about the social and economic conditions in the Ireland of his day, largely epigrammatic and inevitably satiric: 'Whether there be upon earth any Christian or civilised people so beggarly wretched and destitute as the Irish?'

R

Rann (1948–53), a poetry quarterly edited by Roy McFadden* and Barbara Edwards. About the middle of its career it allowed odd bits of prose and reviews. Its concluding number contained a useful mini-dictionary of Ulster writers, compiled by John Boyd*

RATHLIN ISLAND, five miles from Ballycastle, County Antrim, was in 719 the first part of Ireland to be attacked by Vikings. It was the scene of the mythic encounter of Robert the Bruce and the spider in 1306, and of the slaughter of the MacDonnells by Elizabeth I's forces in 1597. Michael McLaverty*, who knew the island well, set part of his novels *Call My Brother Back** and *Truth in the Night* (1951) and several of his short stories there.

Reid, Christina (b. 1942), playwright, was born in Belfast and educated at Girls' Model and QUB. Her play *Did You Hear the One about the Irishman . . . ?* (1983) is a kind of Troubles *Romeo and Juliet.* After *Tea in a China Shop* (1980), about the responsibility of women in preserving common decencies in a violent macho community, she became writer-in-residence at the Lyric Theatre*. Most of her work, including *The Belle of Belfast City* (1987), *Joyriders* (1986) and *My Name, Shall I Tell You My Name?* (1989), deals with the situation of women and young people in the troubled inner city but she has also written versions of *Les Misérables* and Mervyn Wall*'s *The Unfortunate Fursey* (1989).

Reid, Forrest (1875–1947), novelist, was born in Belfast and educated at Inst and Christ's College, Cambridge, where he became friendly with E. M. Forster (1879–1970). He returned to Belfast where he lived for the rest of his life. He wrote fifteen books, mainly about adolescent boys, and his work is noted for its style and its rejection of the normal Ulster values of business success. His best known work is the novel *Peter Waring* (1937), about a teacher's son's upbringing in County Down and his rough Belfast relations, while the last volume of the Tom Barber trilogy – *Uncle Stephen* (1931), *The Retreat* (1936) and *Young Tom* (1944) - won the James Tait Black Memorial Prize. His autobiography, *Apostate* (1926), describes a childhood in an almost rural Belfast, while its sequel, *Private Road* (1940), contains an account of his Cambridge years.

Reid, Graham (b. 1945), playwright, was born in working-class Protestant Belfast and after casual work, unemployment and a spell in the British army, graduated as a mature student from QUB. He taught history until 1980 when the success of his plays encouraged him to become a full-time writer. His work is steeped in the Northern Troubles and their impact on the families who suffer mostly keenly from their violence. *The Death of Humpty Dumpty* (1979) and *The Closed Door* (1980) underline the common inheritance of cruelty and cowardice, though *Remembrance* (1984), about the common ground found, in spite of the bleak disapproval of their warring families, between a Protestant man and a Catholic woman, both of whom have lost sons in the violence, has flickering elements of the need for reconciliation. *The Hidden Curriculum* (1982), based upon Reid's own classroom experiences, considers the effect of the times upon older students. The *Billy* trilogy of television plays (1982, 1983, 1984) about the Martin family, which established Kenneth Branagh as an actor of consequence, remains Reid's most representative work.

Reid, Mayne (pseudonym of Thomas Mayne) (1818–83), writer of children's fiction, was born in Ballyroney, County Down, and educated for the Presbyterian ministry. He settled in America in 1840, having run away to sea, taking a series of typical frontier jobs: storekeeper, teacher, hunter and Indian fighter. He fought as a captain in the Mexican War, being seriously wounded in 1847. Returning to England in 1848, he wrote seventy exciting adventure stories characterised by an unobtrusive but real moral element and authentic backgrounds, which covered locations as far apart as the Rockies and the Himalayas. He was probably the originator of Wild West fiction and his titles speak for themselves: *Rifle-Rangers* (1850), *The Headless Horseman* (1866), *Castaways* (1870). The novel *The Quadroon* (1856), based upon his experiences as a slave-overseer, was the source of *The Octoroon* (1859), the most famous of Boucicault*'s non-Irish plays.

Rising of the Moon, The (1907), a play by Lady Gregory*, first presented on 9 March in the Abbey*, describes the conversation between an RIC sergeant and a rebel, who in the guise of a ragged ballad-monger sits on the very barrel where his 'wanted' poster is displayed. The sergeant allows the rebel to escape and foregoes the £100 reward because the man recalls to him his youthful nationalistic ideals

Robinson, [Esmé Stuart] Lennox (1886–1958), playwright and theatre manager, was born in Douglas, County Cork, and educated intermittently, for reasons of health, at Bandon Grammar School. In spite of fervent Nationalism, caught when the Abbey* company played *The Rising of the Moon** in the Cork Opera House in 1907, he remained, as he wrote in *The Bell** in June 1944, 'a hopeless case from the Catholic point of view'. As manager of the Abbey he decided in May 1910 not to close the theatre when Edward VII died and thus helped speed Miss Horniman* on her way back to Manchester for good. His novel *A Young Man from the South* (1916) is a witty, semi-autobiographical account of literary life in pre-1916 Dublin, but it is as a prolific playwright who could handle realistic drama, light comedies, Ibsenite exposure of provincial mores, and fantasy with equal skill that he is remembered. His work includes *The Clancy Name* (1908), about the prevalence of respectability over common sense, *The Lost Leader* (1918), about Parnell, *The Whiteheaded Boy* (1916), his most popular play, about light-hearted small-town intrigue, *Drama at Inish**, and two plays about the Ascendancy class, *The Big House* (1926) and *Killycreggs in Twilight* (1937). He joined the Carnegie Trust as Organising Librarian in 1915 but returned to the Abbey in 1919 and became a director in 1923. His *Ireland's Abbey Theatre, 1899–1951* (1951) is a useful, matter-of-fact history.

Roche, Billy (b. 1949), novelist and playwright, was born in Wexford and educated locally before working as barman, factory hand and builder's labourer, afterwards working the London clubs as a singer. His novel *Tumbling Down* (1986), based on his experiences working in his father's pub, describes a teenager's year in Wexford. The *Wexford Trilogy* incorporates *A Handful of Stars* (1988), *Poor Beast in the Rain* (1989) and *Belfry* (1991), three distinct plays in character and plot, a trilogy only in that they each portray different aspects of small-town meanness, frustration and longing to be

away, and the persistent but fraying *machismo* of the unsophisticated Irish male. Other work includes *Amphibians* (1992), *Trojan Eddie* (1997) and *Haberdashery* (1998). His first film, *Trojan Eddie*, was screened in 1996.

Rodgers, W[illiam] R[obert] (1909–69), poet, was born in Belfast into a strict Presbyterian family which he magically evoked in his often-repeated radio feature *The Return Room* (1955). He was educated at QUB and Assembly College and called as minister to the parish of Loughgall, near Armagh. He began broadcasting talks on Radio Éireann and in 1945 Louis MacNeice* recruited him for the famous Features Department of the BBC in London. One result was a series of *Irish Literary Portraits* (1947-65) on such writers as Yeats*, Synge*, Shaw* and many others. Rodgers went to America in 1966 and was writer-in-residence and teacher in several campuses. His poetry, in which sensuality and asceticism, the Bible and the ancient classics clash to produce marvellous, troubled statements, was published in *Awake! and Other Poems* (1941), *Europa and the Bull* (1952) and *Collected Poems* (1971).

Rolleston, T[homas] W[illiam] (1857–1920), poet, was born in Shinrone, County Offaly, and educated at St Columba's College, at TCD and in Germany. He was founding editor of the *Dublin University Review*, compiler of *Poems and Ballads of Young Ireland* (1888) and secretary of the influential Irish Literary Society in London (1892).

In January 1896 he suggested in the Press Club that 'Irish was an inadequate instrument for the expression of contemporary thought' but when Hyde successfully translated a piece picked by him from a scientific journal he became a member of the Gaelic League*. When he translated Tórna*'s versions of the stories in Moore*'s *The Untilled Field* back into English, Moore, with characteristically feline charm, said they were the better for their bath in Gaelic. Rolleston was an authority on German literature and became German editor for the newly founded *Times Literary Supplement*. His poetry, including the much-anthologised 'The Dead at Clonmacnoise', is contained in *Sea Spray: Verses and Translations* (1909). His prose works include *The High Deeds of Finn* (1910) and *Myths and Legends of the Celtic Race* (1911).

Ronan, Frank (b. 1963), novelist and short story writer, was born in County Wexford. His novels include the award-winning *The Man Who Loved Evelyn Cotton* (1989) and Lovely (1996). *Handsome Men Are Slightly Sunburnt* is a collection of short stories.

Ros, Amanda McKittrick (1860–1939), novelist, was born in Drumaness near Ballynahinch, County Down, became a teacher and married the stationmaster at Larne, County Antrim, Andrew Ross. She is famous for her oddly phrased romances, *Irene Iddlesleigh* (1897) and *Delina Delaney* (1898), which elevated bathos to high art. Her verse in *Poems of Puncture* (1913) and *Fumes of Formation* (1933) adds surreal vituperation against her favourite targets, lawyers ('Mickey Monkeyface McBlear') and critics, but she also wrote occasional poems, as in 'On Visiting Westminster Abbey' which begins: 'Holy Moses! Take a look!/Flesh decayed in every nook,/Some rare bits of brain lie here,/Mortal loads of beef and beer.' Her work exercised an appalling fascination on such writers as Aldous Huxley and Louis MacNeice*, who started a Ros cult.

Rosenstock, Gabriel (b. 1949), poet in Irish and translator, was born in Kilfinane, Country Limerick, and educated at UCC where he was associated with the *Innti* group of poets, including Michael Davitt*, Liam Ó Muirthile* and Nuala Ní Dhomhnaill*. A former Chairman of Poetry Ireland, he has published ten collections of poetry, the latest being *Rogha Rosenstock* (1994). He is also author of eleven volumes of translations into Irish, including work of Seamus Heaney*, W. B. Yeats*, George Trakl, Gunter Grass, and Peter Huchel. He works for the Irish language publisher, An Gúm*, in Dublin.

Rowley, Richard (pseudonym of Richard Valentine Williams) (1877–1947), poet, playwright and publisher, was born in Belfast and managed the family cotton handkerchief firm until it collapsed in 1931. He then became Chairman of the Assistance Board and in 1943 founded the Mourne Press which published his own work and the short stories of Michael McLaverty* and Sam Hanna Bell*. His poetry about 'ordinary

Ulster folk' was published in *The City of Refuge* (1917) and *Ballads of Mourne* (1940), and his verse-play *Apollo in Mourne* (1944) describes the effect of the high-spoken Olympian on County Down peasants.

Ryan, James was born in County Laois and educated at TCD. He is a teacher at a Dublin comprehensive school. He has published two well-received novels, *Home from England* (1995) and *Dismantling Mr Doyle* (1997).

S

Sáirséal agus Dill (estd. 1945), Irish-language publishing house established by Seán Ó hEigeartaigh and his wife Bríd Ní Mhaoileoin to promote literary writing in Irish. *Nuabhéarsaíocht 1939–49*, edited by Seán Ó Tuama* in 1950, and *Nuascéalaíocht*, edited by Tomás de Bhaldraithe* in 1952, were ground-breaking anthologies, the former poetry, the latter short stories. The imprint subsequently published the leading Irish writers of the day, including Máirtín Ó Cadhain and Máirtín Ó Díreáin. Bought by Caoimhín Ó Marcaigh in 1981, the company became known as Sáirséal Ó Marcaigh.

Sayers, Peig (1873–1958), autobiographer in Irish, was born in Dunquin, County Kerry. As she describes in her own account, *Peig*, she went into service in Dunquin as a young. girl, then lived much of her life on the Great Blasket* after her marriage to islander Pádraig Ó Gaoithín. She bore ten children, only five of whom survived, most to emigrate to the United States, and was widowed while still a fairly young woman. She became famous as a storyteller, attracting folklorists and scholars to the Blasket, and was persuaded to dictate her own story *Peig* (1936) to her son Mícheál. For decades the book was a fixture on the Irish curriculum, its context becoming increasingly remote to the growing number of urban students. A translation by Bryan MacMahon* was published in 1973. Peig Sayers's second book, *Machtnamh Sean-Mhná* (1939) was translated by Seamus Ennis as *An Old Woman's Reflections* (1962). Peg moved to the mainland in advance of the general resettlement of the islanders (1953) and after a long illness died in Dingle.

School for Scandal, The (1777), Sheridan*'s finest play, describes the difficulties of leading an honest life in a polite London society which is dominated by the salon of the malicious Lady Sneerwell. The main characters are the brothers Joseph and Charles Surface, the first a mean, sanctimonious villain, the other an honest, likeable spendthrift, who are tested by their rich uncle Sir Charles Surface as to their worth when he returns from India. Joseph woos Maria, the ward of Sir Peter Teazle who has married a young wife, and he is revealed as a scoundrel when, at the behest of Lady Sneerwell, he tries to seduce Lady Teazle.

Séadna (1904), lively novel by an t-Athair Peadar Ó Laoghaire* which became a classic text in schools and for the teaching of Irish. The eponymous hero sells his soul to the devil ('An Fear Dubh') for financial gain but manages to avoid fulfilling his part of the contract after the granted thirteen years of reprieve have elapsed.

Shadwell, Charles (?1675–1726), playwright, was the son of the Restoration playwright Thomas Shadwell (?1642–1726). He made Dublin his base and mingled insurance with play-doctoring for Smock Alley*. In the breezy manner of the day, he wrote original plays and adapted the writings of others, giving all his work Irish settings. His plays include *The Hasty Weddings* (1716), *Irish Hospitality* (1717) and *The Sham Prince* (1718), which, based upon an actual imposture, was adapted and set in Belfast by Jack Loudan as one of the Festival of Britain plays directed by Tyrone Guthrie in 1951.

Shaw, George Bernard (1856–1950), playwright and Fabian, was born in Dublin and educated at 'Lee's Musical Society [his mother's colleague George Vandaleur Lee], the National Gallery and Dalkey Hill'. He left Ireland in 1876 and became involved in the gradualist left-wing politics of the Fabian Society which he founded with Beatrice (1858–1943) and Sidney (1859–1947) Webb. He became a trenchantly funny critic of music and drama and applied his strictures to his own plays, which became rather more successful than earlier unread (and probably unreadable) novels. He wrote over a long lifetime many plays and volumes of criticism, the political tracts of his earlier years now subsumed as extensive prefaces to the printed editions of his plays. He remained a cranky supporter of Ireland, recklessly defending the various insurrections and consoling Michael Collins's sister with the words: 'Let us all praise God that he had not to die in a snuffy bed of a trumpery cough, weakened by age, and saddened by the disappointments that would have attended his life had he lived.' His plays were Ibsenite in their attack on social evils and Chekhovian in their irony, and full of sometimes wearisome chat. In all his work, even in a serious play like *St Joan* (1923), one is conscious of the astringent, mocking, knowing Dublin voice, enjoying its special appointment as the allowed English gadfly. His most popular plays are *Arms and the Man* (1894) which, like *Pygmalion** (1912), was made into a successful musical comedy, *The Devil's Disciple* (1897), which owes more than is admitted to Boucicault*, *Man and Superman* (1905) and *Heartbreak House** (1921). *The Shewing-Up of Blanco Posnet* (1909), about a gallant horse-thief in a town in the American West, was banned in London for alleged blasphemy, offered to the Abbey* and put on by Lady Gregory* in spite of serious opposition from Dublin Castle. *John Bull's Other Island** (1904) neatly turns the tables on national stereotypes.

Sheehan, Canon [Patrick Augustine] (1852–1913), novelist, was born in Mallow and educated at Maynooth, becoming parish priest of Doneraile,

County Cork, in 1894. He began writing his novels (of which he wrote ten in all) as a counter to certain trends he perceived in the Church. His early novels bore too obviously their sermonic role, but later ones had subjects more congenial mediated through realistic characters in real situations. Among his best known novels are *Miriam Lucas* (1912), about the travails of a Catholic heiress involved in labour strikes in Dublin and journalism in American slums, *Glenanaar* (1905), about agrarian crimes, *The Graves of Kilmorna* (1915), about Fenianism and the Land War, *Luke Delmege* (1901), about an intellectual learning humility in a rural parish, and his most popular work *My New Curate** (1900).

Sheridan, Richard Brinsley (1751–1816), playwright, was born in Dublin and educated at Harrow. He married Elizabeth Ann Linley when both were under-age and she, a professional singer, supported him while he read Law in the Middle Temple. He was unhappy about this arrangement and began to write plays. *The Rivals* (1775), set in Bath, where his family had moved from Dublin, showed him a writer of elegant comedies and creator of memorable characters such as Mrs Malaprop and Sir Lucius O'Trigger. It was followed by *St Patrick's Day* (1775), an efficient farce reminding Drury Lane audiences of the author's origin. *The School for Scandal** (1777), Sheridan's masterpiece, was staged in what was soon to be his own theatre, the Theatre Royal. *The Critic* (1779), a hilarious send-up of the way in which elaborate staging was used to cover up inferior dramaturgy, was his last original play. His long career in parliament was marked by honesty and brilliance of oratory, two rare qualities in the politics of the time. His finances never recovered from the burning down of his Theatre Royal and his last years were debt- and drink-ridden.

Shiels, George (1886–1949), playwright, was born in Ballymoney, County Antrim, emigrated to Canada in 1906 but returned home after being crippled in an accident while working for a railway company in 1913. His early plays, *Away from the Moss* (1918) and *Felix Reid and Bob* (1919), written as by 'George Morshiel', were performed by the Ulster Literary Theatre* but it was the acceptance by the Abbey* of *Bedmates* (about Ulster-Free State relations) in 1921 that led to a career as one of the best known and most popular Irish playwrights of the century. He wrote some thirty plays, mainly mordant comedies set in an unspecified area of the North and concerned with small-town and rural characters, con-men, sharp practice in business, lost wills, family dissension and generation clash. They are mostly naturalistic and tersely eloquent, portraying Ulster life better than the work of St John Ervine* or Rutherford Mayne*. Such plays as *Paul Twyning* (1922), *Professor Tim* (1925), *Cartney and Kevney* (1927) – in which one of the characters defines martyrdom as 'having to live with a saint' – *The New*

Gossoon (1936) and *The Caretakers* (1948) were popular not only with Abbey audiences but also with myriad amateur companies right up till the 1960s. *The Passing Day* (1936), about the last day of life of a miserly shopkeeper, was chosen by Tyrone Guthrie for one of the Festival of Britain drama productions in 1951. *The Rugged Path* (1940) and its sequel *The Summit* (1941) are unusually stark accounts of rural dissension.

Shorter, Dora Sigerson (1866–1918), poet, was born in Dublin, the eldest child of George Sigerson*, and moved to England in 1896 on marriage to Clement King Shorter (1857–1926), pioneer of the English pictorial press, editor of the *Illustrated London News* and founder of the *Tatler* (1903). She was a friend of Alice Furlong and Katharine Tynan* and produced much more verse than either, publishing thirteen volumes of mainly ballad poetry. She was deeply affected by the outcome of Easter Week, as her volume *Sixteen Dead Men* (1919) makes clear.

Sigerson, George (1836–1925), anthologist and physician, was born near Strabane County Tyrone and educated in Letterkenny and at Queen's College, Cork, graduating in Medicine with a special qualification in self-taught Irish. He specialised in neurological problems and was appointed Professor of Zoology at what became UCD. His main work was *Bards of the Gael and Gall* (1897) which, with his founding in 1892 of the National Literary Society,

played an important part in the success of both the literary and the language revival. He was the father of Dora Sigerson Shorter*.

Simmons, James (b. 1933), poet, was born in Derry and educated at Campbell College, Belfast, and Leeds University. He taught in Lisburn, Nigeria and Coleraine University (1968–84) and served as writer-in-residence at QUB (1985–8). In 1969 he founded *The Honest Ulsterman*, a literary and critical magazine meant to challenge the supremacy of Dublin as a cultural centre. His own poetry is prolific, demotic, balladic and often guitar-accompanied. Since his first collection *Late But in Earnest* (1967) he has published at least a dozen other volumes, dealing with childhood memories, love, sex and (not necessarily) local politics. His *Poems 1956-1986* (1986) was edited by Edna Longley.

Sirr, Peter (b. 1960), poet and critic, was born in Waterford and educated at TCD. He lived in Holland and Italy for some years before returning to Dublin. He received the Patrick Kavanagh Award in 1982 and has published four collections of poetry, *Marginal Zones* (1984), *Talk, Talk* (1987), *Ways of Falling* (1991), and *The Ledger of Fruitful Exchange* (1995). He is co-editor of *Graph: Irish Cultural Review* and Director of the Irish Writers' Centre in Dublin.

Smith, Paul (1920–97), novelist, was born in working-class Dublin, the scene of his historical novels *The Countrywoman* (1962), essentially an account of his mother's early married life, and *Esther's Altar* (1959), about Dublin during the 1916 Rising. He had a career of various occupations, including actor, sailor, barman and in-house theatre costumier. His novels, more popular in America than at home, are deeply felt, if marred by florid emotional and sexual description.

Smithson, Annie M[ary] P[atricia] (1873–1948), romantic and patriotic novelist, was born in Sandymount, Dublin, and trained as a nurse. On her mother's remarriage she became a Catholic and a fervent nationalist, an activist in Cumann na mBan during the Civil War*. Her nineteen novels, which reflect elements of her own life, are full of ladylike, ultimately patriotic (that is to say republican) and feminist young women who often succeed in converting their heroic lovers to Catholicism. *The Walk of a Queen* (1922) and *The Laughter of Sorrow* (1925) contain some description of ordinary Dublin life during the Troubles. Her work was once extremely popular, in spite of its decorousness and total lack of irony.

Smock Alley (1662-1786), Dublin's first post-Restoration theatre, was the licensed theatre until Spranger Barry's Crow Street* was opened in 1759. Garrick, Farquhar*, Peg Woffington, Macklin*, O'Keeffe* and Sheridan*'s father Thomas were all part of its history. It fell into disrepair and was finally converted into a corn store.

Smyllie, Robert Maire (1894–1954), editor, was born in Glasgow and educated at Sligo Grammar and TCD, his parents having moved to Ireland. He was interned near Berlin during WWI as an enemy alien, being on a walking tour. Too poor to continue his university career, in 1918 he covered the Versailles talks for *The Irish Times* and stayed with the paper, eventually becoming its editor in 1934. He did much to reconcile the paper to its Irishness and made it liberal and politically independent. It was he who initiated 'Cruiskeen Lawn', Flann O'Brien*'s remarkable column (written as Myles na Gopaleen), and had the w-wit to employ P-Patrick Campbell* as third leader writer. He was a well liked figure in the Dublin of his time, his own blithe column signed 'Nichevo', the Russian for 'nobody'.

Somerville & Ross: Edith Œnone Somerville (1858–1949) and 'Martin Ross' (pseudonym of Violet Martin) (1862–1915), novelists and short story writers. Edith, the elder, was born in Corfu but spent much of her life in Drishane, the family home in Castletownshend*, County Cork. She was educated mainly by governesses and early showed an artistic ability equal to her horsewomanship. She formed a literary partnership with her cousin Violet in 1886 and together they wrote five novels and three collections of comic stories about *An Irish RM** before Violet's death in 1915. Their collaboration was non-specific in its details but a reasonable division was that Edith supplied the humour and equine details, and Violet the darker elements, the Gothic atmosphere and the consciousness of the irreversible decay of the Big House. Her own home of Ross, near Moycullen, County Galway, had had to be closed and her brother had become an entertainer to pay off estate debts. Edith was much more aware of the justice of nationalist claims while Violet, of Catholic ancestry, remained a Wyndhamite unionist. The best of their novels, *The Real Charlotte* (1894), delineates a middle-class Protestant Ireland and its subtle relationship with the aristocratic Big House as no other work has done. Its chief character, Charlotte Mullen, the ruthless aspiring protagonist, her capacity for effective evil somewhat mitigated by an unexpected softness for Roddy Lambert, the worthless man she loves and loses, is one of the most memorable in all of Irish fiction. Edith continued to write after the death of Violet, whom she loved beyond the usual affection of cousins, and insisted on both their names appearing on the published books. The chief book of this ghostly partnership was *The Big House at Inver* (1925), about the decline of the Ascendancy Prendevilles who in their deterioration abandon the social codes of their class and 'go native'. The germ of the book lay in a visit that Violet paid to such a crumbling house in 1912.

Standún, Pádraig (b.1946), novelist, playwright and scriptwriter in Irish and English, was born in Tourmakeady,

County Mayo, educated at Maynooth and ordained priest in 1970. His novels reflect the trials and rewards of his vocation, and the often intolerable strains of celibacy. They include *Súil le Breith* (1983), *Ciocras* (1991), *An tAinmhí* (1992) and *Stigmata* (1995). Many of these appeared later in his own translations. Plays include *T na G 2092* (1992) and *Drama na Páise* (1995).

Stanihurst, Richard (1547–1618), historian and translator, was born in Dublin, son of the Speaker of the Irish Commons, and educated at Kilkenny Grammar School and University College, Oxford, where his tutor was Edmund Campion (1540-81) the Jesuit martyr. He used some of Campion's notes for his Irish contribution to the *Chronicles* (1577) of Raphael Holinshed (d. ?1580). His own history of Ireland, *De Rebus in Hibernia Gestis* (1584), is lively but unreliable. He is best known for a hexameter translation of the *Aeneid* into a kind of Hiberno-English, which was heavily criticised by English contemporaries, and for 'Aqua Vitae', a paean on Irish whiskey as a sovereign panacea that is contained in the *Chronicles*.

Steele, Sir Richard (1672–1729), essayist and playwright, was born in Dublin and educated at Charterhouse, where he met his future colleague Joseph Addison (1672–1719), and at Christ Church and Merton College, Oxford, leaving without a degree to join the Coldstream Guards. A duel fought with another Irishman called Kelly, in which the man nearly died, had a profound effect upon his life and he became a kind of public moralist, determined to make society more refined and to counter the coarseness of Restoration plays. The first he managed by writing with Addison entertaining essays in the *Tatler* (1709–11) and the *Spectator* (1711–12) which tacitly approved good behaviour and contained subtle admonitions to moral improvement. He became for a while the licensee of Drury Lane and his only successful play *The Conscious Lovers* (1722) established a taste for sentimental drama. As with many of his class and insecure position, his fortunes depended on the approval of the government in power and, though knighted by George I in 1713, he was never free from money worries.

Stephens, James (?1880–1950), poet, novelist and short story writer, was born in Dublin, though other details of his early life are obscure. He became a solicitor's clerk in 1896 and began writing stories and novels, including *The Charwoman's Daughter* (1912), *The Crock of Gold** (1912), *The Hill of Vision* (1912), *Here Are Ladies* (1913), *The Demi-Gods* (1915) and *Etched in Moonlight* (1928), in which knowingness, verbal pyrotechnics, quirky humour, patriotism and fantasy were headily mixed. He was a friend of Arthur Griffith (he wrote a biography in 1922) and *The Insurrection in Dublin* (1916) is an eye-witness account of Easter Week and an appeal for Irish freedom and English amity. He was

registrar of the National Gallery of Ireland (1915–25) and then left to live in London, though frequently engaged in successful American tours. Always a brilliant talker and possessing a distinctive voice, he recorded many successful talks for the BBC on poets, poetry and reminiscence. He was friendly with all the great literary names of his day; even the reticent, not to say prickly Joyce suggested that Stephens should finish *Finnegans Wake* if he himself should fail, the authors to be given as J. J. & S. – the initials of the makers of Jameson whiskey. His poetry is as quirky as his prose, his versions of the Gaelic poets in *Reincarnations* (1918) being particularly effective. His poems 'The Snare', 'The Shell' and 'Danny Murphy' usually find their way into children's anthologies.

Stoker, Bram [Abraham] (1847–1911), novelist, was born in Dublin and educated at TCD, where he was a noted athlete, overcoming childhood sickliness. Like his father, he joined the civil service, his first publication being *Duties of the Clerks of Petty Sessions in Ireland* (1878). He became fascinated by the theatre, acting as (unpaid) critic for the *Dublin Evening Mail* and becoming the manager of Henry Irving from 1878 until the great star's death in 1905. His first novel *The Snake's Pass* (1891), set in County Mayo, is about gold, gombeenism and gallantry and is the only one of his books set in Ireland. Though his Gothic romance *Dracula** (1897) is world-famous (like Le Fanu's 'Carmilla', because of its respectable eroticism) some of his short stories, notably 'The Judge's House' and 'The Squaw', are much more chilling and worth their place in any spooky anthology. Other full-length Gothic efforts are *The Jewel of the Seven Stars* (1903) and *The Lair of the White Worm* (1909) which has been filmed several times, the word 'worm' having its medieval connotation of 'serpent'.

Strong, Eithne (b. 1923), poet and fiction writer, was born in Glensharrold, County Limerick and became a civil servant, resigning to rear a large family in 1943. She attended TCD as a mature student and taught in Dublin from 1973 till 1988. She and her husband, the psychoanalyst Rupert Strong (1911-84), founded the Runa Press and published several volumes of poetry, including *Songs of Living* (1961), *Flesh: The Greatest Sin* (1982) and *Spatial Nosing* (1993). She has also published five volumes of Irish poetry, including the early *An Gor* (1942), *Fuil agus Fallaí* (1983) and *Aoife faoi Ghlas* (1990), and two novels, *Degrees of Kindred* (1979) and *The Love Riddle* (1993). *Patterns*, a volume of short stories, many of which first appeared in David Marcus*'s 'New Irish Writing' page, was published in 1981.

Strong, L[eonard] A[lfred] G[eorge] (1896–1958), man of letters, was born in Plymouth of Anglo-Irish parents and spent his summers in Dalkey. He won a scholarship to Wadham College, Oxford, and taught until 1930 when the success of his writing allowed him to retire. Of his twenty novels, *The Garden* (1931), *Sea Wall* (1933), *The Bay* (1941), *The Director* (1944) and *The Light above the Lake* (1958) are set in Ireland. His poetry is collected in *The Body's Imperfections* (1957) and his sketch 'The Brewer's Man' from *Dublin Days* (1921) is often anthologised. Strong wrote biographies of Tom Moore*, John McCormack and Synge* and a study of recurring symbols in the work of Joyce*.

Stuart, Francis (b. 1902), novelist, was born in Australia but was brought home to County Antrim on his father's suicide. He was educated at Rugby and married Maud Gonne's daughter Iseult in 1920, living with her in Wicklow on his release from internment after the Civil War*. He went to Germany in 1939 to work as a university lecturer and was one of several 'neutrals' paid by the Nazis to broadcast during WWII. In 1946 he was interned for a year by the French in Freiburg where he and Gertrud Meissner, his future second wife, lived in near starvation until 1949, a period that inspired his novels *The Pillar of Cloud* (1948), *Redemption* (1949) and *The Flowering Cross* (1950). These are united in the theme of redemption through sufferings, the middle one set in the religious Ireland of the immediate postwar years. Stuart and Gertrud, now married, returned to Ireland in 1959, and he began to write what many regard as his greatest book, the autobiographical *Black List, Section H** (1971). Five experimental novels followed – *Memorial* (1973), *A Hole in* *the Head* (1977), *The High Consistory* (1981), *Faillandia* (1985) and *A Compendium of Lovers* (1990) – all touching in some way upon love, sex, the freedom of the artist, the condition of Ireland (and the world) and the purpose of religion, the last describing the married life of the narrator Joel Samuel and Thérèse Martin, who did not after all enter the Carmelite convent to become the Little Flower. Stuart, who soberly delights in his uncategorisability, remains Ireland's most resolutely original and, in the old sense, crankiest novelist. He is also one of her greatest.

Swift, Jonathan (1667–1745), man of letters, was born in Dublin and educated in Kilkenny and at TCD. Like many another gentleman without means at the time, his career depended upon the ruling party, and his critical adherence to high Toryism and strongly anti-Whig tendencies left him often without any political friends. He left Ireland in 1689 because of the brief period of blatant Catholic Ascendancy during the reign of James II's viceroy, Talbot, and became the private secretary of Sir William Temple. It was at Moor Park, Temple's house, that he met Esther Johnson (1681-1728), the 'Stella' of their long and troubled relationship. He returned to Ireland in 1694 and, taking orders, was appointed curate of the not-very-Anglican parish of Kilroot in south Antrim, moving to the more congenial Laracor in Meath. Returning to England, having put his by now famous polemical tongue and pen

at the service of the Queen Anne Tories, he became a noted literary figure for his satirical verse and spare prose. Giving up hope of better preferment, he accepted the Deanery of St Patrick's Cathedral in Dublin in 1714 and stayed there until his death, 'a poisoned rat in a hole'. He wrote much verse, ranging from extreme scatology to Augustan austerity, but always witty and, strangely for an ultra-conservative who wished to abolish the Irish language, containing some versions of Gaelic poems. His great prose work is *Gulliver's Travels** (1726) meant, like *A Tale of a Tub* (1704), as a blistering comment on contemporary politics and a bleak observation on humankind, but which became, because of the imaginative richness and logic of its fantasy, a children's classic. His anonymous pamphlets, such as those by the 'Drapier' attacking Wood's halfpence (1724) and his brilliantly savage *A Modest Proposal* (1729), showed that the 'Englishman born in Ireland' was being driven by English malpractice to become a 'Hibernian patriot'. His *Journal to Stella* (1766–8) and *Cadenus and Vanessa* (1726) are respectively prose and poetic accounts of his feelings for the two Esthers in his life, Stella and Miss Vanhomrigh (1687–1723). He was buried beside Stella in St Patrick's, secure at last from the *saeva indignatio* of his famous epitaph and the Ménière's disease that made his latter years so frightening.

Synge, J[ohn] M[illington] (1871–1909), playwright, was born in

Rathfarnham of an ecclesiastical family and reared by a mother with severe evangelical beliefs. He rejected religion early in his life and, though often ill as a child, became a great walker and cyclist in the Wicklow glens where the family took holidays. He took a pass degree at TCD but learned Irish in the School of Divinity. This stood him in good stead when, after a period of dilettantism in Paris, he (whether because of a prompt by Yeats* or otherwise) spent four summers (1899–1902) in the Aran Islands*, especially Inis Meáin. The experiences he recorded in *The Aran Islands* (1907) provided him with material for his plays, *In the Shadow of the Glen* (1903), about the rejection of materialism when a woman prefers a free life with a tramp to security with an aged husband or laggardly lover, *Riders to the Sea* (1904) and *The Playboy of the Western World** (1907). The bitter parable *The Well of the Saints*, about a blind couple who prefer to become blind again rather than face the world of sight, was produced in 1905. Two of Synge's plays were not produced in his lifetime: *The Tinker's Wedding* (1909) because of the indignity shown to a priest, and the unfinished *Deirdre of the Sorrows* (1910), a stark poetic version of the saga tale. Synge also wrote sharp, satiric, violent verse, mitigated by poems addressed to Molly Allgood who played Pegeen Mike in the *Playboy* and with whom he was in love. His travel essays, written mainly for the *Manchester Guardian* with illustrations by Jack B. Yeats*, were collected as *In Wicklow and West Kerry* (1911). Synge died of Hodgkin's disease, the tenor of the last ten years of his life heightened by his consciousness of the cancer.

T

Taibhdhearc, An (estd. 1927), Irish-language theatre in Galway, founded by Séamus Ó Beirn with the support of a grant from Minister for Finance Ernest Blythe*. The first production was Micheál Mac Liammóir*'s *Diarmaid agus Gráinne*, with Mac Liammóir playing the lead. Many prominent actors began their careers there, including Siobhán McKenna and Michael Lally.

Tailor and Ansty, The (1942), Eric Cross*'s account of the wit and wisdom of Tim Buckley, the Tailor of Gougane Barra, with interruptions from his short-fused wife Ansty. The salty reminiscences and innocent sexuality of the two proved too much for the Censorship Board, who banned the book, and the two old people were terrorised by bullying local priests into burning their copy. The Tailor's motto *'Glac bog an saol agus glacfaidh an saol bog thú'* [Take life easy and life will be easy on you.] enabled him to weather the agitation but it certainly shortened Ansty's life. Her death is the subject of one of Sean O'Faolain*'s tenderest stories 'The Silence of the Valley' (1947).

Tarry Flynn (1948), Patrick Kavanagh*'s only (and at least emotionally autobiographical) novel, which describes the toil, frustrations and moments of Joycean epiphany of a young Monaghan small farmer as he writes his poetry, sows his potatoes and longs for a suitable wife. Set during the bleak years of the 1930s, it was banned for all the usual reasons.

Tate, Nahum (1652–1715), poetaster and 'improver' of Shakespeare, was born in Dublin, the son of a County Cavan Presbyterian minister, a refugee from the Ulster rising of 1641. His own plays proving unpopular, he gave some of Shakespeare's tragedies happy endings: in his *The History of King Lear* (1681) Cordelia marries Edgar, and Regan's and Goneril's thirds are restored to the wilful king. He wrote the libretto for Purcell's *Dido and Aeneas* (1689) and the often parodied carol 'While Shepherds Watched Their Flocks by Night'. He was appointed Poet Laureate in 1692.

Thackeray, William Makepeace (1811–63), English novelist, essayist and humorist, who visited Ireland to write the commissioned *The Irish Sketch Book** (1843). His first novel *Barry Lyndon* (written in tribute to Henry Fielding and serialised as *The Luck of Barry Lyndon* in *Fraser's Magazine* in 1844) has for its picaresque, eighteenth-century anti-hero an Irishman who began life as Redmond Barry.

Thompson, Sam (1916–65), play-wright and actor, was born in Belfast and apprenticed as a painter in the shipyard in 1930. Encouraged by Sam Hanna Bell*, he wrote such radio features as *Brush in Hand* (1956), *Tommy Baxter: Shop Steward* (1957) and *The General Foreman* (1958). His play *Over the Bridge* (1957), about a failed attempt by a shop steward to oppose sectarianism in the shipyard, was can-celled by the Ulster Group Theatre* and, after a successful suit for breach of contract, was produced with great success by James Ellis in the Empire in 1960. *The Evangelist* (1963) was a tour de force for the actor Ray McAnally (1926–89) as the Pastor Earls of the title, while the teleplay *Cemented with Love* (a traditional Orange banner and arch motto) (1965) described with only minimal exaggeration the chicanery that characterised NI elections. Thompson had a real but limited talent, his 1960s success being as much a function of the relative peacefulness of the period as of his dealing with the hitherto unmentionable.

THRESHOLD (estd. 1957), a literary jour-nal associated with the Lyric Theatre*, founded by Mary O'Malley and having a series of guest editors including John Boyd*, Seamus Deane*, Seamus Heaney*, Brian Friel* and John Montague*. It has been the longest-lasting Ulster journal, with a notable list of contributors including most modern Irish poets.

Thurston, Katherine Cecil (1875–1911), novelist, was the daughter of Paul Madden, a nationalist mayor of Cork. In 1901 she married E. Temple Thurston (1879-1933), a noted anti-Catholic writer whom she divorced nine years later. *John Chilcote MP* (1904), her first successful novel (about politics and impersonation), was dramatised by her husband. Two of her books, *The Gambler* (1906) and *The Fly on the Wheel* (1908), have Irish settings, the second being about the disapproval of divorce in Ireland and the suicide of a woman prevented by this attitude from marrying her lover. Thurston herself probably committed suicide in Moore's Hotel in Cork, where she was found to have died by asphyxia.

Thy Tears Might Cease (1963), a semi-autobiographical novel by Michael Farrell*, unpublished at his death and tailored to manageable length by Monk Gibbon*, describes the career of Martin Matthew Reilly in early twentieth-cent-ury Ireland. His Catholic education makes him bitterly anticlerical and the Easter Rising* kills residual Redmond-ism. He happily joins the IRA but, emer-ging from imprisonment in Mountjoy, regards with little enthusiasm the con-tours of the emerging Free State. The novel's highpoint is the description of idyllic pre-school childhood.

Titley, Alan (b. 1947), novelist, play-wright and critic, was born in Cork and educated at St Patrick's College, Druncondra, where he is Head of the Irish Department. He is the author of nine books including a novel, *An Fear Dána*, a collection of short stories,

Eiriceachtaí Agus Scéalta Eile (1987), a critical study of the novel in Irish, *An t-Úrscéal Gaeilge*, and a collection of essays, *Chur Doirne* (1997). Among his many plays are *Tagann Godot* (1992), an answer to Beckett.. All Titley's works are marked by a keen and original critical intelligence and his fiction by a gleeful, sardonic humour.

Tóibín, Colm (b. 1955), journalist and novelist, was born in Enniscorthy, County Wexford, and educated at UCD. *The South* (1990), his prize-winning first novel, is about an Irish artist's love affair in and with Spain. *The Heather Blazing* (1993) tackled a more difficult subject, the life of Irish people, notably that of Eamon Redmond, a High Court judge whose wife is terminally ill and who is haunted by the events of the '98 rising, which took place where he now lives. *The Story of the Night* (1996) describes in a deliberately unstructured way the life of a gay, HIV-positive Argentine with an English mother during the Falklands War. Tóibín has also written *Homage to Barcelona* (1989) and *Walking along the Border* (1987), a remarkable look at Ulster.

Tomelty, Joseph (1911–95), novelist, playwright and actor, was born in Portaferry, County Down, left school at twelve and became a house-painter in Belfast. His first play *Barnum Was Right* (1940), a broad comedy, was originally a radio play and he was to write much for that medium, especially a Belfast soap, *The McCooeys* (1947-54), which incredibly avoided both religion and politics and in which he played a typical creation, the lugubrious, socially inept and intermittently amorous Bobby Greer. Contrariwise, *The End House* (1944) is set in the sectarian Ulster of the 1930s (the play was begun as early as 1932) and pulls no punches about 'how things were in Belfast' – the wall of the 'end house' marked by the bullets where an informer was shot. The play, which is reminiscent of O'Casey*'s *Juno and the Paycock**, describes the afflictions of the MacAstocker family and ends in almost total gloom, with the daughter seduced and swindled out of money she was holding for a slate club, the son recently out of prison for IRA activity shot by the RUC, the Juno-like mother Sar Alice disallowed her sickness benefit and the self-deluding father accidentally killed. *All Souls' Night** (1948) staged by the Ulster Group Theatre*, which Tomelty helped to found and for which he acted as general manager till 1951, is the best of his thirteen plays. Strangford Lough is the scene of Tomelty's first novel *Red in the Port Light* (1948), about passion and madness and the danger from Strangford rip-tides. *The Apprentice* (1953), also set in the Belfast of the 1930s, draws heavily on Tomelty's own professional experience and describes the rite of passage of a not-very-skilful apprentice. Tomelty's success in George Shiels*'s Festival play *The Passing Day* in 1951 won him a film contract and a busy career as a character actor, which was tragically ended by a serious car crash in 1954. His literary career was effectively finished too.

Tonna, Charlotte (1790–1846), poet and evangelist, was born in Norwich, daughter of the Rev. Michael Browne, and lived in Ulster with her second husband Lewis Tonna. She wrote much material for the Dublin Tracts Society and thirty novels of similar nature. *Derry, a Tale of Revolution* (1839), about the siege, attacks Popery as 'the curse of Ireland'. Her stirring 'The Maiden City' and 'No Surrender' (both on the same subject) still deserve anthological inclusion.

Tracy, Honor (1913–89), novelist and journalist, was born in Bury St Edmunds and educated at the Sorbonne. She settled in Ireland after a wartime career in the WAAF and the Ministry of Information as a Japanese specialist, continuing to write for the posh English Sundays. *Kakemono* (1950) describes a visit to postwar Japan. She worked in the offices of *The Bell** and continued the work of therapeutic criticism of Irish mores begun by her mentor Sean O'Faolain*, with whom she had an affair. Her book of satirical reportage, *Mind You I've Said Nothing* (1956), caused controversy and litigation. *The Straight and Narrow Path* (1958), *The Prospects Are Pleasing* (1958), *The First Day of Friday* (1964) and *The Quiet End of Evening* (1972) are stylish comedies of Irish rural life. Tracy also wrote much about Spain.

Traits and Stories of the Irish Peasantry (1830, 1833), William Carleton*'s early short fiction which, though written as anticlerical propa-

ganda, loses its purpose as the rowdy life of the Ireland of the time takes over. 'Denis O'Shaughnessy Going to Maynooth', 'The Poor Scholar', 'The Lough Derg Pilgrim' and the savage 'Wildgoose Lodge' are among the best of the author's writing.

Treacy, Maura (b. 1946), short story writer and novelist, was born and still lives in Kilkenny. *Sixpence in Her Shoe* (1977) is a collection of stories about the relatively unchanging life of rural farmfolk in the rich Leinster land. Her novel, *Scenes from a Country Wedding*, was published in 1981.

Trevor, William (b. 1928), short story writer, novelist and playwright, was born W. T. Cox in Mitchelstown, County Cork, the son of a frequently transferred bank official. He was educated at St Columba's College, Dublin, and TCD, and after some teaching became for a short while a professional sculptor. He went to live in England in 1954 and published a series of upsettingly comic novels, filled with eccentrics whose bizarre speech matched their personalities. Trevor's gallery of misfits and their predators are as richly comic as anything in Dickens or Firbank. Trevor the Irish writer began to surface in the novel *Mrs Eckdorf in O'Neill's Hotel* (1969), where his descriptions of a seedy Dublin have an even greater authenticity than his London sites. His various collections of short stories, *The Day We Got Drunk on Cake* (1967), *The Ballroom of Romance* (1972), *Angels at the Ritz* (1975) and others, all have their complement of marvellous evocations of Irish life, often from the viewpoint of a reticent child narrator, in the small towns of the south and west. Strongly affected by the Northern Troubles, he began to consider the position of Irish Protestants, a gradually diminishing minority, with regard both to their often honourable past and to their present decay. *The Distant Past* (1979, 1987) is a specially self-chosen collection of Trevor's Irish stories, while in *Fools of Fortune* (1983) he handled a Big House novel with great authenticity. *Reading Turgenev*, one of two novellas in *Two Lives* (1990), set very much in Trevor's Ireland, describes the passion of a Protestant wife for her sickly cousin, expressed only by their mutual reading of Russian authors. Other works with Irish elements are *The News from Ireland* (1986), the novella *Nights at the Alexandra* (1987) and *Felicia's Journey* (1994). *Scenes from an Album* (1981), a play set at different periods of Ulster's history, was produced in the Abbey* and many of his stories have made excellent telefilms.

Trollope, Anthony (1815–82), English novelist, spent much time in Ireland (1841–59) as a Post Office official and found the release there to write, after a miserable childhood and civil service drudgery. Of his forty-seven novels, four, including the unfinished *The Landleaguers* (1883), were set in Ireland. There are no Irish tinges in his great Barsetshire sequence but Phineas Finn, based on several successful Catholic politicians, names the second and fourth of the Palliser novels and is a character in all but the first and third. Trollope was a unionist but understood the Catholic Irish better than any of his peers, and his novels *The Macdermots of Ballycloran** (1847), *The Kellys and the O'Kellys* (1847) and *Castle Richmond* (1860) are splendid sources for the nature of Irish rural life in the mid-nineteenth century, the last full of searing descriptions of the Famine, though the author's diagnosis is flawed. So is his last novel, which, written a quarter of a century after he left Ireland, is totally unsympathetic with the motives of the Land League.

Troy, Una (b. 1918), novelist and playwright, was born in Fermoy, County Cork. She wrote two novels and four plays for the Abbey Theatre* – including *Swans and Geese* (1941) and *The Dark Road* (1947) – under the pseudonym Elizabeth Connor, then fourteen novels under her own name. Her fictional world is that of the country town, her characters, although they may be eccentric or misguided, are fundamentally well-meaning. *We Are Seven* and *Out of the Everywhere* are based on unusual (even implausible) but skilfully rendered domestic situations.

Tynan, Katharine (1861–1931), poet and novelist, was born on the edge of Dublin in her father's Clondalkin farm and educated at Drogheda. She was severely myopic because of a childhood illness but was an enthusiastic constitutional nationalist and feminist, and mistress of a literary salon where she met Yeats*, who became a lifelong friend. *Louise de la Vallière* (1885) was the first of many collections of verse but she is remembered mainly for anthology pieces like 'Sheep and Lambs', 'The Witch' and 'Any Woman', a proud statement of quiet feminism. Her husband Henry Albert Hinkson was appointed RM for Mayo in 1915 but she left Ireland for good on his death in 1919, finding no common cause with Republicanism. In all she wrote 105 novels, twelve collections of short stories, eighteen verse collections and five volumes of reminiscences. Her daughter Pamela (1900–82) was also a writer, living in Ireland for the last two decades of her life.

U

ULSTER GROUP THEATRE (1940–60) was formed by the amalgamation of several existing companies to present a balance of local and international plays. Work by Joseph Tomelty*, Jack Loudan, Sam Hanna Bell*, St John Ervine*, George Shiels* and John Boyd* was presented there, and it started such actors as Harold Goldblatt, Stephen Boyd, Colin Blakely, J. G. Devlin and Denys Hawthorne on distinguished careers. Its board's loss of nerve over the staging of Sam Thompson*'s *Over The Bridge* (1957) led to its collapse, though it had been ailing for some years.

ULSTER LITERARY THEATRE (1902–34) was founded by Bulmer Hobson and David Parkhill as a Belfast version of Dublin's Abbey*. Its playwrights began a kind of tradition of an Ulster play, with effective work by Rutherford Mayne*, Joseph Campbell*, Lynn Doyle*, Gerald MacNamara* and early work by George Shiels*. Many of these playwrights also wrote for the Abbey. The company had no permanent base and staged its plays mainly in the Grand Opera House in Belfast.

Ulysses (1922), James Joyce*'s novel about the events of a single day, 16 June 1904 (the day Joyce first met his future wife), as experienced by three Dubliners. As the title suggests, there are obvious Homeric parallels, not only in its protagonists – Stephen Dedalus being Telemachus, the son in search of a father, Leopold Bloom the returning Odysseus and his wife Molly the ironically patient Penelope – but also in the parodic equivalents of the events of the *Odyssey*. Stephen is the same autobiographical figure as in the *Portrait** but the other two are original creations. The Dublin that Joyce knew so intimately is rendered exactly (he spent much time and postage money having the details checked) and many of the characters are identifiable denizens of the pocket city. The book is long, highly allusive, dazzlingly literary, a great comic and prestidigitatory masterpiece, and the erotic musings of the unfaithful Penelope, which caused the book to acquire a scandalous reputation in the 1920s and 1930s, now seem not only appropriate but quite innocuous.

Ussher, Arland (1899–1980), man of letters and translator, was born in London and educated at TCD and St John's, Cambridge, which he left to manage the family farm in County Waterford. He translated *Cúirt an Mheán-Oíche* (1926) and Mac Conmara's *Eachtra Giolla an Amaráin* (1929). His wise and witty *The Face and Mind of*

Ireland (1949) was a counterblast to the puritanism afflicting the country at the time and his *Three Great Irishmen* (1952) presented a personal view of Shaw*, Yeats* and Joyce*. *Journey through Dread* (1955) is a study of Kierkegaard, Heidegger and Sartre, *The Magic People* (1950) about the Jews and *Enter These Enchanted Woods* (1955) a consideration of the fairytales of the Brothers Grimm. Characteristic of the variety and quirkiness of his writing are *An Alphabet of Aphorisms* (1953) and *The Twenty-Two Keys of the Tarot* (1953).

V

Valley of the Squinting Windows, The (1918), the first novel of Brinsley MacNamara*, which caused a sensational book-burning in the town of Delvin in Westmeath where the author's father was a schoolteacher. It tells of the hopes of Nan Brennan, a woman with a past, that her legitimate son John will become a priest, but the boy is led astray by his dissipated half-brother Ulick Shannon. The new teacher, Rebecca Kerr, with whom John is in love, is hunted from the village of Garradrimna after her affair with Shannon becomes known, and in revenge John kills him. The book was attacked for the grim picture it painted of Irish rural life.

W

Waddell, Helen (1889–1965), medieval scholar, was born in Tokyo, the daughter of a Presbyterian missionary, and educated at Victoria College, Belfast, and QUB. Intended for an academic career, she spent seven years tending an invalid stepmother before going to Oxford. *The Wandering Scholars* (1927) is a history of the medieval 'vagantes' and an anthology, with translations, of the often ribald poetry assigned to them, some of which, otherwise known as the *Carmina Burana*, she included in a later collection, *Medieval Latin Lyrics* (1929). *Peter Abelard* (1933) is a novel about the great French nominalist philosopher (1079–1142) and his tragic love affair with his pupil Héloïse (1098–1164). Like her brother Rutherford Mayne* she was an Ulster Literary Theatre* playwright, contributing the rather esoteric *The Spoiled Buddha* in 1915.

Wadding, Luke (1588–1657), theologian and scholar, was born in Waterford and was ordained a Franciscan priest in Portugal in 1613. He was involved in the politics of the Irish Confederation of the 1640s. His *Annales Minorum* (1625–54) is a thirty-six-volume history of his order, and his critical edition of the works of Duns Scotus was published in 1639. He avoided being made cardinal and died in Rome in the Irish college he founded.

Waiting for Godot (1954), Beckett*'s best known drama, first written in French as *En Attendant Godot* (1952), had its English language première at Dublin's Pike Theatre* (simultaneously with the Arts Theatre in London). It has been described as the play where nothing happens – twice. Two tramps, Vladimir and Estragon, wait on a country road for the coming of the mysterious Godot and pass the time with casual conversation and serious clowning which owes much to French circuses and the films of Laurel and Hardy. They are visited by the loud Pozzo and his roped slave Lucky. In the second act the setting is the same but there are signs of deterioration: Pozzo is dumb and Lucky blind and the single leaf has fallen off the tree. The boy who told them of Godot's coming returns with the same message and, in spite of a voiced determination to move, the last stage direction indicates their philosophical stasis: *They do not move.*

Wall, Mervyn (pseudonym of Eugene Welpy) (1908–97) novelist and short story writer, was educated at Belvedere and UCD and served as a higher civil servant for his whole career, ending as Secretary of the Arts Council. *The Unfortunate Fursey* (1946), about a possessed lay-brother, is an affectionate parody of the received view of Irish monasticism and an effective attack on the contemporary Church. It and its sequel *The Return of Fursey* (1948) became a cult. *Leaves for the Burning* (1953) and *No Trophies Raise* (1956) are darker, sourer accounts of a 'grocer's republic' Ireland, in which public piety and the right connections are essential for success. *Hermitage* (1982) is a well written but glum account of life in the civil service. Wall wrote two Abbey* plays: *Alarm among the Clerks* (1940) and *The Lady in the Twilight* (1941) reflect Wall's perennial themes, the narrowness of all aspects of the Ireland of his young manhood. *Forty Foot Gentlemen Only* (1962) is a short account of the famous Sandycove bathing-place.

Wall, William (b. 1955), poet and fiction writer, was born in Whitegate, County Cork and after education at UCC became a teacher in a Cork boys' school. He has published a volume of poetry, *Mathematics and Other Poems* (1996). His short stories have been published in anthologies and journals and he has also written a historical seafaring trilogy for children.

Waller, John Francis (1809–94), poet and editor, was born in Limerick and studied Law at TCD, becoming Registrar of Rolls in 1867. He took over the *Dublin University Magazine* when Le Fanu* relinquished it and edited (and wrote many entries for) *The Imperial Dictionary of Universal Biography* (1857–63). He also edited the works of Goldsmith* (1864–65) and Tom Moore* (1867). He is still remembered for such lyrics as 'The Spinning Wheel' and 'Cushla Machree'.

Walsh, Edward (1805–50), poet and translator, was born in Derry, the son of a Cork militiaman, and, graduating from a hedge school, became a hedge-schoolmaster. He was imprisoned for taking part in the tithe war and sacked from his position as a national school-master for writing an article for *The Nation** entitled 'What Is Repeal, Papa?' He translated many *aislingí** for *Reliques of Jacobite Poetry* (1844) and in 1847 published *Irish Popular Songs*, which also rendered Gaelic poems metrically while preserving the assonantal qualities of the originals, a typical example being 'The Dawning of the Day'. His lullaby 'The Fairy Nurse' is still in the repertoire.

Walsh, Louis J[oseph] (1880–1942), playwright and fiction writer, was born in Maghera and qualified as a solicitor, serving eventually as District Justice in County Donegal. He wrote many volumes of slightly fictionalised reminiscences with such titles as *Yarns of a Country Attorney* (1917), but his claim to fame is the comedy *The Pope/ Auction in Killybuck* (the title depending on the current political situation) which was first staged by the Dalriada Players in Ballycastle, County Antrim, in

1915 and describes a judicious use of sectarianism for monetary gain. His sister was the early feminist historian Helena Concannon*.

Walsh, Maurice (1879–1964), fiction writer, was born near Listowel, County Kerry. He was educated at St Michael's College, Listowel, and joined the customs service in 1901. Much of his professional life was spent in the Scottish highlands which provided him with themes and settings for such popular romances as *The Key above the Door* (1926) and *While Rivers Run* (1928), which he began writing after his transfer to the Irish service in 1922. His story 'The Quiet Man' from *Green Rushes* (1935) became one of John Ford's most famous films, and another novel, *Trouble in the Glen* (1950), was filmed with Orson Welles in 1954. *Blackcock's Feather* (1932) and *Son of the Swordmaker* (1938) are historical romances.

Webb, Alfred John (1834–1908), Irish biographer, was born in Dublin into a Quaker family and in 1854 set off for Australia, working his way as a deckhand. His *Compendium of Irish Biography* (1878) gave concise biographies of 350 Irish people and was not superseded until that of Crone* in 1928. Of an ecumenical disposition, he tried to build bridges with *The Alleged Massacre of 1641* (1887), an attempt to correct propagandist exaggeration regarding the native uprisings against the Planters.

Welch, Robert (b. 1947), critic, novelist and poet, was born in Cork and educated at UCC and Leeds, his PhD being on translations from the Irish, and is now Professor of English in UU at Coleraine. Among his published works are *Irish Poetry from Moore to Yeats* (1980), *Changing States: Transformations in Modern Irish Writing* (1993), a collection of verse, *Muskerry* (1991), a novel, *The Kilcolman Notebook* (1994), a thriller in Irish, *Tearmann* (1997), and the magisterial *The Oxford Companion to Irish Literature* (1996).

West, Anthony C[athcot] (1910–88), novelist, was born in County Down and brought up in Cavan before living in America (1930–8). He served in the RAF in WWII and then took up farming in Wales. 'Myself and Some Ducks', his first essay, written as by 'Michael Mac Grian' and published in *The Bell** (July 1942), was censored by the printers, but two further pieces were published in February 1947 and February 1948. His first novel *The Native Moment* (1961) describes the adventures of young Simon Green as he journeys to Dublin with a live eel, and his early career in a welter of sex and sectarianism is described in *The Ferret Fancier* (1963). *As Towns with Fire* (1968), the obscure title a quotation from *Love's Labours Lost*, is a semi-autobiographical novel about an RAF navigator from Ulster. *River's End* (1958), West's first book, is a collection of short stories.

Wheatley, David (b. 1970), poet and critic, was born in Dublin in 1970 and educated at TCD where he edited the college literary magazine *Icarus*. *Thirst* (1997), his first collection, reveals a striking and mature talent and was awarded the Rooney Prize in 1998.

White, Terence de Vere (1912–94), novelist, was born in Dublin and educated at TCD while working as an apprentice solicitor. He set up his own law firm, retiring from it to become literary editor of *The Irish Times* (1961–77) and to devote more time to writing. His autobiography *The Fretful Midge* (1959) has all the charm and style of his novels, notable among which are *Lucifer Falling* (1966), about the clash between cultured academics and the new breed, *Tara* (1967), about the final days of a one-shot Irish man of letters, and *The Lambert Mile* (1969), about an Anglo-Irish enclave persisting in south Dublin. *The Distance and the Dark* (1973) mixes social comedy and the Northern Troubles as a Big House landlord discovers that a member of the local FCA is also a member of Gallowglass, a virulent splinter group of the IRA, and can find no one to bring him to justice. White wrote biographies of Isaac Butt* (1946), Kevin O'Higgins (1948), Oscar Wilde*'s parents (1967) and Thomas Moore* (1977), several travel books, a history of the Royal Dublin Society (1955) and *The Anglo-Irish* (1972).

White, Jack [William John] (1920–80), journalist, novelist and playwright, was born in Cork of English parents and educated at Midleton College and TCD. He was features and London editor of *The Irish Times* and later Controller of RTÉ. He wrote three novels: *One for the Road* (1956), a mystery set in the often claustrophobic Dublin of the war years; *The Hard Man* (1958), about the generalised chicanery of Irish life; and *The Devil You Know* (1962), describing the ferment of capital life in the slowly thawing 1960s. His play *The Last Eleven* (1968) is about a decaying Protestant community. *Minority Report* (1973) is an account of Protestantism in the Republic. He died suddenly in Germany.

White, Victoria (b. 1962), short story writer and journalist, was born in Dublin, the daughter of Jack White*, and educated at TCD. She works as a journalist in *The Irish Times* and has published *Raving Autumn* (1990), a collection of stories.

Wilde, Lady (1826–96), poet, was born Jane Francesca Elgee in Wexford, the daughter of a solicitor and granddaughter of Archdeacon Elgee. She was converted to Nationalism at the funeral of Thomas Davis* and as 'Speranza' contributed quite inflammatory verse to *The Nation**, which she edited when Duffy* was imprisoned. She married William Wilde* in 1851 and one of their three children was Oscar Wilde*. She completed her husband's work on Irish antiquities and died while her famous son was in Reading Gaol.

Wilde, Oscar [Fingal O'Flahertie Wills] (1854–1900), playwright and wit, was born in Dublin and educated at Portora Royal School*, Enniskillen, TCD and Magdalen College, Oxford. His mentor at TCD was Mahaffy* and at Oxford, where he won the Newdigate Prize for Poetry, Walter Pater (1839–94), the apostle of aestheticism. His *Poems* (1881) were imbued with his Hellenism, Republicanism and Paterism. Though well known for the brilliance of his wit, it was his *fin-de-siècle* posturing that earned him the Gilbertian parody of Bunthorne in *Patience* (1881), but he was a hard-working journalist and the position of editor of *The Women's World* (1887–9) enabled him to keep his wife and two sons in comfort in a show house in Chelsea. From 1886 he was a practising homosexual but it was his relationship with Lord Alfred Douglas, the spoiled son of the erratic Marquis of Queensbury, that led to the libel action, the charge of gross indecency and the sentence of two years' hard in Reading Gaol. Released in 1897 but broken in health, he lived in Italy and France using the name 'Sebastian Melmoth' (a combination of the famous martyr and the hero of Charles Maturin*'s Gothic novel, *Melmoth the Wanderer*). He was ultimately deserted by 'Bosie', as he called Douglas, but supported by Robbie Ross, one of his first lovers, and died in Paris of meningitis. He was buried in Père Lachaise, commemorated by a monument by Epstein, since defaced. At the time of the ill-advised action urged on him by the defendant's son, Wilde had reached the pinnacle of dramatic success with four brilliant and ultimately serious comedies of class, *Lady Windermere's Fan* (1891), *A Woman of No Importance* (1893), *An Ideal Husband* (1895) and *The Importance of Being Earnest* (1895), which are constantly revived. His lush play *Salome* (1894), first written in French, no longer shocks and *The Happy Prince* (1888) is a children's classic, a collection of stories which he told his own children before helping them to sleep with Irish lullabies learnt from his parents. Other essential Wildeana are *The Picture of Dorian Gray* (1890), a wittily decadent horror story, *De Profundis* (1905), his apologia written in prison, and *The Ballad of Reading Gaol** (1898).

Wilde, Sir William R[obert Wills] (1815–76), surgeon and antiquarian, father of Oscar Wilde* and husband of Lady Wilde*, was born near Castlerea, County Roscommon, and educated at the Royal College of Surgeons. He later specialised in ENT in London, Berlin and Vienna, financed by the proceeds of a book describing a tour of Madeira and Tenerife. He set up his practice in Dublin in 1841, becoming the leading surgeon in his field and official ophthalmologist to the Castle. He was knighted in 1864 but a libel case brought by a former patient (and mistress), which she won with a farthing damages, all but ruined his career. His interest in Irish antiquities was recognised by the award of the RIA medal in 1873 and his antiquarian work was completed by his wife. He was the first to suggest

Ménière's syndrome as the cause of Swift*'s apparent madness.

Williams, Richard D'Alton (1822–62), poet, was born in Dublin, the illegitimate son of Count D'Alton, and studied Medicine at TCD and (after an active period with Young Ireland when he wrote for *The Nation** as 'Shamrock') at Edinburgh. He was arrested for treason-felony in 1848 and successfully defended by Sir Samuel Ferguson*. Emigrating to America in 1851, he first taught literature in a Jesuit College in Mobile and later practised medicine in Thibodaux, Louisiana, where he died of tuberculosis. 'Consumption has no pity/ For blue eyes and golden hair', lines from his poem 'The Dying Girl', became proverbial.

Wilson, Florence M[ary] (*c*. 1870–1946), poet, was born in Lisburn, County Antrim, but lived for most of her life in Bangor, County Down. She was a friend of Alice Milligan* and wrote many pieces for such journals as the *Irish Homestead* and the *Northern Whig*. She is remembered for 'The Man from God-Knows-Where', her poem about Thomas Russell (1767–1803) the United Irishman.

Wilson, Robert MacLiam (b. 1964), novelist, was born in Belfast and educated there and in St Catherine's College, Cambridge. His novel *Ripley Bogle* (1989) is an appallingly eloquent first-person meditation by a hopeless young tramp on his present state, with memories of a sectarian past in Belfast.

Manfred's Plan (1992) is a similar muse upon the past of a dying Jew who was addicted to wife-beating. A third novel, *Eureka Street,* appeared in 1996.

Wogan, Charles (1683/4–1754), Jacobite, was born in Kildare, the son of Patrick Wogan and Marie Dempsey, at a time when the Wogan lands had been much reduced by the wars and confiscations of the preceding century. His unusual career has often been portrayed as that of 'a dashing soldier of fortune' rather than more aptly as an exiled, enterprising Jacobite loyalist. He first gained prominence by taking part in the Jacobite Rising of 1715 in England and escaping from Newgate Prison on the eve of his trial for High Treason. His career indeed can be said to give particular point to his writings. Notable among these are his account, originally written in French, of his role in the selection and entertaining rescue of Princess Clementina Sobieska in 1719 to be the bride of James Stuart, deposed heir to the throne of England (he sent a version of this in 1732 to Jonathan Swift*); next, a long essay in the form of a letter to Swift, on the fate of the exiled Irish on the continent, the misrepresentation of the Irish by English authors, and a vigorous, very royalist interpretation of seventeenth-century English political history; and thirdly his scattered correspondence, often lively and witty, if also in the voice of a loyal courtier. He also wrote some Latin verse and an English version of the penitential psalms and other pieces. Wogan spent most of his life from 1719 as a soldier in Spain. He is not a major literary figure, yet he is a voice from a memorable phase of Irish history.

Woods, Vincent (b. 1960), playwright, was born in County Leitrim and educated in the College of Journalism, Rathmines. He worked as a presenter in RTÉ before much travel. His play *At the Black Pig's Dyke* (1992), which won the Stewart Parker* Prize, is a frightening account of the contagion of terrorist violence in the region of the eponymous Ulster boundary. Effective use was made of dance and the mumming tradition of the area. *Song of the Yellow Bittern* (1994) is based upon an 1829 paternity suit brought by a Protestant woman against a priest, defended by Daniel O'Connell. Woods has also published a volume of verse, *The Colour of Language* (1994).

Y

Yeats, Jack B[utler] (1871–1957), painter and author, was born in London, the younger brother of W. B. Yeats*, and educated mainly in art schools. One of the finest artists of the twentieth century, he wrote a number of unconventional plays, including *La La Noo* (1942) and *In Sand* (1949), and a series of books which might be described as fictionalised reminiscences, notably *Sailing, Sailing Swiftly* (1933), *Ah Well* (1942) and *The Careless Flower* (1947).

Yeats, W[illiam] B[utler] (1865–1939), poet and playwright, was born in Dublin, the son of the impecunious portrait painter John Butler Yeats (1839-1922). As a boy he spent much time with his mother's family, the Pollexfens, who owned mills and a shipping company in Sligo, and it was to there that he returned aesthetically when his early *fin-de-siècle* poetry dissatisfied him. Living in Dublin in the 1880s he came to know Æ*, John O'Leary, a longtime Fenian, and Maud Gonne, the English army officer's daughter who became an Irish nationalist and who was to obsess him romantically for much of his life. He also engaged with George Moore*, Edward Martyn*, Lady Gregory*, Douglas Hyde*, J. M. Synge* and the others who are associated with the Irish Literary Revival*. All the while he dabbled in Theosophy, becoming a member of the Order of the Golden Dawn, and in 1893 his collection of writings *The Celtic Twilight** became a kind of manifesto for the Irish Literary Revival. Already his poetry, focused by an acquired knowledge of Irish mythology and folklore, showed a marked improvement. *The Wind among the Reeds* (1899) contained such 'Celtic Twilight' poems as 'The Hosting of the Sidhe', 'The Host of the Air', 'The Song of Wandering Aengus' and 'The Fiddler of Dooney'. In the same year the Irish Literary Theatre, the first of several avatars that would finally become the Abbey* in 1904, staged *The Countess Cathleen* and persuaded Yeats that he could write plays. *Cathleen Ní Houlihan*, a revolutionary vehicle for Maud Gonne, followed in 1902 and for many years after he immersed himself in theatre, complaining later with *faux-naïveté*, 'All things can tempt me from this craft of verse' in a poem from *The Green Helmet* (1910). He wrote many plays for 'his' theatre, as he with some justice thought of it, but they did not compare with the work of Gregory*, Synge* or O'Casey*. As the century proceeded and Yeats grew in confidence, his verse showed a strength that depended on nothing but its maker's genius, now sharpened by experience and the consideration of many philosophies. He was supported morally and financially by Lady Gregory, finding in her house Coole Park* the necessary leisure and cossetting that the mage he was becoming required, and he celebrated the woman and the place in many poems, notably in the collections *The Wild Swans at Coole* (1919), *The Winding Stair* (1933) and *New Poems* (1938). His marriage to Georgie Hyde-Lees, a woman exactly half his age, in 1917 gave order to what had always been a restless and often worrisome life. The horrors of WWI and the Troubles at home were survived but his imagination grew darker, as such poems as 'The Second Coming' from *Michael Robartes and the Dancer* (1921) make clear. Yet in his home in Thoor Ballylee, near Gort in County Galway (and in his house in Merrion Square in Dublin) he felt himself to be rootedly Irish at last. He won the Nobel Prize in 1923, characteristically asking how much it was worth. He took his duties as a Free State senator seriously, playing his part in debates on the new coinage and on the divorce legislation. He left Ireland in the early 1930s to seek better health in the Mediterranean but continued to write marvellous verse right up till his death in Roquebrunne in France. WWII delayed till 1948 the fulfilment of his wish to be buried in Drumcliffe churchyard, 'under bare Ben Bulben's head' by which time he was celebrated even by late detractors as a great Irishman and a towering literary figure.

Z

Zozimus (pseudonym of Michael Moran) (?1794–1846), balladeer, was born in the Dublin Liberties: 'I live in Faddle Alley/ Off Blackpitts near the Coombe/With my poor wife Sally,/In a narrow dirty room.' He was blind from early childhood and, though having but a poor ear for music, made his living as a writer and performer of his own, mainly topical ballads: '"You put me in a cage/The people to enrage/But I'm once more on the stage"/Says the Dan Van Vought'. His name came from his recitation (written by the Bishop of Raphoe) of the story of the fifth-century St Mary of Egypt who, once a harlot, is rescued after fifty years of desert penance by the Blessed Zozimus. His 'The Finding of Moses' and 'St Patrick Was a Gintleman' are still current. He died at Easter and was buried in Glasnevin, where a monument was unveiled in 1988.